Contents

KU-134-368

Foreword

In 2008, Major General Patrick Cammaert remarked: 'It is now more dangerous to be a woman than to be a soldier in modern wars'. Cammaert made this observation during his period of service as the Deputy Force Commander of the United Nations Mission in Democratic Republic of Congo (DRC). In what had been, and remains, a protracted civil conflict, the DRC gained the unenviable reputation as 'rape capital of the world'. Sadly, while this conflict has been marked by unprecedented levels of sexual violence, gross offences committed against civilian populations including rape, sexual torture and forced pregnancy have been a regular occurrence in warfare for millennia. Often perpetrated as a conscious strategy to 'terrorize, demoralize, injure, degrade, intimidate and punish affected populations', yet for millennia sexual violence has been dismissed as an inevitable consequence of armed conflict and excluded from laws of war designed to prevent the degeneration of men into brutes. Currently, research is making visible the hidden history of sexual abuse against men and boys in conflict zones. As Brenda Fitzpatrick acknowledges, this is important work, but in pursuing new agendas, we should not neglect the continued suffering of women and girls in conflict. In international humanitarian law, the exclusion of women from the category of 'human' has gone unchallenged for far too long, viewed instead as the property of men, and the violation of women deemed a 'property crime'.

The conflict in the former Yugoslavia and the genocide in Rwanda in the 1990s marked a turning point. In the wake of these events, there was significant progress in recognising and confronting conflict related sexual violence. The International Criminal Tribunal for the former Yugoslavia (2000) was particularly important in recognising that such violence might be organised, systematic and perpetrated by states. The Women, Peace and Security Agenda initiated at the Beijing Conference in 1995, United Nations Security Council Resolution 1325 (2000) and subsequent Security Council resolutions, along with developments in international humanitarian law and in the International Criminal Courts, have all contributed to the understanding that sexual violence in conflict might be strategic – undertaken in pursuit of military and political objectives. There is now an international architecture, legal instruments and processes in place to challenge the long-standing culture of impunity, to hold perpetrators to account and to realise justice for survivors.

TACTICAL RAPE IN WAR AND CONFLICT

International recognition and response

Brenda Fitzpatrick

First published in Great Britain in 2016 by

Policy Press
University of Bristol
1-9 Old Park Hill
Bristol
BS2 8BB
UK
t: +44 (0)117 954 5940
pp-info@bristol.ac.uk
www.policypress.co.uk

North America office:
Policy Press
c/o The University of Chicago Press
1427 East 60th Street
Chicago, IL 60637, USA
t: +1 773 702 7700
f: +1 773-702-9756
sales@press.uchicago.edu
www.press.uchicago.edu

British Library Cataloguing in Publication Data
A catalogue record for this book is available from the British Library

Library of Congress Cataloging-in-Publication Data
A catalog record for this book has been requested

ISBN 978-1-4473-2670-0 paperback
ISBN 978-1-4473-2669-4 hardcover
ISBN 978-1-4473-2674-8 ePub
ISBN 978-1-4473-2673-1 mobi

Cover design by Hayes Design
Front cover image: Glow images
Printed and bound in Great Britain by Clays Ltd, St Ives plc
Policy Press uses environmentally responsible print partners

This change would not have been possible without the efforts of many committed individuals, non-governmental organisations (NGOs), advocates and activists in the transnational feminist movements and human rights organisations, and researchers, documenting abuses and reworking the conceptual frames through which we think about and view violence, conflict and security and the subjects of international law of war. Brenda Fitzpatrick has been a part of this project. As both a long-time activist and researcher in many wars and conflicts, she submitted reports to international agencies and the Australian Government, and in her recent academic work, cumulating in the publication of this text, she has made a difference. Her book will serve as an important resource for researchers through her expert surveys and analysis of UN documents, NGO reports, decisions made by international criminal tribunals and the testimonies and judgments from leading experts and opinion formers in the field.

She goes beyond this contribution. While recognising that sexual violence takes many forms in different contexts, perpetrated by different actors, her focus is on rape as a strategic and tactical weapon of war. She reminds us that there is much to do to end this practice and identifies key challenges to negotiate and overcome on the way. We might now meaningfully speak of a global normative discourse and agenda that is helpful to activists and individuals alike in holding states to account, but progress at the national and local level has lagged behind global developments. States have often been slow to implement their commitments, expectations that states will protect their citizens thwarted. Indeed, in many instances states have neglected to pursue, or have shielded, culprits or have continued to act as perpetuators of strategic and tactical rape. From the former Yugoslavia and Rwanda to Sierra Leone and Congo, Sudan and Syria, the obstacles and dangers faced by human rights defenders in war zones and immense difficulties in documenting abuses and collecting evidence are stark. In this book, Fitzpatrick remains true to her longstanding commitment to put theory to the service of rigorous empirical research that can inform practice and so take us a step closer to eradicating an egregious harm that devastates the lives of millions of people worldwide and that threatens our collective security and wellbeing. Her book makes a much needed and most welcome contribution to the field.

Jill Steans
7 January 2016

Acknowledgements

This book has been inspired by experiences related to me by many women and girls encountered in war zones and refugee camps. It is an attempt to keep faith with those who sat on cold, concrete floors and those who sat in the African darkness, who often held my hand and cried as they told me what had happened to women in wars. Sometimes it was couched as, 'this woman I know' or 'my sister' or 'my daughter'. Sometimes it was admitted as the teller's own tale. They were stories of great courage, terrible suffering and of the additional outrage of shame felt by victims. Their specific stories and names are not used, but the stories of others who faced the pain of courts represent them. These women and all those who suffer sexual violence in war are the people who make it important to take action against such violations. They make it important to understand the legal judgements that are the basis for states to recognise their responsibilities to prevent and confront these crimes, and to ensure accountability for those who perpetrate them. These women are the reason why it matters to have United Nations Security Council resolutions and to follow through with sustained actions to implement action that will eventually provide some protection and justice for victims of rape and sexual violence used as tactics in war

ONE

Introduction

Rape in conflict has long been a reality, and has long been accepted as almost inevitable. Now, finally, change is occurring in how the international community recognises and confronts this violation of law and of human rights. It is important to track this change, to understand how it has been achieved, to identify best practice in advocacy, and to understand how such practice can contribute to ongoing work to deal with what remains an ongoing issue. It is important because while there has been significant progress in recognising and confronting rape in conflict, there remain serious and continuing challenges.

In 1992, after visiting refugee camps and women's groups in and around Zagreb, as a member of a team from international aid agencies, I reported a representative of a local church saying that women from conflicting parties were, 'of course', being raped by opposing combatants, and I heard, many times, 'that's war', with accompanying shrugs.[1] It was a comment indicative of the chilling acceptance frequently exhibited to this reality of abuse in war. My report of that visit noted two types of rape that refugee women and women's groups had been highlighting in the conflict between Serbs and Bosnians: rape as a *by-product* of war, and rape as a *weapon* of war.[2] The response from some observers in the international organisation that had assembled my team was to dismiss the term 'rape as a weapon of war' as merely provocative or as an attempt to be clever or strategic in attracting attention to what they deemed as 'just' a women's issue.[3] These workers in humanitarian organisations did not take seriously the reality that rape could be and indeed was a weapon, deliberately planned and systematically implemented. They failed to recognise that such rape was an issue, not only for women, but also for communities including children and men. This was not an uncommon response.

---

[1] Fitzpatrick, B, 1992, *Rape of women in war*, Geneva: World Council of Churches, p 21.

[2] Ibid, pp 21-2.

[3] Ibid.

In 1999, I presented another report to humanitarian organisations and to a cross-party group of women senators in the Australian government.[4] The report highlighted that widespread rape was occurring in the conflict in Kosovo. In 1996, widespread sexual violence had been defined as sexual violence 'committed on a large scale' and directed against a 'multiplicity of victims'.[5] The response this time, from a senior executive in the Australian humanitarian agency that had funded the investigation, was, 'It is not a story – men are being killed'. Despite its long history of prevalence and the work of many feminist scholars, rape in conflict had been largely ignored. Rather than seeing it as a violation of humanitarian law or as behaviour that was preventable, there had been a general acceptance of rape as an inevitable part of conflict. Such a restricted view had centuries of negative implications for women and communities, and facilitated the ongoing use of rape in conflict. This persistent denial and mischaracterisation had:

> ... reinforced its acceptance as a natural, if regrettable, aspect of war rather than as a crime under humanitarian law. Implicit tolerance by military and political leaders signifies implicit permission (and) can lead to condoning it and thereby to an overt strategy that utilises rape as a weapon of war.[6]

The long-standing refusal to confront the strategic, tactical use of rape in war finally gradually began to be overcome in the 1990s, at least in international discourse, although it is a violation that continues.

I spent many years visiting refugee camps and conflict arenas. It was after the response of others involved in humanitarian work – people who were prepared to work to alleviate suffering but who accepted rape in conflict as inevitable – that I joined with many others who protested such acceptance. It is acknowledged that my perspective may at times be influenced by an attempt to keep faith with those women with whom I sat on cold, concrete floors, and those with whom I sat in the African darkness, who often held my hand and cried as they told

[4] Fitzpatrick, B, 1999, *Kosovo – The women and children*, Burwood, VIC: World Vision Australia.

[5] International Law Commission, 1996, *Report of the International Law Commission on the work of its Forty-Eighth Session* (6 May–26 July 1996), Official Records of the General Assembly, Fifty-first Session, Supplement No 10, United Nations Doc A/51/10, New York.

[6] Farwell, N, 2004, War rape: new conceptualisations and responses, *AFFILIA: Journal of Women and Social Work*, 19, 4, Winter, p 389.

of what had happened to women in wars. Sometimes it was couched as 'this woman I know' or 'my sister' or 'my daughter'. Sometimes it was admitted as the teller's own tale. They were stories of great courage, terrible suffering and of the additional outrage of shame and degradation felt by victims. Their specific stories and names are not used in this book, but the stories of others who faced the pain of courts represent them. In this book reference is made to testimonies in international tribunals, as these are formal documents and records of experiences. They are included to ensure that the personal faces of those who suffer rape in conflict are not lost in objective analyses.

These women and all those who suffer rape and sexual violence in war are the people who make it important to take action against such violations. Perpetrators include both state and non-state actors, so it can only be a starting point to consider states' commitments and declarations – but it is a starting point. Tracking and analyses of primary sources such as reports, debates, testimonies and decisions help understand how attitudes did change. While they are not the solution, it is important to understand the commitments made by states and relevant legal judgements. These provided the basis for calling those same states to recognise their responsibilities to desist from using rape as a tactic, to prevent and confront these crimes and to ensure accountability for those who perpetrate them.

It is a further injustice that, as will be seen particularly in Chapters Five and Six, women suffer so often in courts where they should find some recourse and resolution. It is essential that work continue to find alternative methods to hold perpetrators accountable. There is no final resolution and there are significant challenges and gaps in approaches and responses. But the women who have spoken out for themselves and for others who have suffered are the reason why it matters to have United Nations (UN) Security Council resolutions and formal rejection as at least a basis for confronting rape in conflict. These women are the reason why it matters to follow through with sustained actions to implement action, which will eventually provide some protection and justice for victims of rape and sexual violence used as tactics in conflict.

This book focuses on one type of rape in conflict, but recognises that there are various other types of rape in war. There are rapes of individuals by individuals, rapes by out-of-control soldiers or criminals who act without any authorisation. These can be referred to as 'by-products' of conflict within the context of a concomitant breakdown of law and order. They are matters of concern and should be confronted and prevented. There can also be rape offered as a reward for victorious forces. During the Russian army advance through Germany in 1944-45, 2 million women were raped with Stalin's blessing on the grounds that 'the boys are entitled to their fun'.[7] The Japanese Imperial Army enslaved up to 200,000 women and girls from 1932 to 1945.[8] Euphemistically and insidiously known as 'comfort women', they were continuously raped and forced to provide sexual services to soldiers throughout the Pacific, including Portuguese Timor (now East Timor) and the Solomon Islands. Women were kept for months or years on end; most were under the age of 20, but some were as young as 12. Permission for such rape and availability of these women constituted part of the conditions of employment of soldiers.

Recent reports emerging from Syria in 2013 indicated some element of reward in current conflicts as well as authorised rape:

> "They were ordered to take this one, to take 'your portion'," she says. "And they would take it.""We were all blindfolded and raped and we would not know who was raping us," she says, tearing up for the first time in our interview. Before being blindfolded, she could see what she calls the "boss" sit in front of them, teaching them "exactly what to do and say to us."[9]

There are difficulties in documenting violations in this ingoing conflict in Syria, but non-governmental organisations (NGOs), including Human Rights Watch and Amnesty International, are credibly reporting such incidences, and these are considered in Chapter Two. Exchanges such as this one with the comment about combatants having a due 'portion' appear to link with a concept of reward or entitlement. There has been a long tradition of victors claiming the right to rape, and licence to rape has been used as a term of employment for mercenary soldiers.[10]

Christine Chinkin, who has provided numerous insights to the issue of rape and sexual violence, stated in one paper that 'women are

---

[7] Robertson, G, 1999, *Crimes against humanity: The struggle for global justice*, New York: Allen Lane, 1999, p 306.

[8] See www.amnesty.org/en/latest/campaigns/2015/09/70-years-on-comfort-women-speak-out-so-the-truth-wont-die

[9] Wolfe, L, 2013, "Take your portion": a victim speaks out about rape in Syria, 18 June, Women Under Siege.

[10] Chinkin, C, 1994, Rape and abuse of women in international law, Symposium – The Yugoslav crisis: New international law issues, *European Journal of International Law*, 5, 326-41.

attacked in conflicts across the globe by men of all colours, religions, nationalities and ideologies'.[11] While this book focuses on one particular form of rape in conflict, it is not in any way to set one form of violation as more important or more insidious than another. There is no assumption that all men rape, or that all military men rape. There is a case on record where a woman was judged guilty of colluding in the suffering of other women in relation to rape attack in conflict.[12]

The term 'tactical rape'

I use the term 'tactical rape' to refer to rape that is used as a tactic by state or non-state actors to attack individuals, groups and communities deemed to be enemies in conflicts, which may be intra- or inter-state. Tactical rape targets civilians, particularly, although not exclusively, women and girls. Gendered social, political, economic and physical inequity creates gendered vulnerability that is a pervasive precondition for effective use of tactical rape as a specific strategy to control, destabilise and even to destroy the social fabric of civilian communities. It can be a strategy to remove populations from one geographic area to another. It is a widespread, deliberate policy of attack, promoted or condoned by at least one party to a conflict, and it may constitute a war crime, a crime against humanity, and may be used as a weapon of genocide, of torture or of ethnic cleansing.[13]

This definition of tactical rape reflects the growing recognition of widespread, policy-directed use of rape as a deliberate tactic of attack. Since the 1990s, recognition of the full impact of tactical rape and its rejection has evolved into recognition and rejection of sexual violence in conflict situations. The international community has defined sexual violence in a number of key documents. This is a term that is comprehensive but frequently used without specific

---

[11] Ibid, p 328.

[12] On 24 June 2011, the International Criminal Tribunal for Rwanda (ICTR) sentenced Nyiramasuhuko to life imprisonment, after being convicted of conspiracy to commit genocide, extermination, rape, persecution, murder and other inhumane acts. In the summary of the judgement, the tribunal indicated that the former minister 'has agreed with other members of the interim government to commit genocide in Butare', and she 'exercised command responsibility over the Interahamwe [militia] who committed the rapes in Butare prefecture office'. Her appeal was being heard in 2015. See www.trial-ch.org/en/resources/trial-watch/trial-watch/profiles/profile/201/action/show/controller/Profile/tab/legal-procedure.html

[13] Each of these terms is defined in the course of later analysis.

definition, in overlapping and potentially confusing ways. Achuthan and Black pointed out that it is useful to recognise three non-mutually exclusive categories for describing sexual crimes: sexual violence, sexual exploitation and gender-based violence.[14]

In the Rome Statute of the International Criminal Court (ICC) (1998), rape appears in a comprehensive list of acts that are deemed sexual violence. When defining crimes against humanity, the Statute lists 'Rape, sexual slavery, enforced prostitution, forced pregnancy, enforced sterilization, or any other form of sexual violence of comparable gravity'.[15] This list is repeated when defining war crimes and is extended to include 'any other form of sexual violence also constituting a serious violation of article 3 common to the four Geneva Conventions.'[16]

The second term commonly used in discussion is 'sexual exploitation and abuse'. There are two concepts inherent in this term. Sexual exploitation has been defined by the UN Secretary-General as 'any actual or attempted abuse of a position of vulnerability, differential power or trust for sexual purposes including but not limited to, profiting monetarily, socially or politically from the sexual exploitation of another.'[17] Sexual abuse has been defined as 'actual or threatened physical intrusion of a sexual nature, whether by force or under unequal or coercive conditions.'[18] This terminology became particularly relevant in the formulation of UN Security Council resolution 1325, discussed more fully in Chapter Seven later. It reflects the understanding that sexual violence may encompass a variety of forms of attack.

Comprehending the reality, causes and implications of gender-based violence is key to comprehending and responding to tactical rape. Gender-based violence was defined in 1992 with reference to the *Convention on the Elimination of All Forms of Discrimination Against Women* (CEDAW). The monitoring committee of CEDAW referred to the Convention, which in Article 1 defines gender-based violence as:

> ... violence that is directed against a woman because she is a woman or that affects women disproportionately. It

---

[14] Achuthan, M, Black, R, 2009, *United Nations resolution 1820: A preliminary assessment of the challenges and opportunities*, September, New York: International Women's Tribune Centre, p 11.

[15] Rome Statute of the ICC, 1998, Article 7, para 1(g).

16 Ibid, para 2(e).

[17] UN Secretariat, *Special measures for protection from sexual exploitation and sexual abuse*, ST/SGB/2003, 9 October 2003, Section 1.

[18] Ibid, Section 1.

includes acts that inflict physical, mental or sexual harm or suffering, threats of such acts, coercion and other deprivations of liberty.[19]

The recognition that women are made particularly vulnerable because of their gender is of paramount importance. While women may be targeted because of their ethnicity or their political or social grouping, they are often targeted as a result of their gender having been used as part of rendering them more vulnerable. In recent wars, particularly in the Democratic Republic of Congo (DRC) and Darfur, men have been targeted for rape, and further reports from Syria include accounts of men and boys suffering sexual violence.[20] However, overwhelmingly the numbers from conflicts, such as those considered in Chapter Two, indicate that women are disproportionately targeted. Gender-based violence includes violent acts such as rape, torture, mutilation, sexual slavery, forced impregnation and murder and threats of such acts.[21] It can be perpetrated by both state and non-state actors.

In defining tactical rape, there is reference to widespread or systematic abuse as an element of tactical rape and/or sexual violence in conflict. As noted earlier in this chapter, in 1996 the International Law Commission defined widespread sexual violence as sexual violence 'committed on a large scale' and directed against a 'multiplicity of victims'.[22] In 2000, the International Criminal Tribunal for the former Yugoslavia (ICTY) said that systematic violence referred to the 'organised nature of acts of violence' and not 'random occurrences'.[23] In 2008 widespread or systematic violence was deemed to be violence during conflict perpetrated by armed groups 'as a strategy of warfare for obtaining political and military ends', and 'is used to torture, terrorize, demoralize, injure, degrade, intimidate and punish affected populations.'[24] Taken together, these definitions elicited the key elements of widespread and systematic sexual violence.

---

[19] UN Women, 1992, *Convention on the Elimination of All Forms of Discrimination against Women*, General Recommendation No 19, 11th session, New York.

[20] Wolfe, L, 2013, Syria has a massive rape crisis, 3 April, Women Under Siege.

[21] Achuthan and Black, op cit, p 11.

[22] International Law Commission, op cit.

[23] ICTY, *The Prosecutor v Tihomir Bla, Judgement*, Case No IT-95-14-T, 3 March 2000.

[24] Goertz, A-M, Anderson, L, 2008, *Women targeted or affected by armed conflict: What role for military peacekeepers?*, Conference summary, 27-29 May, New York: United Nations Development Fund for Women.

Rape and international law

Numerous analysts have reviewed the place of rape in international law. This has often been a matter of noting the omission of any mention of rape or the lack of understanding the nature of rape, particularly tactical rape. There is some, albeit limited, recognition of rape even when it is not specifically mentioned in international law. It is in the areas of international humanitarian law and human rights law that there is most often reference to rape, especially rape in conflict. Scott defined international law as:

> ... a system of rules, principles and concepts that governs relations among states and, increasingly, international organisations, individuals and other actors in world politics.[25]

Scott highlighted the need to 'appreciate that international law, although an integral part of politics is also to a large extent, autonomous.'[26] She claimed that as there is no international legislature, it is the case that rules, concepts and principles come from a variety of sources. These include treaties, which are 'agreements between states, between states and international organisations or between international organisations'.[27] Treaties may be bilateral such as between an international organisation and a specific state, or between two states. They may be multilateral between states, such as those within a geographic region, or between a larger number of states aiming at global participation. The UN Charter[28] requires member states to register all treaties with the UN Secretariat.[29]

The other source of international law is customary international law, which was once the most important source of international law: 'Custom is created by what states do, where that action is carried out with a view to the rules and principles of international law.'[30] Whatever the source of international law, its enforcement is problematic and it is gendered in content and nature.

---

[25] Scott, SV, 2004, *International law in world politics*, Boulder, CO: Lynne Rienner Publishers, p 1.

[26] Ibid, p 2.

[27] Ibid, p 3.

[28] Charter of the United Nations www.un.org/en/documents/charter

[29] Ibid, pp 4, 5.

[30] Ibid, p 6.

Scott noted that international law operates 'in a state-based system that is anarchical' made up of 'sovereign equals', so enforcing compliance must rely on retortion, 'unfriendly but legal acts', countermeasures, 'acts that would be illegal except that they are carried out in response to an illegal act by the other party' or by rewarding compliance with assistance.[31] There are some limited judiciaries established to enforce compliance. But as Scott noted, it is in the Statute of the International Court of Justice (ICJ) that the sources of international law have been formally articulated. These include treaties (international conventions), international custom, 'general principles of law recognised by civilised nations' and 'judicial decisions and the teachings of the most highly qualified publicists of the various nations'.[32]

The term 'civilised nations' is now understood as 'states', and 'general principles' is understood to refer to:

> ... general principles of law common to a representative majority of domestic legal orders which includes the main forms of civilisation and the principle legal systems of the world.[33]

The definition of states is set out in the 1933 Montevideo Convention:

> A State must have a permanent population, a defined territory and a government capable of maintaining effective control over its territory and of conducting international relations with other States.[34]

This definition becomes particularly relevant as analysis of UN Security Council actions emerges later in this book. It will also become apparent that states are not always willing or ready to maintain effective control over their territory, and that there is an ongoing tension between expectations that states will protect their citizens from tactical rape and the knowledge that in many cases states are perpetrating tactical rape.

Judicial decisions refer to judgements of tribunals and courts and writings of distinguished international lawyers that can be utilised

---

[31] Ibid, p 10.

[32] Statute of the ICJ, Article 38(1), quoted in Scott, ibid, p 11.

[33] Mosler, H, 1995, General principles of law, in *Encyclopaedia of Public International Law*, 2, 511-27, 516-517, and others, quoted in Scott, ibid, p 12.

[34] Scott, SV, Billingsley, AJ, Michaelson, C, 2010, *International law and the use of force: A documentary and reference guide*, Santa Barbara, CA, Denver, CO and Oxford: Praeger Security International ABC-CLIO, LLC, p 14.

to inform judgements.[35] The ICTY and the International Criminal Tribunal for Rwanda (ICTR) are judiciaries that are a particular focus of this book, and their rulings are analysed to understand and evaluate their actual and potential contribution to rejection of tactical rape and sexual violence in conflict. These tribunals were mandated by the Security Council to operate within the limits of existing law. It was by doing this that rulings demanded recognition that tactical rape and sexual violence in conflict violated existing standards and agreements. As detailed in later chapters, they established that no new law was needed because tactical rape and sexual violence in war were deemed to be violations of existing international law.

One area of international law most applicable to tactical rape is international humanitarian law (*jus in bello*), the laws by which war should be fought and which have been codified in numerous legal instruments since the 19th century. Scott pointed out, however, that rules of conducting war had been set out in much earlier times such as in the wars between the Egyptians and the Sumerians in the second millennium BC, and rules prohibiting the use of poisoned arrows by Hindus set out in the ancient Laws of Manu.[36] Scott et al provided a detailed context for modern humanitarian law, and noted that currently, modern humanitarian law has two streams: that pertaining to limitations or prohibitions of specific means and methods of warfare (the Hague laws), and that regarding the protection of civilians and those no longer fighting (the Geneva laws).[37] This second set of laws is the primary focus of this consideration of the legal context for rejecting tactical rape and sexual violence. As later analysis will show, there are grounds for dealing with tactical rape under the Geneva laws, known as the Geneva Conventions and their Additional Protocols.[38] It is Convention IV, concerning the protection of civilians, which will be shown to apply most clearly to tactical rape and sexual violence in war in Chapters Five and Six.

---

[35] Ibid, p 12.

[36] Roberts, A, Guelff, R, 1996, *Documents on the laws of war*, 3rd edn, New York: Oxford University Press, p 29, quoted in Scott et al, op cit, p 245.

[37] Scott et al, ibid, pp 245-6.

[38] UN, 1949, *Geneva Convention I for the Amelioration of the Condition of the Wounded and Sick in Armed Forces in the Field*; UN, 1949, *Geneva Convention II for the Amelioration of the Condition of the Wounded, Sick and Shipwrecked Members of Armed Forces at Sea*; UN, 1949, *Geneva Convention III Concerning the Treatment of Prisoners of War*; UN, 1949, *Geneva Convention IV Concerning the Protection of Civilian Persons in Time of War*.

Scott, among others, acknowledged that the distinction between the two streams became less clear after the 1977 Additional Protocols to the Geneva Conventions, which address both issues.[39] The Additional Protocols are the *Protocol Additional to the Geneva Conventions of 12 August 1949 and relating to the Protection of Victims of International Arms Conflicts* and the *Protocol Additional to the Geneva Conventions of 12 August 1949 and relating to the Protection of Victims of Non-international Armed Conflicts*. There is still a considerable degree of invisibility of women in Geneva law, but Article 76(i) of Additional Protocol I does at least stipulate that 'women shall be the object of special respect and shall be protected against rape, forced prostitution and any other forms of indecent assault.' Women are in need of protection – a double-edged sword, as will be considered later in Chapter Three. Protocol II was the first piece of international law to acknowledge the need for the protection of those in non-international conflicts. This was an important and relevant development when considering events in Rwanda and the former Yugoslavia as well as in more recent conflicts. The ICTY and ICTR built on these protocols and applied interpretations of the other major treaty in international humanitarian law, the 1948 UN *Convention on the Prevention and Punishment of the Crime of Genocide (the Genocide Convention)* (a focus in Chapter Six). As well as the Genocide Convention and the four Geneva Conventions with Additional Protocol II, which are referenced in the statutes of the ICTY, ICTR and ICC, there are some key international agreements that are relevant to tactical rape and sexual violence in war. These include the 1979 UN *Convention on the Elimination of All Forms of Discrimination Against Women* and *Optional Protocol*, the 1948 *Universal Declaration of Human Rights* and the 1993 *Declaration on the Elimination of Violence Against Women*.

It is essential to understand the developments in international humanitarian law in recent decades in order to analyse its relatively recent application to tactical rape and sexual violence in war. Dietrich Schindler outlined two contradictory aspects: enormous progress in attaining almost universal recognition, and the gross violations of that law in inhumane and cruel acts committed in armed conflicts in the same period.[40] He referred to the 'remarkable normative development of international humanitarian law since 1949', and reviewed the phases

[39] Scott et al, op cit, p 246.
[40] Schindler, D, 1999, Significance of the Geneva Conventions for the contemporary world, *International Review of the Red Cross*, 81, 836, December, 715-28.

of this development.[41] He identified five major developments since the end of the Cold War. The first was a realisation by the Security Council, 'that large scale violations of human rights and international humanitarian law and the ensuing magnitude of human suffering can constitute a threat to international peace.'[42] Schindler referred to specific resolutions that included mention of situations in the former Yugoslavia (Bosnia) and Rwanda, where the Security Council determined that violations of international humanitarian law constitute a threat to international peace and security.[43]

The second development was that the distinction between international and non-international conflicts lost much of its significance.[44] Later analysis will indicate that this was certainly applicable when confronting the conflicts in the former Yugoslavia and Rwanda. The third development was the growing importance of customary law in judicial decision-making. The fourth was the increasing influence of human rights law on international humanitarian law. The fifth development was in a judgement of the ICJ, which ruled that the principles of international humanitarian law 'belong to the most fundamental norms of international law, norms which form part of what could be called the unwritten constitution of the international community.'[45]

As the rejection of tactical rape and sexual violence was discussed in international forums, the role of tribunals such as the ICTY and ICTR and their case decisions is a crucial focus. Such focus, however, also reinforces Schindler's acknowledgement of the massive lack of compliance and acknowledgment of the increased levels of violent conflicts in the years since the conflicts in the former Yugoslavia and Rwanda. Much of the analysis in this book is of progress in states' declarations and actions to confront tactical rape, but these are accompanied by ongoing use of tactical rape by at least some of those same states. NGOs and other non-state actors have been crucial in

[41] Ibid, p 716.

[42] Ibid, p 720.

[43] UN Security Council, *Security Council resolution 929 (1994) [on Rwanda]*, 22 June 1994; UN Security Council, *Security Council resolution 770 (1992) [on Bosnia and Herzegovina]*, 18 December 1992; UN Security Council, *Security Council resolution 808 (1993) [on former Yugoslavia]*, 22 February 1993; UN Security Council, *Security Council resolution 827 (1993) [on former Yugoslavia]*, 25 May 1993; UN Security Council, *Security Council resolution 955 (1994) [on Rwanda]*, S/RES/955, 8 November 1994.

[44] Schindler, op cit, p 721.

[45] Ibid, p 723.

achieving this progress, and they will need to continue advocacy and action to sustain further progress.

Review and analysis will show that tactical rape in war is a reality, a strategy that specifically and deliberately targets civilians, which is perniciously effective with immediate and long-term destructive impact. It is a real threat, and the international community of states has increasingly recognised its responsibility and a self-interested motive to confront it, to prevent it, and to hold accountable those who perpetrate it. Yet state actors remain among the perpetrators. It is imperative to recognise that tactical rape as I define it is essentially a military weapon, used to gain political ends. As with any rape, it is not primarily to do with sexuality.

Scope of analysis

The type of rape that is the focus here is not rape as a right or a reward for victory, but rape as a policy and a tactic to effect military or political victory. Tactical rape as a military strategy has an immediate negative physical, emotional and communal impact on women and civilian populations (including men) during conflict. Because of how societies are constructed, there are also long-lasting negative economic, cultural and social impacts on women, men, children and communities. The cases and accounts of the use of rape in conflicts since the 1990s illustrate these effects. There is also consideration of the role of societal values and attitudes, such as patriarchy and perceptions of masculinity, in fostering and increasing the effectiveness of tactical rape. Tactical rape has been recognised as having an impact that hinders transitions from conflict to peace and peacemaking, destabilises communities and states, and can be a threat to international security.

There are increasing reports of rape and sexual violence being used against men and boys as well as against women and girls, and they are referenced in this book. However, overwhelmingly, the constructed gendered inequality of females within societies makes them most vulnerable to attack by tactical rape, and therefore this book concentrates primarily on women and girls.

In 2013, the Security Council noted:

> ... that sexual violence in armed conflict and post-conflict situations disproportionately affects women and girls, as well as groups that are particularly vulnerable or may be specifically targeted, while also affecting men and boys and those secondarily traumatized as forced witnesses of sexual

violence against family members; and emphasizing that acts of sexual violence in such situations not only severely impede the critical contributions of women to society, but also impede durable peace and security as well as sustainable development.[46]

While women and girls are primary victims of tactical rape, there are serious and long-lasting effects on their communities, and these are considered throughout this book. Recognition and understanding of tactical rape can support recognition that this form of sexual violence needs a specific response if women, men, children, communities and states are to be protected from such attacks. It also supports the realisation, implicit in some of the documents to be analysed in later chapters, that if women are made vulnerable to sexual violence in peace, they will be made even more vulnerable in conflict.

Analysis of UN documents will show that in recent decades there has been a significant shift in discourse, debate, resolutions and the institutionalisation of responses around the issue of sexual violence in conflict in the Security Council and other international bodies. There has been recognition of the implications for states' security when rape and sexual violence are perpetrated in conflict. In international policy and practice, the issue of rape and sexual violence in conflict has moved from being regarded as 'just' an issue of security for women, to an issue of human security, and finally to being recognised as an issue for the security of states.

As galling as this may be to workers (such as myself) who are feminists and advocates of justice and protection for women and girls, it has facilitated a more effective response to the issue even though the impact on women and girls actually caught in conflict has been limited. It is important to understand this shift in attitude, to be aware of the grounds and the processes of the shift, and to be cognisant of the commitments made by key stakeholders. This understanding is the basis for ongoing work to ensure lasting rejection, condemnation and prevention of the use of tactical rape and sexual violence in conflict, and to insist on accountability for those who perpetrate this crime. It provides grounds for urging responsible responses in policy and practice from key stakeholders who have committed to resolutions and to upholding international humanitarian law.

---

[46]   UN Security Council, *Security Council resolution 2106 (2013) [on women and peace and security]*, 24 June 2013.

Significant steps in the change process include the findings of international tribunals that provided a body of case law and the debates and resolutions of the Security Council. While there has been considerable separate analysis of case law and of particular UN resolutions (much of this is referenced), it is important to see the interconnectedness of all these developments, to fully understand the foundations and processes of changing attitudes in order to facilitate ongoing responses to this issue. Effective strategies and best practice need to be recognised. The role of international NGOs has been considerable. But while there has been significant progress, ongoing challenges remain.

A key challenge is the need to move from international to national-level policy and practice. Understanding the shift at international level provides a foundation for working for state-level responses, monitoring and urging implementation of stated commitments. Later chapters will review some steps taken to implement international commitments at state levels, and consider the varying degrees of commitment and effectiveness, as evident in a review of some national action plans for the implementation of Security Council resolution 1325. There will also be a specific focus on the tribunal contributions and limitations in the aftermath of the violence in Rwanda and the former Yugoslavia. Additional references and challenges will include more recent conflicts such as Sierra Leone, the DRC, Sudan and Syria. While these state responses (or lack of responses) emanate from the global shift in attitudes, it is the significant shift at international level that is the primary focus here. In the years from the early 1990s until 2014, there were significant international judgements, statements, resolutions and policy decisions that indicated a growing awareness of the implications for state security of the use of rape in war. These have been evident at international criminal tribunals, the ICC, ICJ, Security Council and the UN General Assembly, in UN member states, international NGOs, UN agencies and the G8. For this review and analysis these are the entities that comprise 'the international community'. Discourse between these entities since the 1990s indicates the development of normative rejection of the use of tactical rape and sexual violence in conflict. John Dryzek defined discourse as, 'the sets of concepts, categories and ideas that provide ways to understand and act in the world, whether or not those who subscribe to them are aware of their existence.'[47] The discourse will be analysed in the context of understanding the changing nature of

---

[47] Dryzek, JS, 2006, *Deliberative global politics: Discourse and democracy in a divided world*, Cambridge: Polity Press, p vi.

war. It will consider judicial decisions and applications of international humanitarian law and Security Council debates, resolutions and subsequent institutionalisation contributing to a growing normative rejection of sexual violence in conflict. This is based on the definition of norms as 'collective expectations about proper behaviour for a given identity' as distinct from principled ideas that are defined as 'beliefs about right and wrong held by individuals'.[48] The development of collective expectations within and by communities will be examined in Chapters Three and Four.

Analysis will include consideration of a number of questions – what contributions did the conflicts and ad hoc ICTY and ICTR make to the international community's eventual formally articulated rejection of sexual violence and tactical rape? What degree of understanding and commitment to rejecting sexual violence and tactical rape and understanding the broader concept of sexual violence is reflected in Security Council resolutions since the early 1990s? To what extent do the interests of human security and international stability intersect, and how has realisation of this intersection contributed to a normative rejection of tactical rape and sexual violence? What more is needed to demonstrate a serious international commitment to rejecting sexual violence and tactical rape?

This analysis will show that there has been a gradual move to the international rejection of tactical rape and sexual violence as they represent an issue of international security, because this ongoing form of abuse, which is a threat to human security, is also a threat to international peace and stability. The use of sexual violence and tactical rape as military strategies represents a failure of compliance with accepted international humanitarian and human rights law, and impedes international responses to humanitarian crises. As tactical rape and sexual violence are understood in their totality as strategies for targeting civilians in conflict, contravening accepted international humanitarian and human rights law, there is a consequent imperative to prevent such violations, to hold perpetrators accountable, and to provide justice for survivors. There has been some inconsistent but gradual realisation that accountability and justice must be evident during transitions from war

---

[48] Jepperson, RL, Wendt, A, Katzenstein, PJ, 1996, Norms, identity, and culture in national security, in PJ Katzenstein (ed), *Culture and national security*, New York: Colombia University Press, p 54, cited in Risse, T, Sikkink, K, 1999, The socialisation of international human rights norms into domestic practices, in T Risse, SC Ropp and K Sikkink (eds), *The power of human rights: International norms and domestic change*, Cambridge: Cambridge University Press, p 7.

to peace and in the longer-term post-conflicts because the provision of justice is essential to avoid re-emergence of the same sort of conflicts.

Analysis of Security Council resolutions will show that states have slowly begun to accept responsibility and to respond accordingly. Because tactical rape and sexual violence can destabilise states and hinder peacemaking and peacekeeping, it is in states' interest to respond and take action to confront such attacks. In 1999, the UK Prime Minister, Tony Blair, outlined a new *Doctrine of the international community*, and stated as part of that, 'we cannot turn our backs on conflicts and the violations of human rights in other countries if we still want to be secure.'[49] Political will to confront tactical rape and sexual violence in conflict has followed more from a gradual realisation of it as a threat to international peace and security than from a perception of rape in war as a women's issue.

Analysis of the increasing discourse in Security Council resolutions and debates shows increased global comprehension that the use of rape as a deliberate, multifaceted tactic in conflict is an issue that falls within the mandate and responsibility of the Security Council. It will show an emerging realisation that there is also a multifaceted impact on states, that tactical rape is a threat to human security, to the security of women, to the security of populations and to international security. Confronting tactical rape as a deliberate strategy employed in varying ways by parties to conflicts must be comprehensive and requires state action as one response. This book will show that rape can be a weapon of war or a crime against humanity, a weapon of torture or ethnic cleansing, or a weapon of genocide.[50]

Recognition of the comprehensive range of uses and impact of tactical rape has resulted in a more direct understanding by states of their responsibilities, and recognition that it is in their own self-interest to ensure compliance with international humanitarian and human rights laws. While at least some policies of some states have begun to reflect, in practice, normative rejection of tactical rape, such rejection is still largely limited to the international arena and some states continue to employ tactical rape. At an international level, focusing on the complex totality of tactical rape has resulted in comprehension of tactical rape as one particular strategy among many that constitute sexual violence, and has gradually led to a more comprehensive response to confronting

---

[49] Blair, A, 1999, *Doctrine of the international community*, Hilton Hotel, Chicago, IL, 22 April.

[50] Each of these will be considered in later chapters, including Chapter Six, which specifically deals with genocide.

sexual violence. Relevant Security Council resolutions are now entitled 'women, peace and security', covering concerns for women in conflict situations, and since the 1990s have increasingly recognised that tactical rape and sexual violence relate to human security and international security. Strong calls from the public and pressure from NGOs to respond to widespread tactical rape developed into strong calls to respond to the broader practice of sexual violence in conflict, and eventually to a greater understanding of the links between women's vulnerability in peace and in conflict and human and state security.

While there have been other tribunals, other relevant conflicts and many other relevant UN documents, outcomes from the conflicts in the former Yugoslavia and Rwanda and Security Council resolutions and debates around resolutions 1325 and 1820 particularly moved the understanding of tactical rape into understanding sexual violence. They brought these violations into international consideration in important and major ways. With all their flaws – and there are many – these moments in the development of the discourse have provided the building blocks for normative change, and they warrant particular (although not exclusive) attention and analysis.

Changing context

Consideration of rape in war began to change in the early 1990s with increased recognition of rape in war as a policy-based attack against civilians, requiring it to be considered 'as a weapon, a targeted act of terror, rather than merely as a by-product of the violence surrounding war.'[51] Understanding sexual violence and rape as a tactic in conflict is comprehensible when linked with recognising the changing nature of war in recent decades.[52] Mary Kaldor, in her insightful consideration, wrote of 'new wars' tending to avoid battles between armies and instead aiming at control of territory through 'political, psychological and economic techniques of intimidation.'[53] When referring to wars in the Balkans and Africa, she wrote that in these conflicts, 'warring parties share the aim of sowing "fear and hatred" and "create a climate of insecurity and suspicion".'[54] Kaldor also wrote, 'essentially, what were considered to be undesirable and illegitimate side-effects of old

---

[51] Farwell, op cit, p 390.
[52] A fuller account of the changing nature of war is provided in Chapter Three.
[53] Kaldor, M, 2002, *New and old wars: Organised violence in a global era*, Cambridge: Polity Press, p 8.
[54] Ibid, p 9.

war have become central to the mode of fighting in the new wars.'[55] Tactical rape is an ideal strategy to achieve the aims of these new wars.

While Edward Newman claimed that Kaldor had overstated the differences between old and new wars, he also acknowledged that tactics such as widespread rape characterised current conflicts.[56] Review of the use of rape in conflicts in the former Yugoslavia and Rwanda and more recently in conflicts in the DRC, Sudan, Sierra Leone, Syria and with IS, will show that in these conflicts, violence was, and is, directed against civilian populations. Tactics such as rape and sexual violence are effective ways of targeting women and the communities of which they are part. As part of the civilian population, women and girls (and increasingly men and boys) experience generalised violence. They may be killed, murdered, imprisoned or tortured, but as a result of their gender, women and girls experience additional, more specific violence. They may be raped, forced into prostitution, suffer forced impregnation, be pressured by social and cultural attitudes into abortions, and may suffer particular forms of humiliation, degradation, rejection or exclusion.

This method of waging wars, by attacking civilians and communities rather than directly facing enemies in delineated battles between armies, is fertile ground for the use of rape as a deliberate tactic. Retired Major General Patrick Cammaert, Former Division Commander of the UN Organization Stabilization Mission in the DRC (MONUSCO), said in 2008, in a Security Council debate preceding resolution 1820, that the climate of impunity in most post-conflict contexts allowed the many forms of violence, including sexual violence, to flourish.[57] Further, he noted that the political will to end the vicious cycle of impunity did not exist, and this remained a serious impediment for the prevention of sexual violence. He said, 'it has probably become more dangerous to be a woman than a soldier in an armed conflict'.[58] The use of this particular tactic of waging new wars is an issue for states and entire populations; it is not an issue restricted to concern for one sector of states and populations.

---

[55] Ibid, p 100.

[56] Newman, E, 2004, The "new wars" debate: a historical perspective is needed, *Security Dialogue*, 35, 2, 173-89.

[57] UN, *Security Council demands immediate and complete halt to acts of sexual violence against civilians in conflict zones, unanimously adopting resolution 1820 (2008)*, SC/9364, 19 June 2008.

[58] Ibid.

International action

Growing media and NGO awareness of tactical rape eventually evolved into more widespread rejection of any form of sexual violence in conflict. International law, particularly as case law emerged from the ICTY and ICTR, provided a basis to establish state obligation to prevent, prosecute, hold accountable and disallow impunity for perpetrators of tactical rape and sexual violence in conflict. It became possible to demonstrate where existing law could and should be applied, and to confront arguments against its application. Existing obligations were demonstrated. These required understanding and applying sources of customary law, humanitarian law, human rights law and, importantly, judicial case law.

Emerging case law from the ICTY and ICTR provided a substantial body of definitions and interpretations of international law. While the work of other international courts will be referenced, it was in these two judiciaries that significant normative progress occurred, and it is the outcomes of these two tribunals that will be shown to have been watersheds. Writing in 2003, Kelly Dawn Askin noted, 'ten years ago … there was debate as to whether rape was even a war crime. Since that time, the tribunals have developed immensely the jurisprudence of war crimes, crimes against humanity and genocide.'[59] The tribunals dealt with events in different contexts – one in Africa, one in Europe – but both dealt with arenas where tactical rape was perpetrated. Their similarities and differences helped to ensure a broad understanding of the issue. The extent and nature of the rapes in these two conflict arenas will be identified and judicial rulings and definitions will be analysed with consideration of the key existing instruments of international law and contributions to the discourse rejecting tactical rape and sexual violence.

Key Security Council resolutions also provide grounds for tracking and analysing the development of an international normative rejection of tactical rape. Particular resolutions were, at least in part, stimulated by the findings of the tribunals and built on the two sets of outcomes from those judiciaries. For this reason they are linked together in the development of an international recognition and response to sexual violence in conflict. Relevant resolutions include 1325 (2000), 1820 (2008), 1888 (2009) and others that followed until 2014. These are the

[59] Askin, K, 2003, Prosecuting wartime rape and other gender-related crimes under international law: extraordinary advances, enduring obstacles, *Berkeley Journal of International Law*, 21, 288-349, p 346.

focus of consideration because they reflect the growing attention to sexual violence and tactical rape in conflict, rape in its manifestations as contravention of international law. Tracking progress in these resolutions demonstrates that normative rejection of rape in conflict appears to be accelerating at a global level. This is also reflected in the development of the mandate and focus of the ICC. Resolutions will be analysed to evaluate the extent of progress in understanding the complexity and urgency of having a widely accepted norm rejecting tactical rape. Debates around these resolutions show the extent to which recognition of the security implications of tactical rape was increasingly expressed and increasingly provided motivation for confronting tactical rape specifically and sexual violence more broadly.

Threats to human and international security

The gradual move to the Security Council rejecting tactical rape and sexual violence in conflict can be linked to the increasing degree to which debates aligned tactical rape and sexual violence with security. It is necessary to recognise the links between threats to individuals, to human security and to international stability, peacekeeping and peacemaking. These threats endanger the security of states. Kaldor wrote of the complex relationship between processes of governance, legitimacy and forms of security, which she explained as 'how organised violence is controlled', and she contrasted this with the 'old wars' that were concerned with 'national security' in the sense of protection of territory and protection from external threats.[60] This brings to the fore the need to understand the interplay between the security of individuals, communities and states, states individually, and as a global collective.

The Commission on Human Security has urged increased recognition of human security as an overarching concept of security, broadening the focus from security of borders to security of people and communities inside and across those borders.[61] In its report, *Human security now 2002-2003,* the Commission wrote, 'all societies depend much more on the acts or omissions of others for the security of their people, even for their survival.'[62] Amitav Acharya wrote regarding human security, 'in an era of rapid globalisation, security must encompass a broader range of concerns and challenges than simply defending the state from

[60]   Kaldor, op cit, p 140.
[61]   Commission on Human Security, 2003, *Human security now 2002-2003*, p 6.
[62]   Ibid, p 12.

external military attack.'[63] In the new wars of the former Yugoslavia and Rwanda, security threats extended from the immediate, localised, internal territory to the international community whose laws of war and laws for the protection of the most basic of human rights were flouted, deliberately and extensively. These threats were eventually confronted with international tribunals and some forms of direct intervention into the sovereignty of states.

Between 2000 and 2014 the Security Council recognised the need for action in response to violence against women in conflict. There were significant instances of states' representatives in Security Council debates linking rape in war with the wellbeing and security of states. US Secretary of State, Condoleezza Rice, chairing a debate in 2008, commented that there had long been dispute about whether sexual violence against women in conflict was an issue the Security Council was authorised to address, and concluded, 'we affirm that sexual violence profoundly affects not only the health and safety of women, but the economic and social stability of their nations.'[64] Deputy Secretary-General Asha-Rose Migiro addressed the same meeting, saying that sexual violence had not only grave physical and psychological health consequences for its victims, but also direct social consequences for communities and entire societies: 'impunity for sexual violence committed during conflict perpetuates a tolerance of abuse against women and girls and leaves a damaging legacy by hindering national reconciliation.'[65] The Security Council debates, analysed more fully later in Chapters Seven, Eight and Nine, reflected an important step with states agreeing that rejection of tactical rape and sexual violence was indeed an issue for the Security Council, and could no longer be side-lined or dismissed as a sectoral issue somehow applying to women but not to states.

In 2009, US Secretary of State , Hillary Clinton, urged the Security Council to pursue the fight against sexual crimes, saying that sexual violence in conflict areas could not be separated from broader security issues on the Council's agenda.[66] Bedouma Alain Yoda, Minister for Foreign Affairs of Burkina Faso, averred that sexual crimes created long-lasting enmity between people, making it difficult to bring about

---

[63] Acharya, A, 2007, Human security, in J Baylis and S Smith (eds), *The globalisation of world politics*, 4th edn, Oxford: Oxford University Press, Chapter 28, p 492.

[64] UN Press Release, 19 June 2008, op cit.

[65] Ibid.

[66] UN, *Security Council adopts text mandating peacekeeping missions to protect women, girls from sexual violence in armed conflict*, 30 September 2009.

peace, and degrading the dignity of women reduced their crucial ability to contribute to peacemaking.[67] Recognition and rejection of tactical rape and sexual violence was on the agenda of the Security Council.

Establishing the parameters

This analysis and review focuses on tactical, widespread rape and sexual violence in conflict. There is usually rape of one sort or another on all sides of most conflicts. Women are disproportionately victims, and tactical rape and sexual violence are often employed by at least one side. It is the policy of widespread tactical use of sexual violence and rape in conflict that is the focus of this book. However, I acknowledge the justifiable concerns of those feminist writers who call for attention to all forms of rape, who worry that by putting a focus on one form of rape, other forms are somehow less recognised, or who worry that by focusing on international or state security, the suffering of women generally may somehow be overlooked. Lene Hansen feared that by making a distinction between individual and collective rape, awareness of the needs of the individual who suffers rape may be diminished.[68] This is understandable and a fear shared by many including myself, who would demand the accountability of all rapists. It is understandable because there is such a history and practice of ignoring rape of women in conflict and in peacetime.

This consideration of changed attitudes and responses does, however, limit itself to consideration of tactical rape and sexual violence that is organised and officially promulgated. Furthermore, it focuses on the outcomes of international tribunals and courts, particularly the ICTY and ICTR. This is done recognising the limitations and inappropriateness of how judicial systems can fail to recognise the suffering of women participating in confrontational and antagonistic proceedings that may justifiably be deemed another level of violence against victims. Focusing on legal proceedings is done with recognition of the validity of those who condemn the suffering that women experience when testifying in such courts. The perspectives of scholars who express such concerns regarding legal proceedings will be considered in more detail.

There is a particular focus on two conflicts, although there is a plethora of similar arenas such as the DRC, Sudan, Sierra Leone

---

[67] Ibid.
[68] Hansen, L, 2001, Gender, nation, rape: Bosnia and the construction of security, *International Feminist Journal of Politics*, 3, 1, April, p 63.

and Syria to be referenced.[69] Conflicts in Rwanda and the former Yugoslavia were watershed cases in the development of consideration and action regarding tactical rape. These were conflicts where there was widespread recognition of the use of tactical rape and sexual violence in war. Cases were documented and witness accounts verified, despite difficulties in establishing the exact numbers of rapes. Kaldor referred to the war in Bosnia–Herzegovina as having become 'the paradigm of the new type of warfare' and 'likely to turn out to be one of those defining events, in which entrenched political assumptions, strategic thinking and international arrangements are both challenged and reconstructed.'[70] She highlighted the techniques of population displacement in new wars: systematic murder, ethnic cleansing, rendering an area uninhabitable – physically, psychologically, economically – and noted that a method of defilement is 'through systematic rape and sexual abuse ... or by other public and very visible acts of brutality.'[71] Each technique can be explicitly applied to the conflicts in both the former Yugoslavia and in Rwanda.[72] Tactical rape was a deliberate policy and strategy of attacks on civilians, and rape was widespread.

The work of scholars is referenced in this analysis and reviewed with a strong focus on primary sources such as case judgements from the two tribunals, reports to the Security Council and specific resolutions. Some of these have received extensive scholarly attention, but others have not yet been the subject of extensive academic consideration. With some dearth of scholarly commentary, reports by NGOs, including some written by myself, are sometimes referenced, particularly where they stimulated action by the UN, the European Community, legal advocates and investigators. NGO reports were part of the pressure applied to have UN Special Rapporteurs extend the original areas of investigation, and eventually include reference to rape in the former Yugoslavia and Rwanda. Organisational reports of meetings and encounters in and around Zagreb and Rwanda written by NGO representatives included summary accounts of stories and concerns expressed by refugee women and workers in refugee camps. These were at times accounts from individuals whose identities were not published for reasons of their own security. They included prisoners

---

[69] Gilbert, G, What price justice? Prosecuting crime post-conflict, in U Dolgopol and J Gardam, 2006, *The challenge of conflict: International law responds*, Boston, MA and Leiden: Martinus Nijhoff Publishers, Chapter 22, p 440.

[70] Kaldor, op cit, p 32.

[71] Ibid, pp 99–100.

[72] Ibid, p 99.

who had escaped across the border into Zagreb, representatives of organisations including the UN High Commissioner for Refugees (UNHCR), documentation centres, women's houses, women's support and advocacy groups (such as Mothers for Peace, Help for Children in Croatia, Women of Bosnia-Herzegovina, Women of the Anti-War Campaign), from humanitarian assistance agencies and from church representatives, both Christian and Muslim. There was much input to relevant multilateral agencies and panels, and many reports and articles regarding these experiences were written and submitted to international organisations and activist groups. Insights from recorded and public accounts of personal, professional experience, particularly regarding certain actions taken by international NGOs, are also referenced. On occasion informal narrative can inform and stimulate responses from states, international agencies and judiciaries.

Conclusion

Tactical rape has been defined as rape used as a tactic by state or non-state actors to attack individuals – particularly, but not exclusively, women and girls – and groups and communities deemed to be enemies in conflict that may be inter- or intra-state. There has been significant progress in developing normative rejection of tactical rape and sexual violence in conflict. Progress has been largely at a global level, with recognition and response to this violation of international law as a threat to human security and to state security. However, major challenges remain as tactical rape continues to be perpetrated in international, national and local conflicts. Certain steps have been effective in bringing about change in international understanding, recognition and confrontation of the use of rape in conflict. The aim of this book is to contribute to ensuring that such steps are noted, understood and, where appropriate, replicated to ensure attention to the ongoing problems of the use of rape in conflict. Primary sources are referenced, such as UN and NGO reports and documents, as well as the testimonies and decisions of key international criminal tribunals and opinion and commentary of relevant analysts. Global normative rejection can provide a context for applying pressure at least to states to protect citizens and to bring to account the perpetrators of tactical rape.

TWO

Tactical rape and sexual violence in conflict

Tactical rape is not a new phenomenon. It is deliberate, widespread policy rape implemented with definite intent. Even with the increasing formal recognition of its pernicious effects and its threats to human and state security, tactical rape continues. "In conflicts around the world, armies and armed groups use sexual violence as a devastating tactic of war," said Nisha Varia, women's rights advocacy director at Human Rights Watch.[1] This does not mean that it is useless to insist on all possible steps to prevent it, to offer whatever protection possible against it and to bring perpetrators to account. Laws and normative rejection of other crimes such as murder, theft and corruption do not mean such crimes disappear. As considered in Chapter Three, feminist analysts have serious and credible concerns regarding the gendered nature of legal systems and existing law at international and national levels, and the impact of essentially patriarchal institutions of law on women. In 1991, Hilary Charlesworth, Christine Chinkin and Shelley Wright focused on developing an international feminist perspective, outlined the male organisational and normative structure of the international legal system, and applied feminist analyses to various legal principles.[2]

The notion of law as objective and gender-neutral is questionable, and as such there are limitations to the usefulness of a focus on existing law and legal processes. However, it is a first step – and I argue that it is a useful step – to have a framework of laws as the basis for further progress. Similarly, it is useful to track and recognise progress made at international level such as in the UN Security Council, even though the irony remains that it is states that make UN resolutions and yet they are still often perpetrators of tactical rape. In March 2015, the Secretary-General reported to the UN Security Council:

[1] Human Rights Watch, 2015, *UN: Sexual violence a "tactic of war"*, Nisha Varia, 14 April.
[2] Charlesworth, H, Chinkin, C, Wright, S, 1991, Feminist approaches to international law, *The American Journal of International Law*, 85, 4, October, 613-45.

Sexual violence perpetrated by State actors or armed groups associated with the State remains of grave concern in countries such the Sudan (Darfur), South Sudan, the Syrian Arab Republic and the Democratic Republic of the Congo. Indeed, in recent years, particular emphasis has been placed on the responsibility of Governments to protect the civilian population.[3]

This report highlighted 19 states where sexual violence in conflict continued, and urged that the report should be read in conjunction with six previous reports on conflict-related sexual violence,

> ... which provide a cumulative basis for the inclusion of 45 parties in the list of parties credibly suspected of committing or being responsible for patterns of rape and other forms of sexual violence in situations of armed conflict on the agenda of the Security Council (annex), 13 of which appear for the first time.[4]

It remains imperative to pressure for action against tactical rape. It remains imperative to remember the reality of tactical rape, and that it is about more than numbers and data – it is about the lives and suffering of real victims.

Dr Denis Mukwege at Panzi Hospital, the clinic he set up 15 years ago in the hills above Bukavu in eastern Congo, said in 2015:

> Some of the women arrive naked. Some are only just alive, with knife or gunshot wounds to the thighs, genitals or pelvis. Many have been raped repeatedly by multiple attackers, tied up and brutalised in front of their husbands, parents and children. Sticks are used on some, chemicals on others, doused after the rape to burn and scar, to ensure ruination. It works. Internal injuries can be so extensive as to defy medical solution.[5]

Tactical rape is political but it results in personal impacts and suffering. While there has been an increase in international attention and rejection

---

[3]   UN Security Council, 2015, *Conflict-related sexual violence*, S2015/203, 23 March.
[4]   Ibid.
[5]   Strudwick, P, 2014, Why rape is as deadly a threat as the world has faced: Congo's cheap weapon of mass destruction, *Independent*, 30 December.

of tactical rape and sexual violence since the conflicts in the former Yugoslavia and Rwanda, these abuses continue in other arenas. The list of conflicts where tactical rape has been prevalent is long, and numbers are high:

> In Rwanda, between 100,000 and 250,000 women were raped during the three months of genocide in 1994. UN agencies estimate that more than 60,000 women were raped during the civil war in Sierra Leone (1991-2002), more than 40,000 in Liberia (1989-2003), up to 60,000 in the former Yugoslavia (1992-1995), and at least 200,000 in DRC since 1998.[6]

In September 2013 the Secretary-General provided the Security Council with a list of parties to conflict that were credibly suspected of committing or being responsible for patterns of rape and other forms of sexual violence in situations of armed conflict. This list included the Central African Republic (CAR), Côte d'Ivoire, the DRC, Mali, the Syrian Arab Republic, Afghanistan, Myanmar, Somalia, South Sudan, the Sudan (Darfur) and Yemen. Countries with a record of sexual violence in post-conflict situations, including Bosnia and Herzegovina, Liberia, Libya, Nepal, Sierra Leone, Sri Lanka and Timor-Leste, made it onto another list that also referred to other situations of concern in Angola, Guinea and Kenya.[7]

Oxfam reported in 2011 that 'sexual violence is increasingly being used as a tool of conflict itself.'[8] The Oxfam report highlighted the geographic spread of the abuse across continents, noting the claims made in 2010 by the UN Special Representative on Sexual Violence in Conflict that rape was used in the Côte d'Ivoire for political ends. On 3 October 2011, the Pre-Trial Chamber III of the ICC granted the Prosecutor's request to commence an investigation in Côte d'Ivoire with respect to alleged crimes within the jurisdiction of the Court, committed since 28 November 2010.[9]

Oxfam named other arenas where sexual violence has been prevalent: rape used in Myanmar as a tool in the long-running conflict; in

---

[6] See www.un.org/en/preventgenocide/rwanda/about/bgsexualviolence.shtml

[7] UN General Assembly Security Council, 2013, *Sexual violence in conflict*, S/2013/149, 14 March.

[8] Oxfam, 2011, *Protection of civilians in 2010*.

[9] See www.icc-cpi.int/en_menus/icc/situations%20and%20cases/situations/icc0211/press%20releases/Pages/pr730.aspx

Kyrgyzstan where at least 600 people experienced sexual violence in clashes during the period June to December 2010; and in CAR where one-third of women were victims of sexual violence in conflicts in Bambouti and Mboki.[10] At the same time, the UN Security Council became concerned about sexual violence in the conflicts in Darfur and Columbia, although their response was uneven, with some conflicts attracting attention and others seen as not being on the Security Council agenda.[11]

Other countries where sexual violence has been reported as a significant feature of conflict include Ethiopia, Nigeria, Somalia and Chad.[12] In Chad, rape has been used as 'a deliberate conflict tactic'.[13] Randi Solhjell, John Karlsrud and Jon Harald Sande Lie noted that confronting sexual and gender-based violence in Chad 'involves improving security and is an important element in the imperative to protect civilians under the auspices of international humanitarian law and human rights law.'[14] In the conflict in Conakry, Guinea, soldiers particularly targeted women when suppressing a political demonstration at a stadium, and rapes and attacks 'appear to have traumatized the citizenry.'[15] It was reported in June 2011 that the chief prosecutor of the ICC was likely to add rape to the war crime charges against Muammar Gaddafi (had he lived) following mounting evidence that sexual attacks on women were being used as a weapon in the Libyan conflict.[16] Sexual violence continues to be pervasive in the conflict in CAR. Between January and November 2013, the UN recorded at least 4,530 cases of sexual violence perpetrated by armed men, and 'there were clear indications that conflict-related sexual violence had been a main feature of attacks between March and December 2013.'[17]

By 2015 there were continuing reports of sexual violence against women and girls in conflicts such as those being waged by violent extremist groups. In July 2015, when speaking at the US Institute of

---

[10] Oxfam, op cit, p 16.

[11] Ibid, p 5.

[12] Arieff, A, 2009, Sexual violence in African conflicts, Congressional Research Service, 25 November, p 7.

[13] Solhjell, R, Karlsrud, J, Lie, JHS, 2010, *Protecting civilians against sexual and gender-based violence in Chad*, Oslo: Norwegian Institute of International Affairs, p 5.

[14] Ibid, p 7.

[15] Nossiter, A, 2009, In a Guinea seized by violence, women are prey, *The New York Times*, 5 October.

[16] *Guardian Weekly*, 17 June 2011, p 5.

[17] UN Security Council, 2014, *Conflict-related sexual violence*, S/2014/181, 13 March.

Peace, Special Representative for Sexual Violence in Conflict, Zainab Bangura, argued that the world is:

> ... seeing a new phenomenon – sexual violence being used as a tactic of terror – to displace communities and destroy existing family and community structures, to strike fear into the heart of civilian populations, to extract intelligence, and to generate revenue for trafficking, trading, gifting, auctioning, and ransoming women and girls as part of the currency by which [the Islamic State] consolidates its power.[18]

She continued to highlight, a 'battle that is being waged on the bodies of women and girls' in which sexual violence has become a 'tool of terror'.[19] This is an indication of just how widespread the use of tactical rape is as the 21st century continues.

There are too many ongoing conflicts where tactical rape is still an issue. They cannot all be considered in depth, but this should in no way diminish the importance of any one. As 'new wars' continue, so, too, does the use of tactical rape and sexual violence. The situations in the former Yugoslavia and Rwanda demand particular attention because they were in many ways the beginnings of change in attitudes to tactical rape, but there have been others of significance.

Sudan/Darfur

In early 2015 reports were still emerging of what appeared to be tactical rape in Darfur. Twelve years of fighting between the Sudanese government and rebel groups had ravaged Darfur in western Sudan, despite a political process since 2003 with at least two failed peace agreements. More than 450,000 people were reported to have been displaced in 2014 alone.[20] The report from Human Rights Watch on widespread rapes noted 'the conflict's impact on the civilian population has been horrific', with 'widespread killings, torture and sexual violence against civilians.'[21]

---

[18] Koppell, C, 2015, To fight extremism, the world needs to learn how to talk to women, 12 August, *Foreign Policy*.

[19] Ibid.

[20] Human Rights Watch, 2015, *Mass rape in North Darfur*, 11 February.

[21] Ibid.

In October 2014 Zainab Bangura reported at the end of a visit to South Sudan that women and children had been bearing the brunt of the fighting, and that what she heard from survivors and saw with her own eyes in South Sudan was the worst violence she had seen in her 30-year career:

> 'Survivors feel they have no one to turn to, to report the crimes that have been committed against them,' she told a news conference. 'The character of sexual violence crimes is shocking. In the words of one woman activist I spoke to, it is not just about rape. It is to inflict unimaginable pain and destruction.'[22]

At the same time, Elizabeth Deng, a South Sudan researcher for Amnesty International, reported on the gender-based violence committed during South Sudan's year-long crisis:

> We documented a number of cases of sexual violence including gang rape, brutal acts such as cutting open pregnant women or raping women with objects like sticks.[23]

This is a complex conflict with roots in recent and past history. The use of tactical rape is current and still to be confronted, prevented and its perpetrators to be prosecuted.

The UN Security Council referred the situation in Darfur to the ICC in 2005. The court issued arrest warrants for five individuals, including Sudanese President Omar al-Bashir, for serious crimes in violation of international law committed in Darfur, but it has been unable to proceed in the face of Sudan's resistance. In late 2014, the Prosecutor noted in frustration that 'recent allegations of the rape of approximately 200 women and girls in Tabit should shock this Council into action.'[24] At least 221 women and girls were raped in Tabit over 36 hours beginning on 30 October 2014. The widespread rapes and attacks by Sudanese government forces were carried out 'during three distinct military operations', and two soldiers who had participated in the operations said that superior officers had ordered them to 'rape

---

[22] Bangura, Z, 2014, The "unimaginable pain" of South Sudan's crisis, *Voice of America*, 15 December.

[23] Deng, E, Amnesty International, 2014, in The "unimaginable pain" of South Sudan's crisis, 15 December, *Voice of America*.

[24] Human Rights Watch, 11 February 2015, op cit.

women' because the women were rebel supporters.[25] Human Rights Watch research found that 'the rape was on a large scale and thus could be considered widespread. It was carried out in multiple locations at the same time during the course of three successive attacks on the civilians in the town, indicating it was systematic.'[26] Sexual violence has featured prominently in recent attacks on civilians by Sudanese forces not only in Tabit, but also in the Blue Nile state and elsewhere in Sudan.[27]

Syria

The ongoing conflict in Syria since 2011 demonstrates the difficulty of documenting what appears likely to be tactical rape. In its January 2013 report, the International Rescue Committee described 'rape as a significant and disturbing feature of the Syrian civil war.'[28] However, the Secretary-General reported to the UN Security Council the difficulty in verifying allegations due to lack of access and considerations related to the safety of survivors. He noted that fear of reprisal, social stigmatisation and a lack of safe and confidential response services for survivors had severely limited reporting on sexual violence in the context of the Syrian conflict.[29] This was despite information gathered from displaced civilians outside Syria and reported by the Independent International Commission of Inquiry that indicated that sexual violence has been a 'persistent feature of the conflict and that the fear of rape has served as a driving motivation for families fleeing the violence.'[30]

In its report released in August 2013, the Independent International Commission of Inquiry on the Syrian Arab Republic stated,

> Sexual violence has played a prominent role in the conflict, owing to fear and threat of rapes and by the violence committed. It occurs during raids, at checkpoints and prisons across the country. The threat of rape is used as a tool to terrorize and punish women, men and children perceived as being associated with the opposition. Underreporting

---

[25] Ibid.
[26] Ibid.
[27] Ibid.
[28] IRC, 2013, *Syria: A regional crisis*, January.
[29] UN Security Council, S/2014/181, op cit.
[30] Human Rights Council, 2013, *Report of the Independent International Commission of Inquiry on the Syrian Arab Republic*, A/HRC/23/58, 4 June, para 91.

and delayed reported of sexual violence is endemic, making an assessment of the magnitude difficult.

The report concludes, 'Rape and other inhumane acts, such as crimes against humanity, were committed by government forces and the National defence forces (in Syria).'[31] Reasons for under-reporting are common across many conflict situations. These can include the lack of any opportunity to report, the lack of knowledge of any reliable agency to report, a perceived sense that reporting will achieve nothing, cultural barriers to confiding intimate details and inability to report traumatic events. Often victims refuse to speak about violence they have been exposed to, particularly when the offense has a sexual dimension, as they fear social stigma especially in patriarchal societies such as those discussed later. Although no reliable statistics are available, Syrian human rights groups have expressed deep concerns. 'Rumors of unverified sexual assaults have increasingly spread in Syria, creating a climate of terror for inhabitants and particularly women. Victims of arbitrary arrests and kidnappings are often stigmatized as if they faced sexual abuses.'[32]

Even in 2015, when there is greater awareness of tactical rape, it can be problematic to be sure of the nature of rape and sexual violence in conflicts. In the related conflict in Iraq, Human Rights Watch has also documented:

> ... a system of organized rape and sexual assault, sexual slavery, and forced marriage by ISIS forces. Such acts are war crimes and may be crimes against humanity. Many of the women and girls remain missing, but the survivors now in Iraqi Kurdistan need psychosocial support and other assistance.[33]

The need for support is increasingly recognised. Liesl Gerntholtz, women's rights director at Human Rights Watch, said in the same report:

---

[31] Human Rights Council, 2013, *Report of the Independent International Commission of Inquiry on the Syrian Arab Republic*, A/HRC/24/46, 16 August, paras 95-100.
[32] Euro-Mediterranean Human Rights Network, 2013, *Violence against women, bleeding wound in the Syrian conflict*, Sema Nasar, p 9.
[33] Human Rights Watch, 2015, *Iraq: ISIS escapees describe systematic rape*, 14 April.

ISIS forces have committed organized rape, sexual assault, and other horrific crimes against Yezidi women and girls. Those fortunate enough to have escaped need to be treated for the unimaginable trauma they endured.[34]

Resources need to be allocated for appropriate counselling and psychosocial support as part of an effective response to the reality of tactical rape.

There is growing recognition of this reality. An article in *Le Monde* in 2014 highlighted 'Syria's silent war crime', describing it as:

> ... the most dreadfully silent crime currently perpetrated in Syria. A mass crime, carried out by the regime in the most barbaric ways that relies on the most deep-rooted taboos of traditional Syrian society – and on the silence of the victims, convinced they will be rejected by their own family, or even sentenced to death.[35]

Awareness of the use of rape has reached into the public media, and while there are always dangers of sensationalising and a lack of reliable research, this does bring attention to the issue, and may contribute to global rejection and demands to respond.

Democratic Republic of Congo

One arena that must be mentioned further and that has attracted much attention for the ongoing use of tactical rape and sexual violence is the Democratic Republic of the Congo (DRC). This conflict has earned for the DRC the ignominious title of 'the rape capital of the world'.[36] This intractable conflict, involving seven nations and many rebel groups of armed combatants, all with varying agendas and motives, began in 1996, with a short break between 1997-98 before resuming.[37] Aspects of this conflict are an extension of Rwanda's civil war between the Hutu and Tutsi that continued onto DRC territory. Major causes of the wars

[34] Ibid.

[35] Cojean, A, 2014, Syria's silent war crime: systematic rape, *Le Monde*, 12 March [reprinted in *The New York Times*, 31 August 2015].

[36] Oxfam, op cit, p 16.

[37] For full details of this conflict, see Csete, J, Kippenberg, J, 2002, *The war within the war: Sexual violence against women and girls in Eastern Congo*, New York: Human Rights Watch, and Turner, T, 2007, *The Congo wars: Conflict, myth and reality*, London and New York: Zed Books.

are seen to be long-term, ongoing disputes over land and resources overlaid with significant elements of ethnic conflict. Whatever the causes, any sort of sustainable peace has eluded the DRC as conflicts continue over access to economic and political power. In 2001, the UN described tensions as 'perpetuating the conflict in the country, impeding economic development, and exacerbating the suffering of the Congolese people.'[38] There were renewed outbreaks of fighting again in 2009, despite continued attempts at peacemaking. In March 2009, it was reported that a peace accord had been signed between the government of the DRC and the National Congress for People's Defence (CNDP), which, it was hoped, would 'foresee the end of all hostilities, the transformation of armed groups into political parties and the return of refugees and displaced persons.'[39] However, in April 2009, renewed waves of fighting between splintered rebel factions forced more than 30,000 civilians to flee their homes.[40]

Sexual violence against women and girls continued in the conflict and may even have increased with reports that in South Kivu in the east of the country, some 463 women were raped in the first quarter of 2009, more than half the total number of violations registered for the whole of 2008.[41] At national level, the UN reported that 1,100 rapes per month were registered from 21 November 2008 to 24 March 2009, with an average of 36 per day.[42] Between 35 and 50% of victims were aged between 10 and 17, while more than 10% were younger than 10.[43] A disturbing factor in this conflict was that the use of tactical rape and sexual violence was used by more than one of the warring parties. All sides were using these abuses as strategies of attack: members of all armed groups, rebel groups, the police force and opportunistic criminals have been perpetrators of rape and sexual violence against women and girls in the DRC.[44] There were at least 15,000 cases of

---

[38] UN, *Security Council, in Presidential Statement, condemns plundering of natural resources in Democratic Republic of Congo*, SC/7246, 4441st meeting, 19 December 2001.

[39] UN News Centre, *DR Congo: UN envoy hails new pact with rebels in strife torn east*, 24 March 2009.

[40] UN News Centre, *DR Congo: More that 30,000 flee new attacks by splintered rebel factions*, 7 April 2009.

[41] UN News Centre, *Growing number of women falling victim to rape in DR Congo, reports UN*, 20 May 2009.

[42] UN Security Council, 2009, *Twenty-seventh report of the Secretary-General on the United Nations Organization Mission in the Democratic Republic of Congo*, S/2009/160, 27 March 2009, para 69.

[43] Ibid.

[44] Csete and Kippenberg, op cit, p 23.

sexual violence in the DRC in 2009, and 7,685 cases were reported in the first half of 2010.[45]

By 2011 there had been no lasting resolution to the conflict in the DRC. It has been described as 'Africa's world war', with an estimated 5.4 million deaths and widespread use of rape to strategically shame, demoralise and humiliate 'the enemy'[46] – who may be civilians or non-combatants. A Harvard Humanitarian Initiative report insisted that this use of rape must not be seen as 'collateral damage' but as a deliberate strategy.[47] There have been many instances of mass rapes, rapes in public, the rape of mothers and daughters in front of their families, and forcing victims to have sex with family members.[48] There have been ethnic elements to the use of rape, with combatants purposefully singling out their victims from 'opposing' ethnic groups.[49] Analysis also clearly indicates a spillover into what are termed 'civilian rapes' (rapes committed by non-military personnel), which increased 17-fold between 2004 and 2008, at the same time as military rapes decreased.[50] These findings imply a normalisation of rape among the civilian population, suggesting the erosion of all constructive social mechanisms that ought to protect civilians from sexual violence.[51]

The UN Population Fund reported that:

> ... in 2012 alone there were 15,654 reported cases of sexual violence – a 52 percent increase from 2011. Of these, 98 percent were perpetrated against females. In conflict-affected contexts in DRC, the average age of survivors is less than 21, with a third of all survivors falling between 12 and 17 years of age. In 2012, 82 percent of all survivors had not completed primary school. These are not just abstract numbers; these are children born of rape who are abandoned, women and girls who struggle with the debilitating physical and emotional repercussions day in and

[45] Oxfam, op cit, p 9.
[46] Harvard Humanitarian Initiative, with support from Oxfam International, 2010, *'Now the world is without me': An investigation of sexual violence in Eastern Democratic Republic of Congo*, April, Cambridge, MA: Harvard Humanitarian Initiative, p 7.
[47] Ibid, p 9.
[48] Amnesty International, 2004, *Democratic Republic of Congo: Mass rape – Time for remedies*, 25 October, p 14.
[49] Ibid.
[50] Harvard Humanitarian Initiative, op cit, p 8.
[51] Ibid.

day out, and men and boys who suffer in silence because of the shame and stigma associated with this crime.[52]

During 2015 the government of the DRC recorded 15,352 incidents of sexual and gender-based violence in eastern DRC, and the UN Organization Stabilization Mission in the DRC (MONUSCO) investigated and verified 860 cases of sexual violence committed by parties to the conflict, representing an increase of 13% since the previous report on sexual violence in conflict.[53] If this extended use of tactical rape and sexual violence as part of conflict is ever to end, 'the environment of impunity must end.'[54] This will require ongoing attention and appropriate programme responses from international funders and effective judicial systems to confront and bring perpetrators to account.

Reports from the DRC include the rape of men and boys, and some analysts have expressed concern that there is too much focus on such violence against women to the detriment of concern for men and boys as victims of gender-based sexual violence.[55] As has been discussed earlier in this book, in many situations, the rape of women is an attack on men and communities, but in the DRC now there is a direct sexual attack on males.[56] This, too, is condemned but cannot be used as an argument to lessen the focus on confronting the tactical rape of women and girls, who remain the main targets. Within the government of the DRC, an official was heard to say that 'rape was a women's issue that women needed to deal with on their own'.[57] This attitude did eventually change with initiatives such as those implemented by 2013 with support from MONUSCO and the UN Development

[52]   Osotimehin, B, Bangura, Z, 2013, OP-ED: Act now, act big to end sexual violence in DRC, Inter Press Service, 6 November.

[53]   UN Security Council, 2015, *Report of the Secretary-General on the United Nations Organization Stabilization Mission in the Democratic Republic of the Congo*, S/2015/172, 10 March.

[54]   Harvard Humanitarian Initiative, op cit, p 9.

[55]   Baaz, ME and Stern, M, 2010, *The complexity of violence: A critical analysis of sexual violence in Democratic Republic of Congo*, Uppsala: The Nordic Africa Institute, May.

[56]   Ibid, p 43.

[57]   Pratt, M, Werchick, L, 2004, *Sexual terrorism: Rape as a weapon of war in Eastern Democratic Republic of Congo – An assessment of programmatic responses to sexual violence in North Kivu, South Kivu, Maniema, and Oriental Provinces*, United States Agency for International Development (USAID)/Bureau for Democracy, Conflict and Humanitarian Assistance (DCHA) Assessment Report, 9–16 January, p 30.

Programme (UNDP) – a three-month training programme on the instruction and investigation of sexual violence cases for 60 judicial police officers assigned to a special force for the protection of women and children, and the DRC Commission on Sexual Violence held a technical meeting with the support of the Team of Experts on the Rule of Law and Sexual Violence in Conflict.[58] Training and education are needed to confront elements that render women and men vulnerable, either by direct attack or because social attitudes render one gender particularly vulnerable.

Sierra Leone

During the armed conflict in Sierra Leone from 1991 to 2001, it was reported by Human Rights Watch that:

> ... thousands of women and girls of all ages, ethnic groups, and socioeconomic classes were subjected to widespread and systematic sexual violence, including individual and gang rape, and rape with objects such as weapons, firewood, umbrellas, and pestles.[59]

According to this same report, although both sides in the conflict were guilty of rape, this was mostly committed by the rebel forces, whose use of rape was 'characterized by extraordinary brutality and frequently preceded or followed by other egregious human rights abuses against the victim, her family, and her community.'[60] Victims came from all age groups, but young women, and girls believed to be virgins, were particularly targeted. Many women did not survive the violent attacks:

> ... some bled to death or suffered from tearing in the genital area, causing long-term incontinence and severe infections. Many victims who were pregnant at the time of rape miscarried as a result of the sexual violence they were subjected to, and numerous women had their babies

---

[58] UN Security Council, 2015, *Report of the Secretary-General on the United Nations Organization Stabilization Mission in the Democratic Republic of the Congo*, S/2015/172, 10 March.

[59] Human Rights Watch, 2015, *'We'll kill you if you cry': Sexual violence in the Sierra Leone conflict*, 16 January.

[60] Ibid.

torn out of their uterus as rebels placed bets on the sex of the unborn child.[61]

Sexual violence was often accompanied by the abduction of women and girls who were expected to perform domestic tasks and serve as military porters. This rape was designed to destroy communities as well as individual women and girls. Traditional and cultural values were attacked:

> ... child combatants raped women who were old enough to be their grandmothers, rebels raped pregnant and breastfeeding mothers, and fathers were forced to watch their daughters being raped.[62]

Eventually, conflict ceased, and the government of Sierra Leone requested the UN to set up 'a special court' to address serious crimes committed against civilians and UN peacekeepers during the country's decade-long (1991–2002) civil war.

The Special Court for Sierra Leone was set up in 2002. The structure and mandate of the court represented 'the world's first "hybrid" international criminal tribunal, mandated to try those "bearing the greatest responsibility" for crimes committed in Sierra Leone after 30 November 1996, the date of the failed Abidjan Peace Accord.'[63] The court was the first international tribunal to sit in the country where the crimes took place, and the first funded by voluntary contributions. Prosecution of gender-based crimes was a priority, with 10 out of the 13 accused charged with crimes against humanity of rape and sexual slavery, and the war crime of outrages on personal dignity.[64] This tribunal handed over to the Residual Special Court for Sierra Leone, which was established to oversee continuing legal obligations such as witness protection, supervision of prison sentences and the management of the Special Court archives after 2013. The tribunal for Sierra Leone followed UN Security Council action in establishing tribunals for the former Yugoslavia and Rwanda. These two conflicts

[61] Ibid.

[62] Ibid.

[63] See www.rscsl.org

[64] Oosterveld, V, 2009, Lessons from the Special Court for Sierra Leone on the prosecution of gender-based crimes, *Journal of Gender, Social Policy & the Law*, 17, 2, 407-28.

contributed significantly to international attention finally being paid to tactical rape.

Former Yugoslavia

The acknowledged use of tactical rape in the former Yugoslavia was a key step in beginning international recognition and eventual action to confront this violation of international law. It is worth tracking how such attention was gained. In November 1992, while working at a peak body of church-related humanitarian agencies, I received an informal request from UNHCR to check out rumours of extensive rape of women in the former Yugoslavia. In December 1992, a team of women and I went to the former Yugoslavia with the aim of verifying reports, which were already the subject of many calls for action from the public media.[65] This team and others from NGOs found grounds for a formal international investigation of the use of rape in the conflict, and that 'as part of the overall humanitarian response to physical and emotional needs it is a matter of urgency that adequate and appropriate attention be given to the psychological needs of women raped in war.'[66] There was evidence of the rape of women by all sides in the conflict in Bosnia-Herzegovina, including rape as a by-product of the conflict.[67] The team reported its conviction:

> ... that there is clear evidence of the use of systematic, mass rape as an increasingly sophisticated weapon of war being used, in this instance, by members of the Serbian forces. Survivors speak of "rape on the front line" and "third party rape". These are rapes carried out publicly by Serbian soldiers to demoralise family members and opposition forces compelled to witness them.[68]

This was rape for strategic and tactical purposes, linked with a campaign of ethnic cleansing, systematic and widespread, used by one party to the conflict against civilians. In essence, it was tactical rape.

The team also recorded:

---

[65] Fitzpatrick, B, 1992, *Rape of women in war*, Geneva: World Council of Churches, December.

[66] Ibid, p 24.

[67] Ibid, p 21.

[68] Ibid, p 21.

Women's groups are angered by what they see as prevarication and refusal to accept the accounts of women's suffering. The 'second-layer' of victimisation of survivors by insistence upon legalistic interrogation is being resisted. The team believes that there is sufficient conviction of the truth of reports of mass, systematic rape to, now, place the onus of 'proof' on the international community which claims to condemn it.[69]

There was a dearth of serious attention to the reports of tactical rape and sexual violence, despite widespread media and NGO calls of condemnation.

The report, *Rape of women in war*, was widely shared among UN agencies, NGOs and women's advocates and in press conferences.[70] I was requested to brief Dame Anna Warburton, who was about to lead one of the first formal investigations. The report from this delegation, *European Council investigative mission* in January 1993, accepted the possibility of speaking 'in terms of many thousands. Estimates vary widely, ranging from 10,000 to as many as 60,000. The most reasoned estimates suggested to the Mission place the number of victims at around 20,000.'[71] These numbers and the limited mandate of the mission (to investigate only the treatment of Muslim women) were later criticised by Norma von Ragenfeld-Feldman, but her criticisms and reservations regarding possibly inflated numbers were offset by the acknowledged reluctance of many women to report rapes.[72] The outcome of this and other subsequent investigations later confirmed that rape was widespread and systematic.

Western media attention to the use of rape was maintained for extended periods rather than the more usual, single and often sensationalised story. One could posit that this was due to widely reported use of rape in the conflicts and genocide in the former Yugoslavia and Rwanda that followed closely on one another. The

[69] Ibid, p 22.
[70] The report of this team investigation was later hand-delivered to Slobodan Milosevic by a delegation of the European Council of Churches, and that same delegation eventually submitted a copy to The Hague when Milosevic was on trial.
[71] Warburton, A, 1993, *European Council investigative mission into the treatment of Muslim women in the former Yugoslavia, Report to EC foreign ministers, December 1992-February 1993*, 28 January, para 14.
[72] von Ragenfeld-Feldman, N, 1997, The victimization of women: rape and the reporting of rape in Bosnia-Herzegovina, 1992-1993, Presented at the Fifth Annual Interdisciplinary German Studies Conference, 15-16 March.

complexity of events in both arenas may have meant that it was easy to focus on one aspect of the extensive violence. Distribution of NGO reports exerted effective pressure and kept stories alive. Certainly the sensational nature of the issue of rape and killing may have helped sustain public pressure and consequent pressure on states and the UN to acknowledge what was happening. Events reported in the two arenas interacted to exert pressure to recognise the widespread incidence of rape linked with genocide and ethnic cleansing.

In the final months of 1992, another group of women connected to ecumenical churches visited Belgrade.[73] They met with senior churchmen who, with some exceptions, denied that the widespread rapes being reported could occur on the Serbian side, insisting that media reports were merely propaganda. However, on 16 December 1992, UNHCR issued a statement noting that the agency was 'shocked at reports, over the past several weeks of human rights abuses directed against women in former Yugoslavia', and continued:

> In addition to causing personal physical and mental suffering, rape may be perceived to bring dishonour to the woman and result in marginalisation of both her and her family. Its systematic use can result in the destruction of the social fabric of the persecuted group.[74]

This specific recognition of the use of rape in the conflict and its impact on individual women and on their communities was a development from rape being couched only in terms of 'dishonour' as consistent with the Geneva Convention terminology.

In January 1993, the UN Special Rapporteur made his third visit to investigate human rights abuses in the former Yugoslavia. He reported 'an alarming number of allegations' regarding the use of rape as a weapon of ethnic cleansing.[75] He noted the reports of NGO missions.[76] 'Gravely concerned' by these reports, he sent a team of experts to investigate the allegations.[77] They found that rape had been used on a large scale, predominantly by Serb forces against Muslim women and

---

[73] Raiser, E, 1992, *Women build bridges to the former Yugoslavia*, Geneva: World Council of Churches, quoted in Fitzpatrick, op cit, Appendix 1, p 2.

[74] UN High Commission on Refugees, 1992, *Situation of women in Ex-Yugoslavia*, 16 December, quoted in Fitzpatrick, op cit, Appendix III.

[75] Commission on Human Rights, 1993, *Report of the Special Rapporteur on the situation of human rights in the territory of the former Yugoslavia*, E/CN.4/1993/50, para 82.

[76] Ibid, para 86.

[77] Ibid, para 83.

girls, that rape had been used as an instrument of ethnic cleansing and furthermore, that those in positions of power had made no attempt to stop the rapes.[78]

In December 1994, the Commission of Experts recorded claims that in the former Yugoslavia there were approximately 1,100 reported cases of rape and sexual assault: about 800 victims had been named or were known to the submitting source; about 1,800 victims had been specifically referred to but not named or identified sufficiently by the reporting witness; and witness reports through approximations referred to a possible further 10,000 victims.[79] The report outlined some reasons for survivors of rape being reluctant or unable to report offences against them.[80] They included fear of reprisals for themselves and family members and shame and fear of ostracism. Many women did not have a place to report the assaults or rapes, and refugees had an increasing scepticism about the response of the international community. These reasons are common to women in many conflicts.

The report identified several different categories of rape, and urged a distinction between 'opportunistic' crimes and the use of rape and sexual assault as a method of 'ethnic cleansing'.[81] Rape related to ethnic cleansing could be instances either of a policy of commission or a policy of omission.[82] Patterns of recurring characteristics of rapes and sexual assaults suggested that 'a systematic rape and sexual assault policy exists.'[83] Some level of organisation would have been needed to account for the large number of rapes that occurred, particularly in places of detention. The correlation between media attention and the decline in the number of rapes and assaults suggested, 'that the purposes for which the alleged rape and sexual assault was carried out had been served by the publicity', and that this, in turn, 'would indicate that commanders could control the alleged perpetrators, leading to the conclusion that there was an overriding policy advocating the use of rape and sexual assault as a method of ethnic cleansing.'[84]

There was evidence of the deliberate impregnation of women raped: 'perpetrators tell female victims that they will bear children of

---

[78] Ibid, para 84.
[79] UN Security Council, 1994, *Rape and sexual assault – Final report of the United Nations Commission of Experts established pursuant to Security Council resolution 780 (1992)*, S/1994/674, Annex IX, Vol V, 28 December, Section A.
[80] Ibid, Section A(a)-(f).
[81] Ibid, Section C, para 1.
[82] Ibid, Conclusion, para 3.
[83] Ibid, Conclusion, para 2.
[84] UN Security Council, 1994, op cit, Section D, Annex IX, pp 8, 9.

the perpetrator's ethnicity, that the perpetrators were ordered to rape and sexually assault them' and 'perpetrators tell victims that they must become pregnant and hold them in custody until it is too late to get an abortion.'[85] Bearing children deemed to be children of an enemy, children outside the mother's group, is socially, psychologically and physically damaging. The women who bear these children may be ostracised and denied economic support, inheritance may be contested or denied, and communities may reject the children themselves. All are long-term impacts.

Bassiouni's report (UN Security Council, 1994) was substantiated by other sources including the journalist, Peter Maas, who detailed many individual incidents.[86] The report by Human Rights Watch, *Bosnia and Herzegovina. 'A closed dark place': Past and present human rights abuses in Foca*, also documented many accounts.[87] Foca became known as the site of 'rape camps' where non-Serb women, young Muslim women and girls as young as 12 were detained, abused, raped on a daily basis and enslaved in a context of other crimes such as murder, torture and the destruction of civilian property and religious sites.[88] The perpetrators were members of the Republika Srpska army and police, who, together with soldiers from Montenegro (mainly from the Niksic area) and some individuals (Dragoljub Kunarac, Radomir Kovać and Zoran Vuković), were indicted and charged. The crimes took place in 1992 and the first half of 1993; the indictment was issued in 1996, and the trial began in March 2000.[89]

A witness at the ICTY told how one 'owner' of four women forced these women to dance naked on a table, told them they would be executed at the nearby river, and then took them there. They were subsequently held as sex slaves. Another witness told how her mother and brothers had been killed, and how about 50 men had raped her. When asked by the prosecutor how she felt after the gang rape, she responded, 'I felt dead.'[90] After being raped another witness was told that she would have been hurt much more except that she was about the same age as the rapist's daughter.[91]

---

[85] Ibid, Annex IX, Section C.

[86] Maas, P, 1996, *Love thy neighbour: A story of war*, London: Papermac, Macmillan, pp 51-2, 12-13, 5-7, 53-54.

[87] Human Rights Watch, 1998, *Bosnia and Herzegovina. 'A closed dark place': Past and present human rights abuses in Foca*, 10, 6 (D), July.

[88] Human Rights Watch, 2004, *Foca confronts its past*.

[89] Ibid.

[90] Ibid.

[91] Ibid.

In 1993 and 1994 UN agencies referred to 'the systematic practice of rape' being used in ethnic cleansing,[92] and noted the conviction that 'this heinous practice constitutes a deliberate weapon of war in fulfilling the policy of ethnic cleansing.'[93] In 1995 failures of Dutch UN troops to intervene when they were supposed to be protecting the residents, and failure to send threatened air strikes, strengthened acceptance of the policy of Responsibility to Protect (R2P) perceived to override the concept of sovereignty, and strengthened the Security Council's preparedness to support international legal processes to protect victims of tactical rape and sexual violence.

Rwanda

The genocide in Rwanda followed rapidly on the conflict in the former Yugoslavia. I was in the Rwandan refugee camp, and it seemed to me and to other workers there that the fact of widespread rape as part of the genocide was evident. A Canadian peacekeeper testified: 'It seemed that everywhere we went, from the period of 19th April [1994] until the time we left, there was rape everywhere near these killing sites.'[94] He was one of the professional soldiers who expressed shock at what they had seen of the widespread rape. When Phillip Gourevitch, a prize-winning journalist and author, visited a church where many Tutsi had been killed in mid-April 1994, he saw bodies in varying stages of decomposition, and observed:

> A woman in a cloth wrap printed with flowers lay near the door. Her fleshless hip-bones were high and her legs slightly spread, and a child's skeleton extended between them.[95]

A soldier from the Rwandese Patriotic Front, a Tutsi, told Gourevitch that the dead in this room were mostly women who had been raped

---

[92] OHCHR, 2001, *Rape and abuse of women in the territory of the former Yugoslavia*, Commission on Human Rights resolution 1993/8, 23 February.

[93] UN General Assembly, *Resolution 1994/205, Rape and abuse of women in the territory of the former Yugoslavia*, 6 March.

[94] B Beardsley, assistant to former peacekeeping commander, Roméo Dallaire, giving testimony at the ICTR 2004, quoted in Nowrojee, B, 2005, *Your justice is too slow: Will the ICTR fail Rwanda's rape victims?*, United Nations Research Institute for Social Development, November, p 1.

[95] Gourevitch, P, 2000, *We wish to inform you that tomorrow we will be killed with our families*, London: Picador, p 16.

before being murdered.[96] These were just some of the indications that widespread rape had accompanied the killing. Documentation and evidence at the ICTR, considered later, indicated that rape had also been systematic, and a direct strategy and tactic in the events aimed at destroying the Tutsi.

In January 1996, Rene Degni-Segui, UN Special Rapporteur, reported: 'rape was the rule and its absence the exception.'[97] He reported difficulties in determining the exact number of rape victims, first, because of the social stigma and cultural values, and second, because there was no accurate estimation of 'rapes which took place in refugee camps.'[98] As early as May 1994, I was in conversation with a woman from Médicins sans Frontières in Ngara, who commented that she and many other workers in the refugee camp believed that any Tutsi 'female' (this term was often used to include both women and little girls of any age) who had managed to cross the border to safety had 'probably been raped – and maybe more than once'. This observation was echoed many times by a variety of Tanzanian, Rwandan and European aid workers and medical and relief personnel dealing with the refugees.

Degni-Segui, when considering that not only Tutsi were targeted, referenced a document issued by the General Staff of the Rwandese Army that distinguished between the Tutsi as the main enemy but also referred to 'supporters' defined as 'any person who gives any support to the main enemy.'[99] Accounts of women who survived tactical rape indicate that Hutu women married to Tutsi or Tutsi women married to Hutu were not spared.[100] The reasons for this are linked to the patriarchal belief that women bore children who belonged to the father or father's group. Hutu women were to be 'equally punished for having married Tutsi and having Tutsi children.'[101]

The use of rape was finally recognised as widespread and systematic. Degni-Segui noted that women 'may even be regarded as the main victims of the massacres, with good reason, since they were raped and massacred and subjected to other brutalities.'[102] Human Rights Watch

---

[96] Ibid, p 16.
[97] Degni-Segui, R, 1996, *Report on the situation of human rights in Rwanda*, United Nations Commission on Human Rights, E/CN.4/1996/68, January, para 16.
[98] Ibid.
[99] Degni-Segui, R, 1994, *Report on the situation of human rights in Rwanda*, E/CN.4/1995/7, 28 June, para 47.
[100] See Chapter Six on Rwanda.
[101] Degni-Segui, 1996, op cit, para 13.
[102] Ibid, para 12.

published an extensive documentation of events in Rwanda, and claimed that 'at least half a million people perished' in the 13 weeks after 6 April 1994.[103] Throughout the 771 pages of this documentation there are constant references to the rape of women, although there is no attempt to quantify it. In the publication *Shattered lives*, Binaifer Nowrojee wrote, 'Rwandan women were subjected to sexual violence on a massive scale', and she continued:

> Although the exact number of women raped will never be known, testimonies from survivors confirm that rape was extremely widespread and that thousands of women were individually raped, gang-raped, raped with objects such as sharpened sticks or gun barrels, held in sexual slavery (either collectively or through forced "marriage") or sexually mutilated.[104]

There were also large numbers of pregnancies from the rapes. In a society where children are considered to be of the fathers' groups, there were severe problems for these children and their mothers. Nowrojee mentions terms such as 'children of hate', 'unwanted children', 'children of bad memories' and references the estimates as being conservatively between 2,000 and 5,000.[105] She noted reports of children being abandoned and of infanticide.[106] Degni-Segui supported the reality that reported figures would likely be low estimates, and noted 'that it may never be known exactly how many women were raped.'[107]

The need for data

While the reports noted above are indicative of the widespread and deliberate use of tactical rape and sexual violence, it is recognised that many victims do not or cannot report attacks. Resources to document these reports are likely to be limited. The result is that there is often very little timely or reliable consolidated information on rape and sexual violence despite these being persistent and severe threats faced by women as well as children and men in conflicts.[108] Work is needed

[103] Des Forges, A, 1999, *Leave none to tell the story*, New York: Human Rights Watch, p 1.
[104] Nowrojee, op cit, p 2.
[105] Nowrojee, op cit, p 4.
[106] Ibid.
[107] Degni-Segui, 1996, op cit, para 15.
[108] Oxfam, op cit, p 6.

to estimate and effectively document the numbers and types of rapes in war. Catrien Bijleveld, Aafke Morssinkhofe and Alette Smeulers have argued the case for improved documentation.[109] They have listed some of the reasons given by those arguing that such documentation is not essential: some say it is not important because the number differentials are trivial in the sense that it does not matter if the final figure is 2 million victims or 2.1 million victims; some fear the numbers may overshadow a focus on the causes and nature of a conflict; and others feel the precise number bears little legal relevance.[110]

But it is important to collect data. Figures are important when each figure represents an individual. For planning and delivering post-conflict strategies and resources there is a need to know how many victims there were and their locations. Such data is essential to provide for consequences such as pregnancies and health issues, including HIV/AIDS. To meet the needs of victims and survivors of tactical rape and sexual violence it is necessary to understand if they are able still to bear children, and whether or not they are likely to be able to care for children, emotionally and economically.

For recovery and rebuilding, truth commissions have been shown to be effective. Such commissions proceed from an acknowledgement of victims and the damage done to them. The aim is to 'deconstruct the social reality in which the crimes were committed', so knowing the extent and the nature of suffering matters.[111] It is important to have reliable data regarding current and future conflicts in which sexual violence may be used as a tactic if there is to be an adequate and appropriate response to the protection of civilians and accountability of perpetrators.

From a legal perspective, there is a need to know figures and patterns of the use of rape and sexual violence in order to establish if such use was widespread and/or systematic. This is an element of deciding whether the abuse can be deemed a crime against humanity or a war crime. The extent and nature of the crimes is also important in deciding whether such attacks were deliberate, aimed at a specific group, and whether they constituted genocide.[112] There is recognition of the difficulties in gathering such data, but it has finally been recognised as

---

[109] Bijleveld, C, Morssinkhofe, A, Smeulers, A, 2009, Counting the countless: rape victimisation during the Rwandan genocide, *International Criminal Justice Review*, 19, 2, June, 208-24.

[110] Ibid, pp 209-10.

[111] Bijleveld et al, op cit, pp 209-10.

[112] Ibid, p 211.

a need to be solved. One option proposed is that a self-report for rape victims might be worth considering,[113] although there are immediate difficulties in such a plan. The literacy level of victims varies greatly, and resources are needed to support, design and collate findings. However, documentation and meaningful analysis must be a priority, and it is encouraging to see the moves being made at the UN Security Council (analysed in Chapters Seven, Eight and Nine) to tackle this issue.

Conclusion

It is clear that in 2015 tactical rape and sexual violence in conflict remain persistent and pernicious practices. 'The victims of modern armed conflict are far more likely to be civilians than soldiers' and 'women in particular can face devastating forms of sexual violence, which are sometimes deployed systematically to achieve military or political objectives'.[114] The incidence of tactical rape continues, and it is across continents and cultures. Chapters Seven, Eight and Nine will consider the significant progress made towards UN institutionalisation of commitments to confront, prevent and bring to account perpetrators, because it has been recognised at global level that 'Sexual violence in conflict needs to be treated as the war crime that it is; it can no longer be treated as an unfortunate collateral damage of war.'[115] But despite state members of the UN having made progress in recognising and responding at a global level to tactical rape, state actors are still frequently among those who are complicit or directly responsible for perpetrating tactical rape.

[113] Ibid, p 223.
[114] See www.un.org/en/preventgenocide/rwanda/about/bgsexualviolence.shtml
[115] Ibid.

THREE

Context

The period between 1990 and 2015 was a time of considerable development in global normative rejection of tactical rape and sexual violence in conflict. Many conflicts occurred, with significant humanitarian implications. Social constructions and gendered vulnerabilities contributed to the impact of tactical rape. But normative change can occur, and there are signs of this happening.

Changing nature of war

Herfried Munkler described the process by which war gradually became a state-controlled enterprise, for reasons related to economic costs and the complex weaponry being employed.[1] As war became expensive and required increasingly complex management, states took control, wanting to bring about a rapid end to fighting because shorter conflicts incurred less cost. Munkler said, 'war of this kind was a war of soldiers against soldiers and the civilian population was largely spared from violence and destruction.'[2] He described how as super-powers developed it became increasingly difficult for smaller groups to engage in traditional battles of armies against armies. Guerrilla warfare came to the fore. Guerrillas could take longer to achieve their goals and use methods not requiring complex technology and weaponry. Attacks on civilians increased as, 'the country's civilian population ... falls prey to those who, with the help of their armed henchmen, exercise control over them.'[3] While Munkler highlighted the increased role of children as soldiers, he notably failed to highlight the place of women as particular targets in civilian populations. Yet much of what he says can explain the particular use of rape as a tactic in new wars.

Civilian populations are largely comprised of women, and rape is a means of attacking women. A crucial factor in the emergence of new styles of warfare is 'the fact that they have become cheap to wage.'[4]

[1] Munkler, H, 2003, The wars of the 21st century, *International Review of the Red Cross*, 85, 849, March.
[2] Ibid, p 15.
[3] Ibid, p 16.
[4] Ibid, p 17.

The use of rape and sexual violence as tactics requires no special equipment, no special training, no ongoing maintenance or supply of those capable of employing such tactics for an identified goal. If civilian targets take the place of military objectives, it becomes urgent to clarify rules of engagement regarding attacks on non-combatants, including women.[5] Tolerance of rape as a weapon of war has been an ongoing factor in conflicts throughout history. Christoph Schiessl referred to a pro-Serb organisation that denied the reports of rape by saying they had investigated and found there were no reliable reports of 'more than average war-time rape.'[6] He highlighted the 20th-century focus on targeting civilians. Mary Kaldor noted that at the beginning of the 20th century, 85-90% of conflict-related casualties were military; in the Second World War, approximately half the casualties were civilian; by the late 1990s approximately 80% of casualties were civilians.[7] She added that the numbers of internally displaced people rose from approximately 40,000 per conflict in 1969 to 857,000 per conflict in 1992.[8]

Kaldor referred to the 'new wars' of the 20th century, describing the aim of the new warfare as being 'to control the population by getting rid of every one of a different identity (and indeed of a different opinion)'.[9] Intrinsic to controlling populations is controlling the sectors made most vulnerable, women and girls. New warfare has a gendered nature in that it avoids battle, instead controlling territory through strategies that have a serious impact on women and girls:

> ... the strategic goal of these wars is population expulsion through various means such as mass killings, forcible resettlement, as well as a range of political, psychological and economic techniques of intimidation.[10]

Tactical rape and sexual violence are strategies that fit Kaldor's description. Tactical rape is an attack on women and girls as part of civilian rather than military targets. It has both psychological and physical effects, and can be a means of killing and destroying whole

---

5   Ibid, p 18.
6   Schiessl, C, 2000, An element of genocide: rape, total war, and international law in the twentieth century, *Journal of Genocide Research*, 4, 2, 197-210.
7   Kaldor, M, 2002, *New and old wars: Organised violence in a global era*, Cambridge: Polity Press, p 100.
8   Ibid, p 101, quoting Weiner, M, 1996, Bad neighbour, bad neighbourhoods: an enquiry into the causes of refugee flows, *International Security*, 21, 1, Summer.
9   Kaldor, op cit, p 8.
10 Ibid.

generations of a population. Katrina Lee-Koo provided a clear and comprehensive explanation of the impact of rape:

> Rape attacks women's physical and emotional sense of security while simultaneously launching an assault, through women's bodies, upon the genealogy of security as constructed by the body politic.[11]

Tactical rape is a rational strategy, a sanctioned and systematic means of achieving political objectives. Such use of rape can be based on state-sanctioned representations of non-combatant women that reflect rather than confront traditional conceptualisations of women's realities.[12]

The conflicts in the former Yugoslavia and Rwanda were different but had certain common elements. Carl von Clausewitz recognised that while war is 'a true chameleon', forever changing and adapting its appearance to the varying sociopolitical conditions under which it is waged, it is always distinguished by 'the intrinsic violence of its components, the creativity of its strategists and the rationality of the political decision-makers.'[13] Political objectives are those that 'have at their heart control, compliance of civilians and even genocide.'[14] Tactical rape bears all the hallmarks of modern warfare. If war is 'an act of violence intended to compel our opponent to fulfil our will', then rape and any form of sexual violence are effective and destructive and cannot be ignored.[15] They are gendered tactics aimed at attacking individual women and entire communities.

The impact of rape in conflict

Rape is taken here to be a socially learned form of aggression, as described by Lee Ellis, a form of interpersonal aggression arising from learned and observed behaviour.[16] This sociological theory provides a

---

[11] Lee-Koo, K, 2002, Confronting a disciplinary blindness: women, war and rape in the international politics of security, *Australian Journal of Political Science*, 37, pp 525-36.

[12] Ibid, p 525.

[13] von Clausewitz, C, 1980, *Vom Kriege*, 19th edn, Bonn: Werner Hahlweg, pp 212ff, quoted in Munkler, op cit, p 8.

[14] Farwell, N, 2004, War rape: new conceptualisations and responses, *AFFILIA: Journal of Women and Social Work*, 19, 4, Winter, 389-403, p 393.

[15] von Clausewitz, C, 1968, *On War*, London: Pelican Books, p 1.

[16] Ellis, L, 1989, *Theories of rape – Inquiries into the causes of sexual aggression*, Washington, DC: Hemisphere Publishing Corporation.

political and socioeconomic approach and a construction of societies affected in many conflicts. It is a theory that best helps comprehend the impact of tactical rape on women and communities. Tactical rape is perniciously effective because it relies on social relationships and values, particularly the constructed values inherent in patriarchy.

In 1996 Claudia Card noted that rape as a weapon of war was not new, although it was receiving new attention.[17] When considering the nature and impact of rape, she stated:

> One set of fundamental functions of rape, civilian or martial, is to display, communicate and produce or maintain dominance which is enjoyed for its own sake and used for such ulterior ends as exploitation, expulsion, dispersion and murder.[18]

Sexual gratification could have some role in the perpetration of rape. While not the primary motivation for tactical rape, it facilitates its application.

Cynthia Enloe referred to 'the militarization of rape'.[19] She identified three types of rape in war. One was recreational rape as the alleged outcome of not supplying male soldiers with 'adequately accessible' militarised prostitutes.[20] This could be seen as the attitude underlying the enslavement of women by the Japanese Imperial Army between 1932 and 1945.[21] It would, however, require a degree of twisted logic to accept that such enslavement justified 'recreational rape' because armed forces could not control their sexual urges. Enloe also identified national security rape as an instrument for bolstering a nervous state, and systematic, widespread rape as an instrument of open warfare.[22] Each type occurs in many conflict zones and demands attention, prevention and accountability. Tactical rape falls into the category of systematic, widespread rape.

By the end of the 20th century, scholars were reviewing the emerging law on rape from early customary international law through the post-

---

[17] Card, C, 1996, Rape as a weapon of war, *Special issue: Women and Violence*, Indiana University Press.

[18] Ibid, p 2.

[19] Enloe, C, 2000, *Maneuvers: The international politics of militarizing women's lives*, Berkeley, CA: University of California Press.

[20] Ibid, p 111.

[21] See www.amnesty.org/en/latest/campaigns/2015/09/70-years-on-comfort-women-speak-out-so-the-truth-wont-die

[22] Enloe, op cit, p 111.

Second World War era to late 20th-century responses to Rwanda and Bosnia.[23] Rape had long been an element of war. It was not until international global attention was drawn to the conflicts and genocide in the former Yugoslavia and Rwanda that attitudes began to change.

Tactical rape and sexual violence in conflict had to be recognised as affecting individuals, communities and societies. The ICTY Trial Chamber quoted testimony from a medical worker:

> The very act of rape, in my opinion – I spoke to these people, I observed their reactions – it had a terrible effect on them. They could, perhaps, explain it to themselves when somebody steals something from them or even beatings or even some killings. Somehow they sort of accepted it in some way, but when the rapes started they lost all hope. Until then they had hope that this war could pass, that everything would quiet down. When the rapes started, everybody lost hope, everybody in the camp, men and women. There was such fear, horrible.[24]

People who are raped and people who know that others in their group are being raped are all affected, disempowered. Resistance is attacked. Physical and emotional damage results for victims and survivors, individuals and communities.

In her paper questioning the effectiveness of the ICTR in dealing with Rwanda's rape victims, Binaifer Nowrojee quoted statements to the ICTR by Major Brent Beardsley, a professional soldier and a Canadian member of the UN peacekeeping force:

> One, when they killed women it appeared that the blows that had killed them were aimed at sexual organs, either breasts or vagina; they had been deliberately swiped or slashed in those areas. And, secondly, there was a great deal of what we came to believe was rape, where the women's bodies or clothes would be ripped off their bodies, they would be lying back in a back position, their legs spread, especially in the case of very young girls. I'm talking girls as young as six, seven years of age, their vaginas would be split

---

[23] Ellis, M, 2004, Breaking the silence – Rape as an international crime, Talk given to the United Nations Conference on Gender Justice, 16 September, New York.

[24] ICTY, *Prosecutor v Tadič*, Judgement, Case No IT-94-1-A (ICTY App. CH.15 July 1999), para 175.

and swollen from obviously gang rape, and then they would be killed in that position. So they were lying in a position they had been raped; that's the position they were in.

Rape was one of the hardest things to deal with in Rwanda on our part. It deeply affected every one of us. We had a habit at night of coming back to the headquarters and, after activities had slowed down for the night, before we went to bed, sitting around talking about what happened that day, drink coffee, have a chat, and amongst all of us the hardest thing that we had to deal with was not so much the bodies of people, the murder of people – I know that can sound bad, but that wasn't as bad to us as the rape and especially the systematic rape and gang rape of children. Massacres kill the body. Rape kills the soul. And there was a lot of rape.[25]

This is a powerful description of rape in conflict and the impact it has on survivors as well as victims. Beardsley highlighted the particular violence suffered by women and children and the physical evidence of links to gender. His comment that rape kills the soul is indicative of the long-lasting and widespread negative impact of rape.

Various accounts of rape in conflict and in genocide contribute to understanding this impact. The International Committee of the Red Cross (ICRC) has written that rape is at times used as a method of extracting information and as punishment for actual or alleged actions.[26] Human Rights Watch supports this observation of rape as a punishment, with accounts of Serbian police and military forces raping women as a punishment for their husbands or family members being members of the Kosovo Liberation Army; there were also reports of public rapes, which have an additional impact beyond the suffering of individual women.[27] These attack the fabric of communities and can destroy hopes of any long-lasting recovery. The attack extends beyond the individual and beyond the immediate pain and suffering of the victim. Reports from Syria in 2013 indicated that even by then:

[25] Nowrojee, B, 2005, *Your justice is too slow: Will the ICTR fail Rwanda's rape victims?*, United Nations Research Institute for Social Development, November, p 1.

[26] Lindsey, C, 2001, *Women facing war: ICRC study on the impact of armed conflict on women*, Geneva: International Committee of the Red Cross.

[27] Human Rights Watch, 2000, *Gender-based violence against Kosovar Albanian women*.

> Many victims of sexual violence – if not most of them – chose or were forced to leave their homeland, carrying with them the physical and physiological marks to the country of asylum where they are subjected to deprivation of their economic, health, and cultural rights, and face more risk of sexual violence and exploitation through very early marriages, trafficking or forced labor, which forms a new burden on the female refugee who already suffers anxiety, depression and other mental issues due to their tragic memories of violations.[28]

With this conflict continuing in Syria, the possible impact of rape and sexual violence will likely intensify.

Bulert Diken and Carsten Bagge Laustsen noted that in Bosnia-Herzegovina family members were at times forced to rape each other or to witness the rape of family members.[29] After such rapes, victims and perpetrators would have severe difficulty in facing each other. For some men raping was a rite of initiation, forced into a brotherhood of guilt.[30] This is not opportunistic rape by rogue individuals making the most of a breakdown of law and order. This is a deliberate attack on the community as well as on individual women. Diken and Laustsen noted that as well as immediate degradation, pain and terror, rape survivors frequently experience long-term physical injury, psychological trauma, sexually transmitted diseases and pregnancy. Intense cultural pressures can come into play, especially when there is cultural opposition to abortion but rejection of a child conceived by rape, and abortion in a context where health provision was likely to be disrupted.[31]

Hilary Charlesworth and Christine Chinkin noted the ways in which rape in war has an impact on women and their communities:

> As well as the immediate degradation, pain and terror, rape survivors frequently experience long-term physical injury and psychological trauma. Fear and shock are also

---

[28] Euro-Mediterranean Human Rights Network, 2013, *Violence against women, bleeding wound in the Syrian conflict*, Sema Nasar, November.

[29] Diken, B, Laustsen, CB, 2005, Becoming abject: rape as a weapon of war, *Body and Society*, 11, 1, 111-28.

[30] Ibid.

[31] Ibid.

experienced by women who were not themselves subjected to attack.[32]

It is essential to understand that fear and shock are experienced by survivors and victims and by those in their collective group. Charlesworth and Chinkin recognised several allied impacts on women raped in conflict, including the risk of sexually transmitted diseases and pregnancy, with the possibility of facing childbirth or seeking an abortion 'at a time of great dislocation, with reduced health care and intense social and cultural pressures, sometimes against abortion and sometimes against keeping a child conceived by rape.'[33] Physical damage may last a long time after an attack, and can have serious health implications for childbirth, at the very time when health services are least available.

Women forced to flee conflict zones are made vulnerable to rape and sexual violence. Charlesworth and Chinkin referred to attacks 'in refugee camps, in foreign countries or as displaced persons in their own countries' and to demands for sex amounting to rape when such demands are exploiting the economic need of women, and are made as requisites for provision of food and necessities for survival.[34] The definitions of rape in war developed in the ICTY and ICTR began to come to terms with rape that was not specifically the result of physical force and violent attack, but the result of coercion. Charlesworth and Chinkin were voicing the concerns about rape necessitating violent force, and the international community gradually confronted these concerns.

Charlesworth and Chinkin also recognised that war-related rape may continue after a conflict. They noted, 'a rape epidemic was reported in Kuwait after "liberation" at levels worse than during the Iraqi occupation', where the attitude of men perpetrating the rapes was that the women targeted 'deserved' their treatment for 'supporting' the Iraqis.[35] The government took no action against these crimes, 'especially where rapes were committed by men in uniform.'[36] Tactical rape can leave a legacy of using rape for a variety of reasons and a variety of expressions of power relations.

---

[32] Charlesworth, H, Chinkin, C, 2000, *The boundaries of international law: A feminist analysis*, Manchester: Manchester University, p 252.

[33] Ibid, p 253.

[34] Ibid.

[35] Ibid, p 262.

[36] Ibid, p 262.

Rape, always an expression of power relationships, can in conflict express power over a collective as well as over an individual. A report relating to the former Yugoslavia in 1992 noted that there was mounting evidence of 'systematic rape', with survivors speaking of what they called 'rape on the front line' and 'third-party rape', which were reported as rapes carried out publicly by Serbian soldiers to demoralise family members and opposition forces compelled to witness them.[37] This report was based on accounts given by women and workers in a refugee camp. The stories were accepted as sufficiently convincing for legal and formal investigations to consider them, and I was requested to brief a European Council investigative team that travelled to Zagreb immediately after the report's distribution.[38]

The report of the European Council mission substantiated the earlier report:

> ... the delegation frequently heard – including from several
> individual witnesses and sources – that a repeated feature
> of Serbian attacks on Moslems towns and villages was the
> use of rape, often in public.[39]

This public rape was perceived as having an impact both on the victim and on her community. The collective impact of tactical rape must be traced back to collective social relationships.

Collective social relationships

The vulnerability of women and communities to tactical rape and sexual violence could be lessened by clear recognition of the interaction of conflict with social attitudes and norms, and by subsequently attempting to change those attitudes and norms that are part of collective values and sense of identity. There is a real need to 'un/ recover the experiences of women.'[40] It has been said that 'culture

---

[37] Fitzpatrick, B, 1992, *Rape of women in war*, Geneva: World Council of Churches, December, p 21.

[38] Warburton, A, 1993, *European Council investigative mission into the treatment of Muslim women in the former Yugoslavia, Report to EC foreign ministers, December 1992-February 1993*, 28 January.

[39] Ibid, para 2.

[40] Lee-Koo, op cit, p 526.

constitutes one's political self.'[41] If, as Munkler claimed, 'the defence of cultural identity could also become a recurring reason for going to war', then attacks on cultural identity can be an effective and strategic way to wage war.[42] Attitudes to women are part of cultural identity, and patriarchy is an attitude that affects both men and women, rendering whole communities vulnerable to the destructive force of tactical rape and sexual violence in war. Adrienne Rich provided one definition:

> Patriarchy is the power of the fathers: a familial–social, ideological, political system in which men – by force, direct pressure or through ritual, tradition, law and language, customs, etiquette, education and the division of labour determine what part women shall or shall not play and in which the female is everywhere subsumed under the male.[43]

The definition articulates many features of patriarchal societies, even though these may be interpreted differently between cultures.

Nancy Farwell provided valuable insights to the links often demonstrated between patriarchal attitudes and militarisation of rape.[44] Protectionist values inherent in patriarchal relationships promote the view that women are the property of men and as such are to be defended.[45] A female may be 'viewed as a vessel for a male seed', and this can provide 'a construct that is central to the use of rape in ethnic cleansing.'[46] In patriarchal societies women are perceived as protecting the honour of the community through marriage and cultural practices that maintain a pure lineage and pure ethnic-cultural heritage.[47] This explains how 'rape and sexual violence during ethnic conflict become strategies for infiltrating or destroying those boundaries and attacking

---

[41] Wildavsky, A, 1989, Choosing preferences by constructing institutions: a cultural theory of preference formation, in AA. Berger (ed), *Political culture and public opinion*, New Brunswick, NJ: Transaction, pp 21-46, quoted in Finnemore, M, Sikkink, K, 2001, Taking stock: the constructivist research program in international relations and comparative politics, *Annual Review of Political Science*, 4, 391, p 408.

[42] Munkler, op cit, p 12.

[43] Rich, A, 1986, *Of woman born: Motherhood as experience and institution*, New York: Norton, p 57, quoted in Puechguirbal, N, 2010, Discourses on gender, patriarchy and resolution 1325: a textual analysis of UN documents, *International Peacekeeping*, 17, 2, 172-87.

[44] Farwell, op cit.

[45] Ibid, p 394.

[46] Ibid, pp 394-5.

[47] Ibid, p 395.

the honour of the community and the purity of the lineage.'[48] The individual victim suffers direct physical and emotional pain. The community suffers from a perceived attack on the holder of its values and its lineage, an attack on a member the community perceives it has a responsibility to protect.

Patriarchy damages women and girls by restricting their access to many rights. It can facilitate acceptance of sexual violence against women and girls. When men restrict the freedom and rights of women, when they condone or commit sexual violence, indirectly they are also making their own communities vulnerable to attacks such as tactical rape and sexual violence in conflict. In Rwanda, before the genocide, women were traditionally deemed to be dependents of men. A 1996 report on the status of women in Rwandan society said:

> Throughout their lives, women are expected to be managed and protected by their fathers, their husbands and their male children. Traditionally, the role of the Rwandan woman in society centred on her position as wife and mother.[49]

Women were valued as belongings, and the value a woman placed on herself was largely determined by male expectations and attitudes. Patriarchy damages women's self-esteem and makes them liable to doubt their own strengths and capacity. Such an attitude gives males power but also pressures males to protect 'their' women. Any failure to do so could contribute to a sense of social disintegration and could intensify the defeat of an 'owner' unable to protect 'his' property. Testimonies in Chapter Six demonstrate the damage done to women as a result of such attitudes. But they also demonstrate the strength of women who survived violation and who faced the insensitivity of courts and legal personnel, and who placed themselves at further physical and emotional risk from parts of their own communities. In 1992, the UN Committee monitoring the *Convention on the Elimination of All Forms of Discrimination Against Women (CEDAW)* commented:

> ... traditional attitudes by which women are regarded as subordinate to men or as having stereotyped roles perpetuate widespread practices involving violence or coercion, such as family violence and abuse, forced marriage, dowry deaths,

---

[48] Ibid.

[49] Nowrojee, B, 1996, *Shattered lives: Sexual violence during the Rwandan genocide and its aftermath*, New York: Human Rights Watch, September, p 14.

acid attacks and female circumcision. Such prejudices and practices may justify gender-based violence as a form of protection or control of women.[50]

The combination of patriarchal attitudes and women's gender is a potent factor in the effectiveness of tactical rape and sexual violence in conflict.

Jill Steans, in her monograph *Gender and international relations*, provided valuable insight to understanding how patriarchy and the notion of 'protectors' and the 'protected' intersect with the suffering of women in conflicts.[51] Women are always seen as those needing protection politically, socially and physically, and while this is at odds with the strengths demonstrated by women and their role as carers, it can be a pervasive attitude. Steans' chapter on understanding 'how gender is central to the processes involved in constructing the boundaries of the nation–states, specifically war' underscored the bases of many societies that render women vulnerable when those 'protectors' are unable or unwilling to fulfil the constructed role.[52] It is helpful to see her analysis of the relationship between military participation and citizenship concluding with the implications of the relationship between women and 'the state, the military- and state-sanctioned violence'.[53]

The distinction between the perceived 'protectors' and 'protected' disguises the particular ways women suffer in wars: they are made vulnerable to tactical rape; their health is damaged; lives and livelihoods are disrupted; and many become refugees and are at further risk of sexual violence in camps.[54] When I was in refugee camps, women who had to walk considerable distances for water or firewood were at risk of attack. It was something of a breakthrough when UNHCR finally realised that lighting around toilet facilities at least lessened the risk of night-time attacks within camps. Refugee women were most often without their 'protectors' and were fending for themselves. This might be seen as somehow liberating, but for women who had been convinced they were better off with protection, this was part of the whole trauma of being displaced geographically as well as socially and

[50] UN Women, 1992, *Convention on the Elimination of All Forms of Discrimination against Women*, General Recommendation No 19, 11th session, New York.
[51] Steans, J, 1998, *Gender and international relations*, New Brunswick, NJ: Rutgers University Press.
[52] Ibid, Chapter 4.
[53] Ibid, p 8.
[54] Ibid, p 100.

emotionally. Steans quoted J.H. Stiehm who had noted that 'protectors usually control those whom they protect',[55] and Jan Pettman, 'the protector/protected relationship makes women vulnerable to other men's/states' violence.'[56]

My experience and observation leads me to agree with Steans that patriarchal attitudes underlie and exacerbate women's vulnerability in wartime, particularly their vulnerability to rape. Steans also highlighted that 'rape in warfare does not occur as an isolated incident' but, as she claimed feminists had long argued, attitudes to rape 'should be viewed as an accepted part of the code that governs the fighting of wars rather than as an individual act of wrong'.[57] This was echoed in situations such as my exchanges noted earlier in Chapter One, where a churchman said, 'of course' women were being raped because 'that's war'. Steans concluded convincingly, 'war, violence and women's oppression all grow from the same root'.[58] The notion of women as victims with little capacity to protect themselves and participate in peacemaking and peacekeeping has been soundly debated and been contradicted by many survivors of tactical rape. Steans contributed to the debate by explaining the societal underpinnings that can make tactical rape and sexual violence effective forms of attack.

So, too, did Christine Chinkin, who wrote that the potency of rape as a weapon is often due to the fact that for men, the rape of their women encapsulates the totality of their defeat as they are demonstrably unable to protect 'their' women.[59] It is somewhat ironic that by making women vulnerable and controlling women, men create a route to their own sense of failure. Military men often assume that their violent roles extend to their sexual rights, as Hilary Charlesworth and Christine Chinkin noted when quoting B. Reardon: 'sexually manifested violence' is 'connected to ideas of male soldiers' privileges, to the power of the military's line of command as well as by class and ethnic differences among women.'[60] Women are made vulnerable by the codes

55 Stiehm, JH, 1982, The protector, the protected and the defender, *Women's Studies International Forum*, 5, 3/4, 367–76, quoted in Steans, op cit, p 101.

56 Pettman, JJ, 1996, *Worlding women: A feminist international politics*, London: Routledge, quoted in Steans, op cit, p 100.

57 Steans, op cit, p 101.

58 Ibid, p 102.

59 Chinkin, C, 1994, Rape and abuse of women in international law, Symposium – The Yugoslav crisis: New international law issues, *European Journal of International Law*, 5, 326–41.

60 Reardon, B, 1985, *Sexism and the war system*, New York: Teachers College Press, p 39, quoted in Charlesworth and Chinkin, op cit, p 254.

around males' expectations. This flows on to the broader group that accepts that code. Charlesworth and Chinkin also quoted R. Seifert: 'to rape a woman is to humiliate her community.'[61] Patriarchy and gendered vulnerability form a context to be understood for its implications regarding tactical rape and sexual violence in conflict.

Charlesworth and Chinkin also wrote, 'Sexually manifested violence in armed conflict is an aspect of the subordinate position of women globally.'[62] Writing in 1998, they noted:

> ... the entirely unacceptable situation in international law is that the fundamental norms which all states must observe include systematic racial discrimination but not discrimination against women or even widespread gender-based violence. Women have had to mount a campaign to have violence against women, in all its forms, recognised as an international legal wrong.[63]

They are among the feminist analysts who highlight the links between rape in conflict and underlying gender relationships often most clearly determined in recognition of patriarchy. Tadeusz Mazowiecki, Special Rapporteur of the Commission on Human Rights, said that rape was used in the former Yugoslavia, to humiliate, shame, degrade and terrify an entire ethnic group.[64] This reflects the reality that communities see women as belonging to the group, as requiring protection, and as holders of what Farwell called 'the purity of the lineage'.[65] Social constructions regarding the perceived damage by rape to a woman's value come into play. There is a complex and damaging effect on individual women and on women as part of a group.

Binaifer Nowrojee has also described the group impact of rape:

> The humiliation, pain and terror inflicted by the rapist are meant to degrade not just the individual woman but also to strip the humanity from the larger group of which

---

[61] Seifert, R, 1994, War and rape: a preliminary analysis, in A Stigelmayer (ed), *Mass rape: The war against women in Bosnia-Herzegovina*, Lincoln, NE: University of Nebraska Press, p 82, quoted in Charlesworth and Chinkin, op cit, p 254.

[62] Charlesworth and Chinkin, op cit, p 254.

[63] Ibid, p xi.

[64] Mazowiecki, T, 1993, Special Rapporteur of the Commission on Human Rights, Report pursuant to Commission resolution 1992/S-1/1 of 14 August 1992, UN Doc E/CN. 4199/50, 10 February.

[65] Farwell, op cit, p 395.

she is a part. The rape of one person is translated into an assault upon the community through the emphasis placed in every culture on women's sexual virtue: the shame of the rape humiliates the family and all those associated with the survivor.[66]

Patriarchal attitudes damage whole communities, males and females, although this in no way diminishes the suffering of individual women victims of tactical rape and sexual violence. Their suffering is intensified in a community that is culturally patriarchal. As accounts from women in Rwanda and the former Yugoslavia make clear, physical attacks and violations of women are exacerbated by their feelings of shame and their perception of themselves as being less valuable as well as of being less valued. Tactical rape has a long-term communal, as well as an immediate individual, capacity to damage.

Lynda Boose posited that the way rape is socially constructed makes it 'primarily' a violation defiling male members of families and communities, and concluded, 'the more patriarchal the culture, the more vulnerable it becomes, all the more likely are the women to become targets for enemy rape'.[67] While rape may be a violation of males, it is questionable that it is 'primarily' a violation of those males in any society.

In 2006, Diana Milillo specifically referred to rape as a tactic of war, and linked the devastating impact of rape on individuals and societies with patriarchy:

… the systematic nature of rape as a tactic of war exists against a backdrop of rigid cultural norms of gender and women's sexuality, social dominance and power within conflicting groups and a soldier's identity as a man and as a member of a particular military group.[68]

Milillo's linking of tactics and rape in war was an advance in understanding causes and motivations. On the one hand, she challenged the notion that all men have a drive to use their genitalia as a weapon,

[66] Nowrojee, 1996, op cit, p 2.
[67] Boose, LE, 2002, Crossing the River Drina: Bosnian rape camps, Turkish impalement and Serb cultural memory, *Signs*, 28, 1, Gender and Cultural Memory, Autumn.
[68] Milillo, D, 2006, Rape as a tactic of war – social and psychological perspectives, *AFFILIA: Journal of Women and Social Work*, 21, 2, p 196.

saying that not all men rape, and in fact, not even most men rape.[69] On the other hand, Milillo quoted H. Tajfel and J.C. Turner, who believed that individual men desire a positive social identity and will do what is needed to enhance the status of the group perceived as the 'in-group' and/or to discriminate against the 'out group'.[70] This can be a double-edged sword. Chapter Six on genocide in Rwanda indicates how many men were involved in violent attacks as a result of such a desire or need to belong to the dominant group.

Lee-Koo highlighted the 'extreme insecurity' of women in war, and the failure of mainstream approaches to international relations theory to identify this extreme insecurity of individual women and their experiences in inter-state war.[71] She criticised the realist and neo-realist traditions of international relations theory for rendering women unseen and unheard in international relations, trapping them in gendered and subordinate roles. She acknowledged some positive developments: international recognition of the socially constructed and gendered reality identifying vested interests in the subordination of women, and awareness of multiple subjectivities of women helping to dispel the 'essential women' myth.[72]

As members of patriarchal societies, women themselves may share their society's value of them. A report from the Government of Rwanda in 1995 reflected that society's value of women:

> ... the ideal image of a woman is still generally viewed through the perspective of her maternal role. The woman must be fertile, hard-working and reserved. She must learn the art of silence and reserve.[73]

Rwandan women could share this view, explaining why many would be reluctant to speak of their experiences of being raped. Silence and reserve were honoured. Those who were physically damaged and no longer likely to be able to bear children were likely to fear being

---

[69] Brownmiller, S, 1975, *Against our will: Men, women and rape*, New York: Simon & Schuster, quoted in Milillo, op cit, p 198.

[70] Tajfel, H, Turner, JC, 1986, The social identity theory of inter-group behaviour, in S Worchel and WG Austin (eds), *Psychology of inter-group relations*, Chicago, IL: Nelson Hall, 7-24, quoted in Milillo, op cit, p 201.

[71] Lee-Koo, op cit, pp 525-36.

[72] Ibid, p 527.

[73] Government of Rwanda, 1995, *Rapport national du Rwanda pour le Quatrième Conférence Mondiale sur les Femmes*, Beijing, September, p 19.

rejected as no longer fertile and valuable. In the report, *Shattered lives*, Nowrojee said:

> In Rwanda, as elsewhere in the world, rape and other gender-based violations carry a severe social stigma. The physical and psychological injuries suffered by Rwandan rape survivors are aggravated by a sense of isolation and ostracisation. Rwandan women who have been raped or have suffered sexual abuse generally do not dare reveal their experiences publicly, fearing that they will be rejected by their family and wider community, and that they will never be able to reintegrate or marry.[74]

This statement would likely hold true for women in many other patriarchal societies. The silence of women who have survived rape of any form has been a long-standing issue, and there are many reasons for such silence.

Testimonies from victims and survivors in Rwanda and the former Yugoslavia are particularly illustrative of the impact of tactical rape on women, an impact that goes beyond the agonising physical suffering they experienced and that reflects the constructed sense of self as a member of a society. One woman, 'Goretti', was raped for days by various groups and had her legs held open while the sharpened end of the stick of a hoe was pushed into her.[75] After this she found some temporary refuge before being raped again. In the telling of these horrific events she said that after the last rapes:

> I was left alone and naked. I decided to try and escape. I couldn't walk properly and so was on all fours. When people passed me, I sat down and stopped walking so they wouldn't know I had been raped because I was ashamed.[76]

The fact that she felt shame was an addition to her plight that goes beyond the terrible physical attack and reflects an imposed constructed value of herself. The same sense of imposed degradation and heartbreaking sorrow was reflected when she said, 'you can't ever

[74] Nowrojee, 1996, op cit, p 3.
[75] Ibid, pp 28–9.
[76] Ibid, pp 28–9.

forget. Until I die, I'll always be sad.'[77] There have been many stories of such dire suffering.

Another victim and survivor, 'Josepha', said, 'rape is a crime worse than death.'[78] 'Jeanne', who was abducted and kept in sexual slavery as a 'wife', said, 'rape is a crime worse than others. There's no death worse than that.'[79] 'Nadia', who was 11 when the militia attacked her house, was still severely traumatised two years after seeing them hack her brothers to pieces in front of her, was then taken and raped at least five times. She said:

> He threatened to kill me with his machete. He would keep the machete near the bed while he raped me. I have never told anyone before what happened to me. I am ashamed and scared that people will laugh at me.[80]

Shame such as this is socially constructed and imposed. Medical practitioners have reported rape victims being reluctant to seek medical treatment because of the fear of being judged because 'society is looking at you' and they feel such shame.[81] The effects of tactical rape are not some unfortunate by-products. One interviewee stated, 'many women begged to be killed during the genocide', continuing, 'they were refused and told, you will die of sadness.'[82] The rapes were often accompanied by severe torture and mutilation, particularly of sexual organs, which emphasised degradation and violation:

> Sexual mutilations included the pouring of boiling water into the vagina; the opening of the womb; to cut out an unborn child before killing the mother; cutting off breasts; slashing the pelvis area; and the mutilation of vaginas.[83]

---

[77] Ibid, p 29.

[78] Ibid, p 28.

[79] Ibid, p 35.

[80] Ibid, pp 34–5.

[81] Ibid: FIDH interview, E Rwamasirabo, Director, Kigali Central Hospital, Kigali, 16 March 1996.

[82] bid: FIDH interview, Ester Mujawayo, Association for Widows of the April Genocide, 18 March 1996.

[83] Ibid: Coordination of Women's Advocacy, *Mission on gender-based war crimes against women and girls during the genocide in Rwanda: Summary of findings and recommendations*, p 7.

Such actions are more than torture. As well as savage personal physical attacks, they are a destructive attack on future generations, and are considered to be a direct demeaning of the value of women. This is a potent attack in societies where women are valued as holding the purity of lineage.

The impact of tactical rape is often greater when rapes result in pregnancies. This is heightened when there is the added belief in strongly patriarchal societies that children 'belong' to their fathers. During the visit of an international team to refugee camps in and around Zagreb in 1992, a woman in Zagreb said, 'one part of me – deep inside – believes that my children belong to their father.'[84] She explained the struggle that a community would have in accepting the children of rapes as part of the mothers' communities. As a strategy to attack the civilians of opposing groups, rape is frighteningly effective.

Nowrojee explained the rights of men in Rwanda, noting that in Rwanda, customary law accords men the role of head of the family.[85] They inherit property, name children and transmit the family name. Before the genocide, when ethnicity was registered it was the father's ethnicity that was transmitted. If the husband dies, children can be taken from the wife by the husband's family as the children 'belong' to the husband and his family.[86] This has serious implications for inheritance laws and recognition of children. They are the children of their fathers even when the result of rape:

> Pregnant women, including those of Hutu origin, were killed on the grounds that the foetuses in their wombs were fathered by Tutsi men, for in a patrilineal society like Rwanda, the child belongs to the father's group of origin.[87]

Other testimonies heard, especially that of Major-General Dallaire, also show that there was an intention to wipe out the Tutsi group in its entirety, since even newborn babies were not spared.[88]

One witness testified regarding the rape of Tutsi women married to Hutu men. She described encountering on the road a man and woman, whom she knew to be a Tutsi married to a Hutu and who

[84] Fitzpatrick, op cit, p 20.
[85] Nowrojee, 1996, op cit, pp 48–50.
[86] Ibid, pp 48–50.
[87] ICTR, *The Prosecutor v Jean-Paul Akayesu*, ICTR-96-4-T, Decision of 2 September 1998 [The Akayesu decision], para 121.
[88] Ibid.

was 'not exactly dead' and still in agony.[89] She continued to describe the Interahamwe (a Hutu paramilitary organisation) forcing a piece of wood into the woman's sexual organs while she was still breathing, before she died. However, the witness believed that in most cases Tutsi women married to Hutu men 'were left alone because it was said that these women deliver Hutu children.'[90] She believed that there were Hutu men who married Tutsi women to save them, but that these women were sought, taken away forcibly and killed.[91] One accused at the ICTR was quoted as saying to a Tutsi woman that 'when rats are killed you don't spare rats that are still in the form of fetus'.[92] She had been pregnant and miscarried after being beaten by the police and Interahamwe. Of her nine children, only two survived the events of this period.[93]

There was another savage attack on a woman called 'Alexia' who was pregnant. The Interahamwe threw her to the ground and climbed on top of her, saying 'now, let's see what the vagina of a Tutsi woman feels like.'[94] Alexia gave the Interahamwe, named Pierre, her Bible before he raped her and told him, 'take this Bible because it's our memory.'[95] Then one person held her neck, others took her by the shoulders and others held her thighs apart as numerous Interahamwe continued to rape her. When she became weak she was turned over, and lying on her stomach she went into premature delivery during the rapes.[96]

When a woman is physically damaged to the point of not being able to be sexually active nor to have children, she, as well as the community, may judge her as devalued, not worthy of being a marriage partner. An international team interviewing refugees and workers in camps in Zagreb in 1992 was told that there had been calls within the Muslim community to accept women who had been raped as 'heroes' and 'to maintain marriage as a continuing option.'[97] Motivation behind the call was to be supportive and to ameliorate community judgement of raped women as being of less value. However, as women workers at the time said to one another and to the team, there would be many women who would not welcome any sexual relationship after their

---

[89] Ibid, para 429.
[90] Ibid.
[91] Ibid.
[92] Ibid, para 428.
[93] Ibid.
[94] Ibid, para 473.
[95] Ibid.
[96] Ibid.
[97] Fitzpatrick, op cit, p 23.

attacks, and so would be caught between the choice of entering into an unwelcome marriage or being seen as less than a natural woman, with a less secure place in their society.

In Rwanda, 'Maria', an 18-year-old Hutu student, 'does not like to see or be near men.'[98] She saw her grandparents, two aunts and her brother killed before she was gang raped and her vagina was slashed with knives by militia who shouted, 'We are going to kill you so you will want death.'[99] What may seem at first as a nonsensical statement actually reflects a different form of killing for a woman, a form of attacking so that a quick death would be welcome. When Maria eventually reached medical help, reconstructive surgery was performed, but she will never be sexually active or bear children, and she is HIV positive. She said, 'They have ruined my future. I am not the only one. What they did to me they did to many others. But what can I do?'[100] In a society that values a woman for bearing children, Maria is deemed valueless. Such is the destructive impact of rape when patriarchy is prevalent. Societal attitudes are constructed, so they can be changed. It is important to understand how such change can be effected.

Changing societal attitudes

Key stimuli for changing existing attitudes and relationships may come from international or transnational sources. NGOs can be key agents, working within global and national civil society. The Prosecutor of the ICC noted: 'global civil society, as a network of domestic and transnational non-governmental organisations is able to shape the values and the priorities of the international community.'[101] He said, 'when domestic and trans-national NGOs work together in consensus with a common message, new international norms are established and justice can more easily be recognised.'[102] This was certainly the case in drawing attention to the widespread use of rape in both the former Yugoslavia and Rwanda in the 1990s. Many NGOs and multilateral agencies had for many years highlighted situations of tragic sexual abuse and rape in conflicts. In the early 1990s, they seemed finally to attract due attention, supported by individuals and organisational leaders within

---

[98]   Nowrojee, 1996, op cit, p 40.

[99]   Ibid.

[100]   Ibid, p 41.

[101]   Moreno-Ocampo, L, 2010, *OTP-NGO Roundtable: Introductory remarks*, The Hague, 19 October, p 5.

[102]   Ibid, p 5.

and beyond country borders, civil society groups within country and regional structures. Pressure for a response to the reports of widespread rape came from sustained attention and publicity from public media and NGOs, and eventually from the UN's own rapporteurs. It became difficult for states to ignore the use of rape. Events in the former Yugoslavia and Rwanda were being perceived as pressing by the public media. Action was demanded of the UN Security Council, and even some states themselves demanded more than statements of rejection and called for resolutions and action to confront tactical rape and sexual violence in conflict.[103]

An idea's degree of persuasion may originate in the perceived legitimacy of the advocate as well as in the international support it receives. Thomas Risse, Stephen C. Ropp and Kathryn Sikkink recognised the role of 'transnational advocacy networks', agreeing with other analysts that these are networks of 'those relevant actors working internationally on an issue, who are bound together by shared values, a common discourse, and dense exchanges of information and services'.[104] Risse et al acknowledged the essential role of international NGOs and foundations that are loosely connected to human rights organisations (international and domestic), and the role of international institutions such as UN bodies and related treaties drafted and ratified under the auspices of UN and regional institutions.[105] Such transnational advocacy networks were instrumental in sustaining attention and responses to tactical rape and sexual violence in war.

Risse et al posited processes by which states are socialised and norms become entrenched in domestic policy and practice, moving beyond rhetoric when ideas and norms become habitualised and internalised.[106] Attitudes need to become part of the rule of law in states as well as at international level. Shirley V. Scott commented that the principle of the rule of law 'serves as a normative basis for law: it establishes what the law should do, even though it does not always do so'.[107] Rejection of tactical rape and sexual violence in conflict must be translated from global rhetoric into state institutions, policy and practice, so that changed attitudes become part of the rule of law.

---

[103] See Chapter Six regarding UN Security Council resolution 1820.

[104] Risse, T, Ropp, SC, Sikkink, K, 1999, *The power of human rights: International norms and domestic change*, Cambridge: Cambridge University Press, p 18.

[105] Ibid, p 21.

[106] Ibid.

[107] Scott, SV, 2004, *International law in world politics*, Boulder, CO: Lynne Rienner Publishers, p 13.

Risse et al also highlighted that normative change influences political change through a socialisation process: 'norms become relevant and causally consequential during the process by which actors define and refine their collective identities and interests.'[108] Furthermore, they identified three types of socialisation process: first, the processes of adaptation and strategic bargaining; second, the processes of moral consciousness-raising, 'shaming', argumentation, dialogue and persuasion; and third, the processes of institutionalisation and habitualisation.[109] These stages may overlap or occur in parallel time.

States may first endorse a norm for strategic motives in a desire to win approval from other states, and consequently political and economic benefits. Risse et al note that to 'endorse a norm not only expresses a belief, but also creates an impetus for behaviour consistent with the belief'.[110] So whatever the motive, there can be moves to the second stage, accompanying or raising moral consciousness. Norms adopted or given rhetorical support by some leaders may eventually become internalised as those leaders, used to hearing the rhetoric, come to believe and accept what have become collective expectations. Consequently, 'the goal of socialisation is for the actors to internalise norms, so that external pressure is no longer needed to ensure compliance'.[111] When international actors and organisations such as those at the UN Security Council and General Assembly began to reject certain behaviours, even rhetorically, it is possible that eventually change occurred in normative attitudes. However, no significant change can be deemed to have taken place if apparent acceptance of an attitude or value is not reflected by ratification of relevant international conventions and optional protocols; is not reflected in constitutions and domestic law; does not provide some mechanisms for citizens to call for redress of abuses; and if states do not comply without complaint of 'interference in internal affairs.'[112] Reliance on states to institutionalise norms such as rejection of tactical rape and sexual violence is in itself problematic, as many feminist scholars have highlighted that there is an inherent legitimising of 'a model of (male) dominance and (female) subservience within states as immutable'.[113]

---

[108] Risse et al, op cit, p 9.
[109] Risse et al, op cit, p 11.
[110] Ibid, p 7.
[111] Ibid, p 11.
[112] Ibid, p 29.
[113] Charlesworth and Chinkin, op cit, p 164.

J.T. Checkel similarly agreed that not only do different states react differently to the same international norms, but mechanisms for internalising norms within states also differ.[114] Change happens slowly in social, communal attitudes and responses to events, and is often eventually encapsulated in the development of new social and community attitudes and values. The working of international tribunals and the Security Council are relevant because international law and international organisations are the primary vehicles for stating community norms and for collective legitimation.[115]

As moral consciousness occurs and is shared, allied processes of argumentation, dialogue and persuasion come into play. Shaming agents or entities, which do not comply with articulated and accepted standards, may be effective in applying pressure for compliance. As the expectations of collective behaviour are integrated into the operations and expectations of institutions, they are simultaneously strengthened. By making judgements and legal clarifications, the ICTY and ICTR institutionalised international standards and demonstrated that tactical rape and sexual violence were contraventions of acceptable attitudes. Engaging in moral discourse can contribute to eventual conviction that these standards are justified. Adaptation of behaviour can follow. It is also possible, however, that, 'actors might actually agree on the moral validity of the norm, but disagree whether certain behaviour is covered by it.'[116]

Moral attitudes can be misappropriated, used as excuses for behaviour that would otherwise be condemned. Countering terrorism or extremism may be invoked to cover behaviour against groups or governments that are perceived to be oppositional. Risse, Ropp and Sikkink acknowledged that persuasion itself can be conflictual, and often involves 'not just reasoning with opponents, but also pressures, arm-twisting and sanctions'.[117] There is a long way to go before rejection of tactical rape and sexual violence in war is fully institutionalised by states, until it is 'incorporated into standard operating procedures of domestic institutions' and 'actors follow the norm because it is the

---

[114] Checkel, JT, 1997, International norms and domestic politics: bridging the rationalist-constructivist divide, *European Journal of International Relations*, 3, 473–95; Checkel, JT, 1998, The constructivist turn in international relations theory, *World Politics*, 50, 324–48, 1998; Checkel, JT, 2001, Why comply? Social learning and European identity change, *International Organisation*, 553–88, quoted in Finnemore and Sikkink, op cit, p 397.

[115] Risse et al, op cit, p 8.

[116] Ibid, p 11.

[117] Ibid, p 14.

normal thing to do'.[118] However, a strong motivation for states to institutionalise the rejection of tactical rape and sexual violence in conflict can be the belief that it is in a state's own interest to conform to international norms for economic, political or security reasons.

An important step towards real rejection of tactical rape and sexual violence in conflict is changing and challenging existing law to have it respond to a feminist analysis. In 1991, Hilary Charlesworth, Christine Chinkin and Shelley Wright focused on developing an international feminist perspective, outlined the male organisational and normative structure of the international legal system, and applied feminist analyses to various legal principles.[119] This required 'looking behind the abstract entities of states to the actual impact of rules on women within states'.[120] They concluded that modern international law is both andro-centric and Euro-centred in its origins, and includes legal institutions that are essentially patriarchal and based on questionable assumptions that law is objective, gender-neutral and universally applicable. Understanding and challenging the patriarchal base that applies in many situations must be a foundation for an emerging change of attitude and to non-acceptance of tactical rape and sexual violence in war.

Conclusion

Social attitudes can have serious consequences on the degree of vulnerability constructed for women in conflict. Such attitudes can and should be confronted. Patriarchy and a sense of male 'ownership' of women contribute to women's vulnerability and, importantly, can also contribute to women undervaluing their own worth, strengths and capacities. Patriarchy and the control that accompanies the sense of ownership renders women vulnerable to attack when male combatants set out to find ways to attack each other. As L.R. Jefferson said, 'the patterns of social dominance and deeply engrained gender-specific roles get violently expressed in wartime'.[121] Normative change is possible, and understanding the processes and steps in such possible change forms an integral part in working to effect that change. Strategies to achieve social relationships and women's access to rights, to ensure

---

[118] Ibid, p 17.

[119] Charlesworth, H, Chinkin, C, Wright, S, 1991, Feminist approaches to international law, *The American Journal of International Law*, 85, 4, October, 613-45.

[120] Ibid, p 614.

[121] Jefferson, LR, 2004, *In war as in peace: Sexual violence and women's status*, New York, Human Rights Watch, January, p 3.

women's strengths and capacity to participate fully in decision-making in peacetime and during and post-conflict, will result in greater real protection from tactical rape and sexual violence in war.

FOUR

Critical commentary

Feminist commentators, NGOs and political advocates condemn the use of rape and sexual violence. Critical analysis includes reservations regarding theorising on rape in conflict, recognises legitimate concerns about the limitations and inappropriateness of judicial systems and gendered international law. It recognises the suffering of women in adversarial court proceedings, and notes the omission of mention and lack of understanding of tactical rape. Despite these legitimate concerns, I am convinced that imperfect and incremental normative change is significant.

Critical analysis

Hilary Charlesworth and Christine Chinkin examined the boundaries of international law from a feminist perspective.[1] They believe that international law excludes appreciation of women's concerns. Gendered attitudes inherent in law, supposedly applying to both men and women, really ignore or fail to recognise the differing needs of the two genders. International law is 'a mechanism for distributing power and resources in the international and national communities.'[2] Quoting Elizabeth Grosz, Charlesworth and Chinkin argued the 'international' in international law is a 'veiled representation and projection of a masculine which takes itself as the unquestioned norm'.[3] While I argue that international law is a logical starting point in achieving recognition and response to tactical rape, it does have serious limitations when applied to women. Charlesworth and Chinkin have informed this understanding by providing sound feminist analysis of international law.

They are convinced that feminist analysis has two major roles: 'one is deconstruction of the explicit and implicit values of the international legal system, challenging their claim to objectivity and rationality

---

[1]   Charlesworth, H, Chinkin, C, 2000, *The boundaries of international law: A feminist analysis*, Manchester: Manchester University Press, p 252.

[2]   Ibid, p 1.

[3]   Grosz, E, 1994, *Volatile bodies: Towards a corporeal feminism*, Sydney, NSW: Allen & Unwin, p 103, quoted in Charlesworth and Chinkin, op cit, p 60.

because of the limited base on which they are built'.[4] This conviction could lead to elemental revision of all international law. The second role is reconstructing explicit and implicit values, which 'requires rebuilding the basic concepts of international law in a way that they do not support or reinforce the domination of women by men'.[5] Gendered formulation and application of international law impedes justice for women, but there has been at least some progress in applying international law more inclusively.

Geneva Convention IV says that state parties must protect women 'against any attack on their honour, in particular against rape, enforced prostitution or any form of indecent assault'. Not explicitly prohibiting offences but calling for the protection of women and designating rape as a crime against 'honour' rather than of violence, it presents women as the property and responsibility of males and family.[6] Protocol I portrays women needing special respect and protection, and Protocol II identifies rape in non-international conflicts as an outrage on personal dignity, and not a violent attack on personal integrity.[7] Chapter Three has highlighted that deeming women always in need of protection exacerbates women and their communities' vulnerability to tactical rape. Charlesworth and Chinkin's analysis highlighted that 'grave breaches of the Geneva Conventions are made subject to universal jurisdiction exercisable in national courts' and are 'regarded as the most significant violations of international humanitarian law'.[8] They point out that, 'rape, enforced prostitution and sexual assault are not explicitly designated grave breaches.'[9] It is possible to use the wording of Protocol I, which lists grave breaches as 'degrading practices involving outrages on personal dignity based on racial discrimination', for prosecuting cases of tactical rape and sexual violence in war. Non-grave breaches can be deemed war crimes. But this is a less than satisfactory formulation in international law.[10] Even in Common Article 3 to the Geneva Conventions, it is not explicit that sexual assault and violence are covered by listed prohibitions.

Charlesworth and Chinkin also noted that human rights law 'challenges the traditional state-centred scope of international law, giving individuals and groups, otherwise with very restricted access to

4   Ibid.
5   Ibid, p 61.
6   Ibid, p 314.
7   Ibid, p 315.
8   Ibid.
9   Ibid.
10   Ibid, p 316.

the international legal system, the possibility of making international legal claims'.[11] This reading of human rights law provides greater opportunity for women to negotiate and use international legal systems. The *Universal Declaration of Human Rights*[12] requires that states do not engage in acts such as torture, arbitrary deprivation of life, liberty and security – recognising that states could be perpetrators.

However, as Charlesworth and Chinkin pointed out, 'mainstream human rights institutions have tended to ignore the application of human rights norms to women.' They referred to the 1993 work of the UNHCR Special Rapporteur on Torture, finding that 'he rarely considered the application of norms of international human rights law or international humanitarian law (IHL) to women.'[13] In the Special Rapporteur's work, 'well documented cases of torture and ill-treatment of women went un-investigated or were treated in a desultory fashion'.[14] The Special Rapporteur's condemnation of rapes in Bosnia–Herzegovina focused on the harm resulting to ethnic communities, and failed to acknowledge the harm inflicted on women as individuals because of their sex and gender.[15]

Similarly, the UN's fact-finding missions in Rwanda did not detect 'systematic sexual violence against women until nine months after the genocide when women began to give birth in unprecedented numbers', exemplifying the reality that 'methods of investigating and documenting human rights abuses can often obscure or even conceal abuses against women'.[16] The failure to report formally on the evidence of widespread tactical rape and sexual violence was incomprehensible to NGO workers such as myself. While human rights law could be invoked, it was as difficult an exercise as applying international humanitarian law.

In 1998, Judith Gardam considered the growing focus on women's human rights, particularly in relation to the criminalisation and

[11] Ibid, p 201.
[12] UN General Assembly, *Resolution 217A(III) (1948)*, *Universal Declaration of Human Rights*, 10 December 1948.
[13] International Human Rights Law Group, 1993, *Token gestures: Women's human rights and UN reporting: The UN Special Rapporteur on torture*, Series of reports, Washington, DC: International Human Rights Law Group, pp 5-6, quoted in Charlesworth and Chinkin, op cit, p 218.
[14] Ibid, pp 10-11, 14-15.
[15] Ibid, pp 7-8
[16] Gallagher, A, 1997, Ending the marginalisation: strategies for incorporating women into the United Nations Human Rights system, *Human Rights Quarterly*, February, 283-333, p 292, quoted in Charlesworth and Chinkin, op cit, p 219.

punishment of sexual violence against women in armed conflicts.[17] Developed principles comprising human rights law had a major impact on international humanitarian law, and indeed on international law generally.[18] While events since 1998 indicate that the impact was not major, Gardam is correct that there was a shift in attitudes, and an impact could be seen 'primarily in developments regarding the criminalization and punishment of sexual violence against women in armed conflict'.[19] Gardam concluded quite correctly that scrutiny by human rights groups of sexual violence against women in armed conflicts had translated into 'a new perception that such acts must be addressed by mainstream bodies dealing with enforcement of international humanitarian law.'[20] There is a dual need to ensure equality of women's human rights and to ensure due attention to war crimes and crimes against humanity when perpetrated against women. There is some hope that when this is achieved at international forums of states such as the UN Security Council, there will eventually be similar application at national and local levels.

Gardam noted that the International Committee of the Red Cross (ICRC) had 'given increasing recognition to the fact that the situation of women in armed conflicts poses distinctive challenges for humanitarian law'.[21] She referred specifically to a resolution of the ICRC adopted by consensus in 1995.[22] This condemned sexual violence against women in armed conflict, reaffirmed that rape in the conduct of hostilities was a war crime and highlighted the importance of enforcing the relevant provisions.[23] This was progress, but it had not led to 'a general acknowledgement that women's human rights warrant a special place in humanitarian law'.[24] This left the option of using mainstream humanitarian law, elaborated where possible by reference to human rights law, to enforce justice for survivors and victims of tactical rape and sexual violence.

---

[17] Gardam, JG, 1998, Women, human rights and international law, *International Review of the Red Cross*, 324, 421-32.

[18] Ibid, p 421.

[19] Ibid, p 422.

[20] Ibid, p 431.

[21] Ibid, p 432.

[22] ICRC, 1995, 26th International Conference of the Red Cross and Red Crescent Movement, 07-12-1995, Resolution, 2(B), 3-7 December, Geneva.

[23] Gardam, op cit, p 432.

[24] Ibid.

In 2001, with Michelle J. Jarvis, Gardam highlighted the need to view sexual violence in conflict in the broader context of generalised discrimination:

> ... violence against women is perhaps one of the clearest examples of how discrimination against women that exists in all societies during peace-time is exacerbated during periods of armed conflict.[25]

Gardam and Jarvis rightly highlighted that discrimination against women in society is reflected in international humanitarian law, and that the 'unequal status of women also exacerbates what appear initially to be neutral factors experienced by both men and women'.[26] Their commentary provided a basis for deeper understanding of the linkage between gender discrimination, gendered laws and violence against women in conflict.

Even though human rights law can be applied to women's rights, experience shows it can be applied selectively. Georgina Ashworth charted responses by women's human rights movements to 'the built-in selectivity' of the human rights regime.[27] These included NGO activism and the Declaration and Programme for Action for adoption at the Vienna World Conference on Human Rights (1993). Activists wanted to demonstrate that recognition of women's human rights had been suppressed.[28] Ashworth concluded that women's groups had begun to use the 'mainstream' human rights systems more effectively, and that 'while not abandoning the Women's Convention, they aspire to see the equality promises in the major conventions become real for themselves and their sisters'.[29]

Jane Connors listed international conferences at which the issue of gendered discrimination of women's access to their human rights had been confronted.[30] She argued that the international community

---

[25] Gardam, JG, Jarvis, MJ, 2001, *Women, armed conflict and international law*, Netherlands: Kluwer Law International, p 25.

[26] Ibid, p 134.

[27] Ashworth, G, 1999, The silencing of women, in T Dunne and N Wheeler, *Human rights in global politics*, Cambridge: Cambridge University Press.

[28] Ibid, p 265.

[29] Ibid, p 271.

[30] Connors, J, 2000, Using general human rights instruments to advance the human rights of women, in K Adams and A Byrnes (eds), *Gender equality and the judiciary: Using international human rights standards to promote the human rights of women and the girl-child at the national level*, London: Commonwealth Secretariat, p 37.

had openly acknowledged that the body of international law and mechanisms established to promote and protect human rights did not take into account the concerns of over half the world's population, but states had finally formally recognised the human rights of women as 'an inalienable, integral and indivisible part of human rights'.[31] This may seem so obvious that it would not warrant explicit statements, but it indicated the degree of obfuscation that held sway in international discourse for so long.

However, progress was never undiluted, as Connors noted. She identified ongoing limitations: human rights were conceptualised and defined without significant participation of women's groups; many issues including systematic violence had not been defined as human rights issues or made the subject of legally binding norms; international human rights law effectively excluded many actions by non-state actors and by the private sphere; and discrimination against women was justified by governments on the basis of culture, religion and ethnicity.[32] Connors named the Committee on Torture as having done less than other treaty bodies to reflect the importance of gender consideration.[33]

Distinctions made between public and private spheres often have an impact on where, when and how international law is interpreted and applied. Karen Engle mapped 'onto public international law the public/private distinction that demarcates bodily autonomy as private, and this distinction carries different implications for legal intervention'.[34] The implications for women are serious when they are perceived as part of private ownership. Karen Knop also referred to feminist debates over the public/private distinctions made in interpreting international law.[35] She argued that feminist legal analysis showed women as more vulnerable in the private sphere, but the public/private distinction had been applied to prevent relevant law from remedying the situation.

This distinction, intended as a critique of international law, had been questioned for possibly being more 'mystifying than useful' by Patricia

---

[31] Ibid, p 37.

[32] Ibid, p 39.

[33] Ibid, p 45.

[34] Engle, K, 1993, After the collapse of the public/private distinction: strategising women's rights, in DG Dallmeyer (ed), *Reconceiving reality: Women and international law*, New York: American Society of International Law, p 143, quoted in Knop, K, 2004, *Gender and human rights*, Oxford: Oxford University, note 16, p 7.

[35] Knop, op cit.

Viseur-Sellers.[36] It was a notional division deeming legal regulation appropriate to the public sphere and ordinarily inappropriate to the private sphere, where the line between public and private is most often drawn either between the state and civil society or within the civil society so as to mark off the domestic space of family life as private.[37] Viseur-Sellers focused on individuals' liability for collective violence with particular attention to work of the ICTY reviewed in the context of the public/private distinction.

She also emphasised that international law prohibited crimes against humanity, yet when these crimes were committed against women, they were deemed to be in the private sphere and not really the subject of international humanitarian law. She made what she called a self-evident point:

> All international humanitarian law, or in modern terminology, the laws of armed conflict, is public not private law. To accentuate the obvious, war crimes, crimes against humanity and genocide reside only in the very public domain that obligates state action and, more recently, galvanized the international community to establish the ad hoc Tribunals and the ICC.[38]

War crimes, whether perpetrated against men or women, are in the public domain and demand a response. Women are frequently, although not exclusively, found among non-combatants in conflicts.

Julie Mertus provided some insights to the mention of rape, albeit limited, in codes of conduct for combatants.[39] She reviewed the work of Hugo Grotius in *De Jure Belli* (1623-24), and his conclusion that the rights of combatants and non-combatants alike should be protected.[40] She noted that 'Eighteenth-century Enlightenment thinkers further refined the rights of non-combatants and the limitations placed on warfare' and 'rape was not viewed as strategy to further war aims nor was it regarded as necessary to winning a war'.[41] By the 19th century, codes of conduct for armed forces still deemed rape in peace or in war a crime against a man, 'an assault on male property', and even when

---

[36] Viseur-Sellers, P, 2004, Individual('s) liability for collective sexual violence, in K Knop, *Gender and human rights*, Oxford: Oxford University Press, 153-95, p 7.

[37] Knop, op cit, p 6.

[38] Viseur-Sellers, op cit, p 7.

[39] Mertus, J, 2000, *War's offensive on women*, Bloomfield, CT: Kumarian Press.

[40] Ibid.

[41] Ibid, p 73.

rape was seen as a theft of chastity and virtue, the crime was against the man or the family 'who was entitled to the woman's chastity and virtue, not against the woman herself as an independent individual'.[42] There was the 'existence of international customary law prohibiting rape during armed conflict' but 'political will to prosecute and punish violators of such rules' did not exist.[43] Political will to prosecute and punish violators remains problematic.

Existing law appropriately interpreted and applied could provide a framework for justice. Mertus identified prohibition against wartime rape in many international instruments as well as in customary international law.[44] Rape is listed as a simple breach of obligation under Article 27 of the Geneva Convention IV, which calls for women to be 'especially protected against any attack on their honour, in particular rape'; however, rape constitutes a grave breach of the Geneva Conventions if classified as inhuman treatment or great suffering or serious injury to body or health.[45] This matters because only grave breaches fall under universal jurisdiction, meaning that they can be tried by any court, irrespective of where the offence occurs. Rape can also fall under Common Article 3 of all Geneva Conventions and the two 1977 Additional Protocols to the 1949 Geneva Conventions. These 'offer greater protection as they apply to all women in the territory of the conflict, regardless of whether their states are parties to the convention'.[46] These international laws could provide protection to victims with political will for prosecution and accountability. In 1992 the ICRC deemed that rape fell under the provisions of both Articles referenced in Mertus.[47] Clearly it was necessary to strengthen the protection of women who may also be the victims of rape.[48] It was progress to have recognition that existing law encapsulated the rules for confronting tactical rape and sexual violence in conflict.

Mary Kaldor described new wars as, 'in a sense, a mixture of war, crime and human rights violations', so it is understandable that tactical rape, a strategy of these new wars, required reference to a range of

---

[42] Ibid.

[43] Ibid, p 74.

[44] Ibid, p 79.

[45] Ibid.

[46] Ibid, p 83.

[47] See the notes to Thomas, DQ, Ralph, RE, 1994, Rape in war: Challenging the tradition of impunity, *SAIS Review*, 82-9.

[48] Sandoz, Y, Swinarski, C, Zimmerman, B (eds), 1987, *ICRC commentary on the Additional Protocols of 8 June 1977 to the Geneva Conventions of 12 August 1949*, Geneva: Martinus Nijhoff Publishers, p 1375, para 4539.

law.[49] Kaldor argued that 'all types of warfare are characterised by rules; the very fact that warfare is a socially sanctioned activity, that it has to be organised and justified, requires rules'.[50] Warfare has an impact on women and girls, so it is reasonable to expect the rules should apply to them. Kaldor stated, 'there developed rules about what constituted legitimate warfare which were later codified in the laws of war'.[51] These codified laws constitute international humanitarian law. Kaldor noted that after the Second World War human rights norms were added to what was known as international humanitarian law, and the difference 'between humanitarian and human rights law has to do largely with whether violation of the law takes place in war or peacetime'.[52] The ICTY and ICTR ruled that actions illegal in conflict could not escape accountability by manipulating definitions of war. Even though existing law is gendered and has serious limitations concerning women, there is progress in obviating some legal avoidance in applying it to crimes against women. This should be the case even as the nature of wars changes.

Chris Brown re-examined war and the states system, noting the move away from decisive battles and women's place in the public and private spheres.[53] He omitted any real focus on attacks on civilians, where attacks on women become apparent, although he did offer insights into human rights law and norms. Human rights laws frequently represent norms purportedly held by many states.[54] Brown considered the term 'settled norms' used earlier by Mervyn Frost, and stated 'a norm is "settled" if states endorse it even when their behaviour is apparently in contradiction to it'.[55] A norm has been developing.

In 2003 Kelly Dawn Askin highlighted the limited attention previously paid by international judicial proceedings to rape in war.[56] She provided comprehensive background and analysis, noting that

---

[49]   Kaldor, M, 2002, *New and old wars: Organised violence in a global era*, Cambridge: Polity Press, p 11.

[50]   Ibid, p 17.

[51]   Ibid.

[52]   Ibid, p 116.

[53]   Brown, C, 2002, *Sovereignty, rights and justice: International political theory today*, Cambridge: Polity Press, pp 110–14.

[54]   It is recognised that there are ongoing debates around the universality of human rights, but these are not considered to negate this general statement.

[55]   Brown, op cit, p 65, quoting Frost, M, 1996, *Ethics in international relations*, Cambridge: Cambridge University Press.

[56]   Askin, KD, 2003, Prosecuting wartime rape and other gender-related crimes under international law: extraordinary advances, enduring obstacles, *Berkeley Journal of International Law*, 21, 288-349, p 288.

progress had to be measured against a prior dearth of attention and focus.[57] In the Hague Conventions one single article prohibits sexual violence as violation of 'family honour'; in 723 pages of reports at the Nuremberg Trials, rape was not even indexed; at the Tokyo Trial, with five supplementary indexes to 22 volumes, rape is mentioned only four times, under 'atrocities'; in the four Geneva Conventions, of the 429 sentences, only one mentions prohibition of rape, although a few others could be interpreted as including rape; the UN 1974 *Declaration on the Protection of Women and Children in Emergency and Armed Conflict* includes no mention of rape; in the 1977 two Additional Protocols to the Geneva Conventions, only one sentence explicitly prohibits sexual violence.[58] Linkages between rape and international law were being clarified by the international community – slow progress, but progress nonetheless.

Legal definitions

While gendered law is recognised, I argue that ensuring the application of international law matters, knowing how acts are defined and ensuring non-discriminatory interpretation for women. A UN legal study summarised key issues for states dealing with rape.[59] It stated, 'a single act suffices to constitute a war crime'.[60] Individual rapes can be war crimes. The study noted, 'crimes against humanity can be committed by anybody and come with universal jurisdiction'.[61] State involvement must be proved, 'at least in terms of tolerance', and acts must be part of a widespread or systematic attack based on national, political, ethnic or religious grounds.[62] Accountability for individual rapes can be required when part of a tactical strategy and the possibility of state involvement are recognised. Geoffrey Robertson argued, 'an act which is wicked in itself, becomes especially wicked (that is a crime

---

[57] Askin, K, 1999, Sexual violence in decisions and indictments of the Yugoslav and Rwandan Tribunals: Current status, *The American Journal of International Law*, 93, 1, January, 97-123.

[58] Ibid, p 295.

[59] UN Security Council, 1994, *Rape and sexual assault – Final report of the United Nations Commission of Experts established pursuant to Security Council resolution 780 (1992)*, S/1994/674, Annex II.

[60] Ibid, Annex II, VI A.

[61] Ibid.

[62] Ibid.

against humanity) when deployed systematically and for political ends.'[63] The idea of certain acts being 'especially wicked' when compared with other acts is somewhat troubling, but this is an important distinction between rape as a 'by-product' of war and rape as a tactic of war.

The ICTY and ICTR contributed definitions now generally accepted in international law. Many are reflected specifically in the Treaty of Rome and the Statute of the ICC adopted in 1998, which came into force in 2002 ratified by 60 states.[64] The Statute of the ICC Article 7 defined a crime against humanity as any of a comprehensive list of acts committed as part of a known widespread or systematic attack directed against a civilian population:

> ... rape, sexual slavery, enforced prostitution, forced pregnancy, enforced sterilisation, or any other form of sexual violence of comparable gravity; persecution against any identifiable group or collectivity on political, racial, national, ethnic, cultural, religious; gender or other grounds that are universally recognised as impermissible under international law.[65]

The specific note that such acts are 'recognised as impermissible under international law' sets them within the existing, established parameters.

Article 8 gives jurisdiction over war crimes 'when committed as part of a plan or policy' or when acts are committed on a large scale. It defines war crimes as 'grave breaches of the Geneva Conventions of August 12 1949', and lists specific acts that include wilful killing, torture or inhuman treatment and wilfully causing great suffering or serious injury to body or health.[66] A second category of war crimes are acts that constitute 'serious violation of laws and customs applicable in international armed conflict' and include (inter alia): intentionally attacking civilian populations or individuals not taking direct part in hostilities; committing outrages on personal dignity in particular humiliating or degrading treatment; and committing rape, sexual slavery, enforced prostitution, forced pregnancy or any other form of sexual violence constituting a breach of the Geneva Conventions.[67] In

---

[63] Robertson, G, 2008, *Crimes against humanity: The struggle for global justice*, New York: Allen Lane, p 393.

[64] Rome Statute of the International Criminal Court, 1998, UN Document A/ CONF.183/9, came into force 1 July 2002.

[65] Ibid, Article 7, para 1.

[66] Ibid, Article 8, para 2a.

[67] Ibid, Article 8, para 2b.

an armed conflict not of international character, the Statute includes as war crimes violations of Common Article 3 of the Geneva Conventions and violations of laws and customs applicable in armed conflicts not of international nature.[68] The conflicts in the former Yugoslavia and Rwanda were clearly covered. Article 6 refers to the definition and requirements of acts of genocide, as set out in the 1948 Convention.[69] The ICTR made a key ruling linking tactical rape and genocide.[70]

There is often confusion regarding 'genocide' and 'ethnic cleansing'. Genocide is defined according to the *Genocide Convention*, a legal term based on agreed international law describing the annihilation of a race. It is essential to establish the key elements of genocide as determined by the international Convention.[71] Raphael Lemkin may not have been fully satisfied with the final text, but this Convention has widespread application.[72] Lemkin was appalled that the banner of 'state sovereignty' could shield men 'who tried to wipe out an entire minority', and argued that 'sovereignty cannot be conceived as the right to kill millions of innocent people'.[73] There is no legal requirement for conflict to be occurring for events to be deemed genocide. Helen Fein noted that besides mass killing, genocide may include murder through starvation and poisoning of air, water or food and the involuntary transfer of children.[74] Rape is a notable omission from her list, and its inclusion may still be disputed by some analysts, but as will be seen in Chapter Six, there is a judicial precedent for recognising genocide by rape.

Ethnic cleansing is a political concept rather than a legally defined term. It was a term coined during the dissolution of Yugoslavia and more widely applied.[75] It refers to situations or stratagems by which minority ethnic groups are driven from a territory so that 'a majority group can assemble a more unified, more contiguous, and larger

---

[68] Ibid, Article 8, para 2c.

[69] Text of the 1948 Genocide Convention, in Andreopolous, GJ, 1997, *Genocide: Conceptual and historical dimensions*, Philadelphia, PA: University of Pennsylvania.

[70] See Chapter Six, this volume.

[71] UN, 1948, *Convention on the Prevention and Punishment of the Crime of Genocide (the Genocide Convention)*.

[72] Power, S, 2003, *A problem from hell: America and the age of genocide*, London: Flamingo, HarperCollins.

[73] Ibid, p 19.

[74] Fein, H, 1994, Genocide, terror, life integrity, and war crimes, in GJ Andreopolous, *Genocide: Conceptual and historical dimensions*, Philadelphia, PA: University of Pennsylvania, pp 96, 102.

[75] Griffiths, M, O'Callaghan, T, 2002, *International relations: The key concepts*, London: Routledge, pp 93-4.

territory for its nation–state'.[76] Ethnic cleansing seeks to 'cleanse or purify' the territory of an ethnic group 'by use of terror, rape and murder to convince the inhabitants to leave'.[77] In contrast, genocide seeks to destroy the group.

In 1993, the UN Economic and Social Council (ECOSOC) expressed outrage at rape being used as a weapon of war.[78] In 1994, General Assembly resolution 1994/205 expressed alarm at 'the continuing use of rape as a weapon of war'.[79] Both resolutions recognised rape as an instrument of ethnic cleansing, and noted that the abhorrent policy of ethnic cleansing was a form of genocide. This was not a legal definition. Ethnic cleansing had been defined by the UN Commission of Experts as 'rendering an area ethnically homogeneous by using force, or intimidation to remove from a given area persons from another ethnic or religious group'.[80] Ethnic cleansing is a general expression of a strategy, while genocide is a legal term with consequent legal implications. The two terms are sometimes wrongly used as if they are interchangeable.

Elisabeth Jean Wood highlighted other differences:

> Sexual violence during war varies in extent and takes distinct forms. In some conflicts, sexual violence is widespread, yet in other conflicts – including some cases of ethnic conflict – it is quite limited. In some conflicts, sexual violence takes the form of sexual slavery; in others, torture in detention.[81]

Chapters Five and Six review how rape in conflict differed and could be confronted under a range of legal definitions.

---

[76]   Ibid, p 94.

[77]   Ibid.

[78]   OHCHR, 2001, *Rape and abuse of women in the territory of the former Yugoslavia*, Commission on Human Rights resolution 1993/8, 23 February.

[79]   UN General Assembly, *Resolution 1994/205, Rape and abuse of women in the territory of the former Yugoslavia*, 6 March 1994.

[80]   UN Security Council, 1994, *Rape and sexual assault – Final report of the United Nations Commission of Experts established pursuant to Security Council resolution 780 (1992)*, S/1994/674, 27 May, vol 1, annex IV, para 84.

[81]   Wood, EJ, 2009, Variation in sexual violence during war, *Politics & Society*, 34, 3, 307–42.

The UN Security Council and its resolutions

In the absence of a global parliament or government, any change in political attitudes and expectations of states by states usually finds its roots in debates and deliberations at the UN. Hedley Bull defined international society as existing:

> ... when a group of states, conscious of certain common values, form a society in the sense that they conceive themselves to be bound by a common set of rules in their relations with one another, and share in the working of common institutions.[82]

In the UN, rules and values are debated and shared and become international law. Michael Barnett and Martha Finnemore pointed out that 'rules, norms and principles that define what counts as legitimate international order' are not fixed in stone but are subject to debate.[83] UN debates are 'most intense when there is shift, shock or challenge in world politics that potentially destabilises the existing standards'.[84] There was shock and challenge as world media and NGOs decried events in the former Yugoslavia and Rwanda in the 1990s.

The Security Council bears 'primary responsibility for the maintenance of international peace and security'.[85] It is the most powerful UN organ. Its decisions are binding on all member states when adopted under Chapter VII of the Charter of the UN.[86] The ICTR and ICTY were established under Chapter VII of the Charter, allowing the tribunals to claim primacy over domestic courts and demand 'legally cognizable cooperation' from UN member states.[87]

---

[82] Bull, H, 1995, *The anarchical society: A study of order in world politics*, Basingstoke: Macmillan, p 13, quoted in Birdsall, A, 2007, Creating a more "just" order: the ad hoc International War Crimes Tribunal for the former Yugoslavia, *Cooperation & Conflict*, 42, 4, 397–418, p 398.

[83] Barnett, M, Finnemore, M, 2008, Political approaches, in TG Weiss and S Daws (eds), *The Oxford handbook on the United Nations*, Oxford: Oxford University Press, p 51.

[84] Ibid.

[85] Charter of the UN, Article 24, Security Council, Chapter VII.

[86] Malone, DM, 2007, Security Council, in TG Weiss and S Daws (eds), *The Oxford handbook on the United Nations*, Oxford: Oxford University Press, p 117.

[87] Goldstone, R, 2007, International Criminal Court and ad hoc tribunals, in TG Weiss and S Daws (eds), *The Oxford handbook on the United Nations*, Oxford: Oxford University Press, p 465.

These demonstrated the powers of the Security Council to remove threats to international peace and security.[88]

The Security Council now operates in a context of globalisation or 'increased connectivity' of states and organisations, facing new expectations of humanitarianism and new understandings of sovereignty. The sovereignty of states came increasingly to include 'a modicum of respect for human rights'.[89] However, Jana Bufkin quotes Green and Ward (2004), arguing that state crime is organisational deviance involving human rights violations by sovereign and proto-states to fulfil organisational goals, and that all states are capable of violating human rights and women's rights.[90] The UN is based on sovereign equality of all member states,[91] but in reality, not all member states are equal, and some states fail. So while borders remain crucial, sovereignty seems considerably less sacrosanct today than in 1945.[92]

In the early 1990s attitudes to humanitarian intervention shifted. In 2001, the report of the International Commission on Intervention and State Sovereignty (ICISS) moved the emphasis from the traditional right of states to non-interference in their affairs within their own borders to the responsibility of states and the international community to protect citizens within those borders.[93] Ongoing debate around this concept is generally seen as illustrating the power of 'a strong normative concept in responding to massive atrocities'.[94]

Although the concept 'Responsibility to Protect' (R2P) developed from a sense of hope that it would end mass atrocities 'once and for all', Hilary Charlesworth argued that R2P had 'developed without adequate attention to the lives of women'.[95] While she noted the ambivalent attitudes of feminist scholars to international law, sometimes invoking it and 'sometimes worrying that invoking it may legitimate oppressive state structures', she concluded that R2P should be framed 'as one strand of a complex response that draws inspiration and ideas

---

[88]   Ibid, p 466.

[89]   Weiss and Daws, op cit, p 8.

[90]   Bufkin, J, 2005, Book review of *State crime: Governments, violence and corruption*, *Western Criminology Review*, 6, 1, 161-62, quoting Green, P, Ward, T, 2004, *State crime: Governments, violence and corruption*, London: Pluto.

[91]   Charter of the UK, Article 2 (1).

[92]   Weiss and Daws, op cit, p 9.

[93]   Malone, op cit, p 126.

[94]   Charlesworth, H, 2010, Feminist reflections on the responsibility to protect, *Global Responsibility to Protect*, 2, 232-49.

[95]   Ibid, p 233.

from everyone affected by violence', and that was valuable.[96] I share such ambivalence. Law is gendered and it needs to be more inclusive of women's realities. But until this changes, using existing law remains a pragmatic strategy. R2P has influenced the context in which normative rejection of tactical rape and sexual violence in conflict began to emerge. Theoretically it should improve women's chances of protection from tactical rape.

Reservations about theorising rape and judicial processes

Theorising about rape in conflict, developing principles and frameworks around such pernicious practice can be, and has been, questioned. There is disagreement about the relevance of feminist theory to women raped in war and the extent to which theorising creates tensions given it is often perceived to be culturally driven by feminists in situations markedly different from women in conflict. This debate highlights differences in attitudes, considering women as victims or as having agency in their own right. Positively, it keeps the issue in the public and academic consciousness.

On one side of the debate is Beverley Allen, who noted that after spending time in Croatia and in Bosnia-Herzegovina with 'people who had been affected by the war, including those affected by genocidal rape', she found that 'the relevance of contemporary theory grew pretty distant' and she 'stopped reading feminist theory pretty much altogether'.[97] She was disappointed by the cognitive dissonance between reality in the Balkans and US academia, and her response was to rely on her experience and observations, admitting more anecdotes and less theory, even while noting the deficiencies of doing so. So few academics had direct experience of the Balkans, when so much of what was being studied – ethnicity, gender, nationalism – had become matters of life and death there.[98]

Also engaging in the debate was Janice Haarken, who wrote of 'the seductions of theory' exploring the ambiguities at the borders of the politics of rape which risk victim blaming.[99] An approach to politics of sexual violence should encompass the complexity of women's

---

[96] Ibid, p 249.
[97] Allen, B, 2002, Towards a new feminist theory of rape: a response from the field, *Signs*, 27, 3, Spring, 777-81.
[98] Ibid.
[99] Haarken, J, 2002, Towards a new feminist theory of rape: the seduction of theory, *Signs*, 27, 3, Spring, 781-86.

experience and the subjective and objective barriers to women's emancipation from patriarchal dominance. One issue bridging rape politics and feminist cultural theory centres on 'how we understand the gap between experience and representation', and 'it is important to recognise that there is an inevitable disjuncture between rape as a metaphor and rape as a concrete act of violence'.[100] This seems, at least in part, to support Allen's call to remember that rape in war affects real people in real ways, and cannot always be dealt with without some subjective emotional response.

Carine Mardorossian took both Allen and Haarken to task. She rejected Haarken's 'theory/experience opposition', and insisted that academic theories could make sense of Allen's experience.[101] Mardorossian claimed that Allen wrote about victims of 'genocidal rape' and assembled their stories, while Mardorossian herself addressed ethical and theoretical questions arising when feminists document, explain or work to alleviate the suffering of rape victims. She claimed academic feminists write about victims, make sense of their subjectivity and import their stories so as to interpret them.[102] I am convinced that theoretical understanding cannot and should not be divorced from experiential understanding. Nor should the human personal dimension of an issue be excluded in consideration and analysis. Theory and analytical frameworks may make sense of the chaos of conflict provided that humanity is not lost in objective considerations.

Also writing in 2005, Karen Engle reviewed progress in criminalising wartime rape.[103] Highlighting a further aspect requiring caution, Engle recognised two 'camps' engaged in feminist theory and strategising in the early 1990s: those who focused on rapes being genocidal and in some respects different from what was referenced as 'everyday rape' or even 'everyday wartime rape', and others who believed that as rape in war had long been a reality, the focus should not be genocide but rapes. Engle acknowledged that the debate faded as feminists joined forces to achieve what was certainly progress in the ICTY. However, she warned that pushing the limits of the ICTY might be counterproductive.

---

[100] Ibid.

[101] Mardorossian, CM, 2002, Theory, experience and disciplinary contentions: A response to Janice Haarken and Beverley Allen, *Signs*, 27, 3, Spring, pp 787-91.

[102] Ibid.

[103] Engle, K, 2005, Feminism and its (dis)content: Criminalizing wartime rape in Bosnia and Herzegovina, *American Journal of International Law*, 99, 4, October, 778-816.

Judicial systems

Another debate is whether or not judicial proceedings are appropriate responses to tactical rape and sexual violence in conflict. Advocates including myself argue that even imperfect judiciaries contribute to justice for victims and survivors of tactical rape, and decry the lack of attention paid to such crimes. Julia Hall commented, 'I think the reticence [of international courts to try cases of rape] is a combination of classic gender discrimination that manifests itself in the attitude that crimes of sexual violence against women are so-called lesser crimes.'[104] Her calls for courts to deal with cases of rape in conflict, typical of many NGOs and women's advocates, have been challenged by feminist writers, highlighting the additional suffering and pain in insensitive judicial proceedings. Suffering and pain cannot be denied. Any benefits come at considerable cost for women who testify. In the ICTR, a woman victim of multiple rapes was cross-examined:

> As lawyer Mwanyumba ineptly and insensitively questioned the witness at length about the rapes, the judges burst out laughing twice at the lawyer while witness TA described in detail the lead up to the rape. Witness TA had undergone a day and a half of questioning by the prosecutor, before being put through a week of cross-examination by the counsel of the six defendants. One of the more offensive questions put by defence lawyer, Mwanyumba, included reference to the fact that the witness had not taken a bath, and the implication that she could not have been raped because she smelled. The three judges [named] never apologised to the rape victim on the stand, nor were they reprimanded in any way for their behaviour.[105]

There are, indeed, insensitive, unjustifiable and antagonistic strategies used in the name of formal investigation.

In a case before the ICTY, the defence counsel called for a woman judge, Florence Mumba, to be disqualified for apparent bias.[106] This

---

[104] J Hall, lawyer with Human Rights Watch, in an interview reported by A Poolos, 1999, Human rights advocates say rape is war crime, Radio Free Europe, 25 May.

[105] Nowrojee, B, 2005, *Your justice is too slow: Will the ICTR fail Rwanda's rape victims?*, United Nations Research Institute for Social Development, November, p 24.

[106] ICTY, *Prosecutor vs Furundzija*, Judgement IT-95-17/1-A, 21 July 2000, para 164 (fourth ground of appeal).

judge had represented Zambia on the UN Commission on the Status of Women, and by implication was therefore predisposed to promote a feminist outlook. The court eventually deemed that opposition to rape and supporting accountability did not render the judge biased. In another case the testimony of one witness was initially disallowed because she had undergone counselling for her trauma, and her testimony was therefore claimed to be unreliable. It was eventually judged that there were no grounds for excluding a witness because of her suffering extreme trauma.[107] However, the defence had seen some potential to exclude a witness account of a traumatic event because she was traumatised. This would seem a long way from justice or even logic.

It is therefore essential that feminist analysts highlight the negatives associated with women's treatment and experiences in court. Julie Mertus, in 'Shouting from the bottom of the well', listed disadvantages for women victims of rape being involved in international courts.[108] She based her case around the experiences of women involved in the trials of the three men indicted in the ICTY Foca case.[109] Many people witnessing criminal court hearings of rape crimes will agree with Mertus' analysis that the adversarial process can result in further violation of survivors and victims. But here is the ambivalence of pragmatists such as myself. While there is real sympathy for Mertus' opinion, a desire for an ideal situation may endanger even the slow and tiny progress made in confronting the impunity of those who rape in conflict. Without legal prosecution, impunity continues or increases. There may be some compromise in insisting that processes and practices are needed that recognise the pain of victims and survivors and their right to protection and understanding. Too often it seems that the rights of the accused take precedence over the rights of the accuser. Advocacy for greater sensitivity in courts is a justifiable, essential strategy.

Other feminist analysts focus on the way crimes of rape are still interpreted. Dorothy Thomas and Regan Ralph wrote of the long-standing impunity of those who rape in conflict, despite the act of rape being universally condemned, providing examples of rape being 'mischaracterised and dismissed by military and political leaders.'[110] Rape has been, and is still in many penal codes, seen as a crime against the

---

[107] Furundzija Trial Chamber Judgement, para 109.

[108] Mertus, J, 2004, Shouting from the bottom of the well: the impact of international trials on wartime rape on women's agency, *International Feminist Journal of Politics*, 6, 1, March, 110-128.

[109] ICTY, Gagovic & Others ('Foca') Indictment, confirmed 26 June 1996, IT-96-23-1322, 332.

[110] Thomas and Ralph, op cit, pp 82-9.

honour of males rather than as an attack on a victim. Attitudes towards women that prompt rape (in war) and fuel its mischaracterisation as a personal matter are reinforced and even shared by those in a position to prohibit and punish the abuse. Thomas and Ralph highlighted that many women suffer further violation when crimes against them are made public and denounced, for political purposes rather than to prevent abuse or to see justice done. The dangers of misappropriation of women's suffering and of bringing perpetrators to account are always possibilities when there is political mileage to be gained.

Even trying to increase the visibility of particular rapes by soldiers can be a political act. Cynthia Enloe wrote of the invisibility of many rape victims, saying that 'the women who suffer rape in wartime usually remain faceless'.[111] She referred to Atina Grossman for an explanation of the trap of assuming that increasing the visibility of rape 'is a simple undertaking to reveal "the truth" about militarized rape, even brutal war-time rapes or mass-scale rapes.'[112] Grossman wrote about the widespread rapes of German women, mostly by Soviet troops in 1945-46, explaining that the telling of a rape experience is affected by many factors:

> Women's rape stories were framed in incredibly complicated ways, shaped by their audience and the motives behind their telling. Their experiences were ordered and given meaning within a complex grid of multiple images and discourses.[113]

For courts to recognise this complexity and still deliver justice is not easy.

Enloe considered militarised rape, the political implications when soldiers rape.[114] Militarisation is 'a step-by-step process by which a person or thing gradually comes to be controlled by the military or comes to depend for its well-being on militaristic ideas'.[115] There was sometimes a need for organising by women for women to uncover

---

[111] Enloe, C, 2000, *Maneuvers: The international politics of militarizing women's lives*, Berkeley, CA: University of California Press, p 108.

[112] Ibid, p 109.

[113] Grossman, A, 1995, A question of silence: The rape of German women by occupation soldiers, *October Magazine*, 72, Spring, p 55, quoted in Enloe, op cit, pp 108-9.

[114] Enloe, op cit, Chapter 4.

[115] Ibid, p 3.

soldiers' systematic political uses of rape.[116] Exposing militarised rape did not automatically serve the cause of demilitarising women's lives.[117] Enloe provided the example of a woman outside the military raped by someone else's soldiers, who could be remilitarised if her ordeal were made visible chiefly for the purpose of mobilising her male compatriots to take up arms to avenge her and their alleged lost honour.[118] Strategies of making women vulnerable and then using that constructed vulnerability are apparent. Charlesworth and Chinkin quoted Gibson: 'the vulnerability of women to sexual attack is appropriated by government, military and the media' for the purpose of justifying international responses to conflict. During the Iraqi invasion of Kuwait, for example, 'the construct of the virile, white male defender of women and children' was projected.[119] Tactical rape and sexual violence in war may be highlighted for short-term, political gains and then fade from public attention, eliciting little or no response to the specific needs of women, and underlying the reasons why tactical rape and sexual violence are effective. This presents a strategic dilemma for feminist advocacy.

The use of women's suffering for political gain is abhorrent. Yet, I argue that the ongoing secrecy and practice of ignoring tactical rape must be countered. By publicising events and indicting those who commit rape in conflict, some greater security, albeit extremely limited, may be achieved for women, individually and collectively. Women refugees in Kosovo in 1999 were 'unusually' prepared to report rape because the expectation was reticence based on rape often being 'seen as such a big shame, a mark for their whole lives'.[120] A lawyer taking formal statements from victims suggested: 'sadly when many women have been raped, it may be easier for each one to cope and to speak about her experiences'.[121] It is possible that Kosovar women knew what had happened to others in Bosnia-Herzegovina, and felt they

---

[116] Lerner, S, 1998, Haitian women demand justice, *MS Magazine*, July–August, 10–11, quoted in Enloe, op cit, p 109.

[117] Enloe, op cit.

[118] Ibid.

[119] Gibson, S, 1993, The discourse of sex/war: thoughts on C MacKinnon's 1993 Oxford Amnesty lecture, 1, *Feminist Legal Studies Journal*, 179-88, p 179. The lecture referred to is MacKinnon, C, 1993, Crimes of war, crimes of peace, in S Shute and S Hurley (eds), *On human rights: The Oxford Amnesty lectures 1993*, New York: Basic Books, p 83, quoted in Charlesworth and Chinkin, op cit, p 255.

[120] Fitzpatrick, B, 1999, *Kosovo – The women and children*, Burwood, VIC: World Vision Australia, p 14.

[121] Ibid, p 15.

would be believed and not made to suffer for being victims. They may also have thought that there was a chance of the perpetrators being held accountable. The lawyer continued that the women were, 'first interviewed at border points but they really WANT to give evidence again'.[122] At the time, recognition and rejection was beginning to be considered, and tactical rape was accorded a degree of credibility.

There are concerns regarding the suffering incurred when well-meaning activists 'interview' women. There are times when women want to tell their stories, but as Cynthia Enloe highlighted, unnecessary additional pain can be inflicted. One woman had been questioned by 12 interviewers.[123] Shana Swiss and Joan E. Giller noted:

> The very process of human rights documentation may conflict with the needs of the individual survivor. Recounting the details of a traumatic experience may trigger an intense reliving of the event and, along with it, feelings of extreme vulnerability, humiliation and despair.[124]

Re-telling can have significant repercussions socially, emotionally and psychologically. However, much as those outside a society may decry the cultural value of chastity, these are often imbedded in the psychology of women as much as in the psychology of the men in their societies. I heard many stories from women in refugee camps, but names and identifications were always protected. Details were the purview of authorised and formally authenticated documentation. Many interviews were with workers in camps rather than actual victims and survivors.

There is, however, a balancing view. Rosalind Dixon noted the emerging imperative for recognition of victims and survivors as well as for a more ordered international community.[125] She posited that prosecution alone would not provide due redress for violations, and proposed that compensation might be needed as the concept of 'justice' moved beyond the existing ICTY and Rome Statutes. This is a justifiable proposition given that much domestic law now compensates victims and survivors of many crimes.

---

[122] Ibid.

[123] Enloe, op cit, p 133.

[124] Swiss, S, Giller, JE, 1993, Rape as a crime of war: a medical perspective, *Journal of the American Medical Association*, 270, 4 August, p 614, quoted in Enloe, op cit, p 133.

[125] Dixon, R, 2002, Rape as crime in international law: where to from here?, *European Journal of International Law*, 13, 3, 697-719.

As international tribunals come to an end, there remain many crimes that are handed over to national or traditional courts, such as the Gacaca courts in Rwanda. There are many limitations to these courts just as there are to international courts. The ICTY has handed over to a national judiciary with an acknowledged need to train personnel, to build capacity and sensitivity. National and traditional courts are subject to cultural, social and political values and constructs and the same criticisms.

The ICTY and ICTR were ad hoc courts limited in an operating time frame and geographic focus. After considerable lobbying and advocacy by some states and international NGOs, agreement emerged that an independent permanent criminal court was needed.[126] The Rome Statute was adopted by 120 states in 1998 as the legal basis for the establishment of the ICC,[127] which is:

> ... an independent judicial institution, charged with carrying out investigations into and trials of individuals allegedly responsible for the most serious crimes of international concern, namely genocide, crimes against humanity and war crimes.[128]

Although not part of the UN system, it is funded primarily 'by states parties as well as by governments, international organisations, individuals, corporations and other entities.'[129] The ICC has built on the work of tribunals and UN Security Council resolution 1325 in 2000. By January 2015:

> ... 123 countries are States Parties to the Rome Statute of the International Criminal Court. Out of them 34 are African States, 19 are Asia-Pacific States, 18 are from Eastern Europe, 27 are from Latin American and Caribbean States, and 25 are from Western European and other States.[130]

---

[126] See www.icc-cpi.int/en_menus/icc/Pages/default.aspx
[127] Ibid.
[128] UN General Assembly, 2011, *Report of the International Criminal Court*, 19 August, A/66/309, para 1.
[129] See www.icc-cpi.int/en_menus/icc/Pages/default.aspx
[130] Ibid.

The ICC has a particular mandate to consider sexual violence in conflict. In 2009, the ICC prosecutor, Luis Moreno-Ocampo, outlined the approaches to gender crimes, particularly as they are committed in conflict.[131] He highlighted the explicit mandate to deal with crimes of gender, specifically in Articles 42(9) and 54(1)(b).[132] He made the connection with the former Yugoslavia:

> The efforts since the mid-1990s to obtain accountability for atrocities committed against women in Bosnia helped establish how rape and other sexual violence could be instrumentalised in a campaign of genocide. This equally contributed to the expanding understanding of gender or sexual violence as war crimes or crimes against humanity.[133]

He referred to the Akayesu case at the ICTR, described as, 'the most ground breaking decision advancing gender jurisprudence world-wide', noting that 'for the first time in history, rape was explicitly recognised as an instrument of genocide.'[134] By recognising the foundational work of the ICTY and ICTR, the ICC was providing permanent codification of the progress in the normative rejection of tactical rape and sexual violence.

Moreno-Ocampo highlighted some ICC cases. In the CAR, one party to the conflict had 'used rape as a primary weapon of war to terrorise and punish the civilian population ... and to create a politically pliable situation'.[135] Moreno-Ocampo recognised that there had been an 'evolution' regarding gender crimes.[136] With reference to the Application for the Arrest Warrant for al-Bashir, President of Sudan, he noted that, 'crimes of rape and sexual violence committed in the Darfur area are an "integral part" of attempts to destroy' certain groups and 'should be charged as genocide'.[137] The connection with work of ICTY and ICTR are clear. He concluded that his office 'is part of a new system to end impunity'.

Perhaps not surprisingly, in October 2014 the General Assembly expressed support for the work of the ICC, but with some reservations,

---

[131] Moreno-Ocampo, L, 2009, *Sexual violence as international crime: Interdisciplinary approaches to evidence*, The Hague: International Criminal Court, 16 June.

[132] Ibid, p 3.

[133] Ibid, pp 4, 5.

[134] Ibid, p. 5.

[135] Ibid.

[136] Ibid, p 4.

[137] Ibid, p 7.

'delegates alternatively praised its effectiveness in prosecuting crimes against humanity and criticized what they viewed as its partiality'.[138] There was affirmation that the ICC was essential for the enforcement of global peace and justice, with commendation for its record of arrests, criminal cases and preliminary investigations, particularly in light of the number of cases of genocide and impunity for perpetration of atrocities in recent years. Criticism came from several members, 'especially some representing African States, who said the Court was partial to interfering with the crimes committed on their continent', with Sudan's representative stating:

> ... the Court had become a tool in international conflicts and political action by focusing on Africa and targeting its leaders, while ignoring atrocities in other regions, an idea echoed by Syria's representative, who said some countries had prevented the adoption of a Security Council resolution to hold Israel responsible for crimes against humanity. Senegal's representative said the Council must act responsibly and in a non-politicized way to avoid being suspected of selectivity and double standards.[139]

There is further considerable criticism regarding the apparent emphasis on prosecuting African offenders. Janie Leatherman reiterated that African states are not the only arenas where sexual violence occurs in conflict, and this is borne out by the incidences reviewed in Chapters Two and Five (this volume).[140] In January 2015, President Robert Mugabe of Zimbabwe, the African Union rotating chair for 2015, threatened to push for African ICC members to withdraw from the court, but this was opposed by Malawi and Botswana, which consistently offered support for the court.[141] One-sidedness is also perceived at local levels. In the four years since investigations began in Côte d'Ivoire, the only opened cases relate to alleged crimes committed in Abidjan, the country's economic capital, by forces affiliated with one side of the conflict.

[138] UN, *International Criminal Court receives mixed performance review, as General Assembly concludes discussion of body's annual report*, 31 October 2014, 69th session.
[139] Ibid.
[140] Leatherman, JL, 2011, *Sexual violence and armed conflict*, Cambridge: Polity Press.
[141] Human Rights Watch, 2015, *AU: ICC members should lead on justice*, 9 June.

The victims' high expectations for impartial justice before the ICC – fuelled by the fear, especially among the victims of crimes by the Ouattara-allied forces, that they would never get it at home – have given way to frustration regarding a lack of progress in prosecuting all sides. Where the ICC truly needs to matter is in the countries – and indeed in the communities – affected by the crimes the court will try.[142]

Criticism comes from a perceived need to maintain a balance between the jurisdiction of the ICC and the prosecution of serious crimes in national courts, with representatives referring to a principle of complementarity as the 'backbone of criminal justice'.

States are also criticised for failure to meet their responsibilities to surrender accused perpetrators of crimes to the ICC. Many arrest warrants issued by the court are outstanding, 'a result of a lack of cooperation among some Member States to apprehend individuals, undermining the Court's ability to deliver justice'.[143] This will always be an issue for an international judiciary taking up unfulfilled national responsibilities for bringing criminals to justice. However, I argue that the ICC is of some significance for all its limitations, even if only as a potential deterrent factor for perpetrators. The challenge is to make it effective. Other criticisms arise from the structure and mandate of the ICC itself. It is dependent on voluntary contributions from states; states have capacity to withhold support, and there is no effective enforcement mechanism, even when states have ratified the court. It is restricted to prosecuting cases only when states either will not or cannot do so effectively. There are discrepancies in global and national legal systems, causing controversy about sentences. The ICC's capacity to try heads of state has been criticised as interfering with peacemaking. When ICC arrest warrants were issued for Sudanese President Omar al-Bashir in 2009, some critics,

> ... predicted that criminal charges would imperil, if not destroy, prospects for implementation of the Comprehensive

---

[142] Evenson, E, 2015, ICC success depends on its impact locally, *Open Democracy*, 26 August.

[143] UN, *International Criminal Court receives mixed performance review, as General Assembly concludes discussion of body's annual report*, 31 October 2014, 69th session.

Peace Accord (CPA) between Sudan and an emerging South Sudan.[144]

Despite these fears, 'the catastrophic consequences never materialized'.[145]

Conclusion

Critical analyses focus on the limitations and dangers as well as the achievements of judicial processes dealing with tactical rape and sexual violence in conflict. Courts are demonstrably insensitive, and subject many women to additional levels of trauma and humiliation. Judiciaries and law are gendered, not acknowledging the reality of women's experiences. But despite the many reservations, there have been incremental, less than perfect, moves towards normative rejection of tactical rape and sexual violence in war. While working to change gendered laws and adversarial proceedings, the transitional and accompanying step would be changing the attitudes and functioning of courts. In many ways, thanks to the courage of women survivors, there have been some albeit limited advances in bringing perpetrators to account.

---

[144] Dicker, R, 2015, Throwing justice under the bus is not the way to go, *Open Democracy*, 11 December.
[145] Ibid.

FIVE

Tactical rape in the former Yugoslavia

The conflict in the former Yugoslavia demonstrated a style of warfare where civilians were targeted, where international intervention happened within a context of new understandings of the limits on sovereignty, where a tribunal that was deliberately an ad hoc entity extended judgments regarding tactical rape and sexual violence as contraventions of established international law. It became:

> ... the paradigm case, from which different lessons are drawn, the example which is used to argue out different general positions, and, at the same time, a laboratory in which different ways of managing the new wars are experimented.[1]

The judgments of the ICTY provided a base in international law for recognising that tactical rape and sexual violence were issues of security for women, for communities and for states.[2] The rate of convictions has been criticised, and as will be seen later in this chapter, handover to national judiciaries has been problematic. International law is justifiably criticised for being male-centric and for setting a context that neither recognises the needs, capacities nor the realities of women.

While acknowledging this essential nature of international law and the many shortcomings of the international tribunals (detailed later), I argue that it was due to working with established law that significant progress was made in recognition and response to tactical rape and sexual violence in conflict. There is much still to achieve, but this was a beginning. The establishment of legal precedents was not an end to bringing perpetrators to account, but it did open one route to doing so.

---

[1]   Kaldor, M, 2002, *New and old wars: Organised violence in a global era*, Cambridge: Polity Press, p 6.

[2]   UN Security Council, 1993, *Statute of the International Tribunal for the Prosecution of Persons Responsible for Serious Violations of International Law Committed in the Territory of the Former Yugoslavia since 1991*, UN Doc S/25704 at 36, Annex (1993) and S/25704/Add.1 (1993), 25 May, UN Doc S/RES/827

The conflict in the former Yugoslavia between 1992 and 1995 concerned Bosniaks (Bosnian Muslims), Serbs and Croats. Muslim nationalists wanted a centralised independent Bosnia-Herzegovina. Serb nationalists wanted a Belgrade-dominated Yugoslavia. Croats wanted an independent Croatian state. In March 1992, Bosnia declared independence, conflict broke out and the Serb Republic was proclaimed. The Serbs then began a process of 'ethnic cleansing'. In April 1992, a report by the Secretary-General to the UN General Assembly and Security Council noted:

> Ethnic cleansing is the direct cause of the vast majority of human rights violations which have occurred in Bosnia and Herzegovina since the present human rights emergency began in March and April 1992.[3]

In early August 1992, reputable media reports were widely published about the Omarska Prison Camp in Northern Bosnia, telling of violations including torture and rape.[4]

This conflict exemplified the development of 'new wars'. This was not a war in which armies confronted and battled other armies, not a battle across international state borders. The battle was for control of territory, and methods and strategies focused on control of civilian populations. Achievement of the goal depended on 'getting rid of all possible opponents', creating 'an unfavourable environment for all those people it cannot control', and on 'continuing fear and insecurity and on perpetuation of hatred of the other'.[5] Before the conflict, different groups in the disputed areas were living together in shared communities. Some observers believed that attacking forces were 'determined to "kill" the city [Sarajevo] and the tradition of tolerance and ethnic harmony that it represents'.[6]

Mary Kaldor identified specific techniques for gaining territorial control: systematic murder, ethnic cleansing, and rendering an area uninhabitable – physically and economically: defilement through

---

[3] Note of the Secretary-General, *Human rights questions: Human rights situations and reports of the Special Rapporteurs and Representatives, Situation of human rights in the territory of the former Yugoslavia*, A/47/666 and S/24809, 17 November 1992, para 8.

[4] Vulliamy, E, 1992, Shame of camp Omarska, *The Guardian*, 7 August.

[5] Kaldor, M, 2002, *New and old wars: Organised violence in a global era*, Cambridge: Polity Press, pp 98–99.

[6] Report on the situation of human rights in the territory of the former Yugoslavia, United Nations, E/CN.4/199/S-1-9, New York, 28 August 1992 para 17.

systematic rape and sexual abuse.[7] In effect, Kaldor provided a summary of the strategies employed in the conflict. The full nature and impact of all the strategies, particularly tactical rape and sexual violence, took time to be recognised and understood. However, this conflict proved something of a watershed in that such strategies were even noted and condemned rather than accepted as unfortunate but ultimately inevitable in war.

In October 1992, the Security Council established a Commission of Experts to analyse and examine events relating to 'violations of humanitarian law, including grave breaches of the Geneva Conventions.'[8] The Commission reported grave breaches and violations of international law including rape.[9] It recommended the establishment of an ad hoc tribunal and the Security Council agreed to establish the ad hoc ICTY.[10]

The International Criminal Tribunal of the former Yugoslavia

Faced with condemnation and strong international cries for action including calls from NGOs, public media and its own UN agencies such as the UNHCR and Human Rights Commission, the Security Council could no longer ignore the contravention of common humanitarian values and rules in the former Yugoslavia. However, any solution needed to take into account opposition to overriding the sovereignty of individual states. Resolution 764 (13 July 1992) reaffirmed obligations to respect international humanitarian law, and set down the principle of individual responsibility for grave breaches of the Geneva Conventions. Resolution 771 (1 August 1992) applied Chapter VII of the Charter of the UN, demanding that all states desist from all breaches of international law. Then resolution 827 (27 May 1993) approved the Statute of the ICTY, under the Charter of the UN.

The ICTY was established with 'the power to prosecute persons responsible for serious human rights violations of international humanitarian law committed in the territory of the former Yugoslavia

---

[7]   Kaldor, op cit, pp 99–100.

[8]   UN Security Council, 1994, *Rape and sexual assault – Final report of the United Nations Commission of Experts established pursuant to Security Council resolution 780 (1992)*, S/1994/Paragraph 2.

[9]   UN, 1993, *Report of the Secretary-General pursuant to paragraph 2 of Security Council resolution 808.*

[10] Ibid.

since 1991.'[11] The Statute covered powers to prosecute grave breaches of the 1949 Geneva Conventions, violations of the laws or customs of war, crimes against humanity and of genocide. It outlined areas of responsibility regarding superior command, planning, instigating, ordering or committing violations and territorial and temporal jurisdiction. A head of state did not have impunity from prosecution. The decision to establish such a court 'constituted a response to the threat to international peace and security posed by those crimes'.[12] Juan Jose Quintana pointed out that by acting under the application of Chapter VII of the Charter, the Security Council had:

> ... the major advantage that all States would be under a binding obligation to take whatever action is required to apply the decision of the Security Council, since it was a measure approved under Chapter VII.[13]

Quintana listed the distinctive features of the ICTY: it was an independent organ, not subject to any kind of authority or control by the Security Council; it was a temporary organ, the existence or maintenance of which depends on the restoration of peace and international security in the former Yugoslavia; it was an ad hoc jurisdictional mechanism not directly related to the establishment of an international criminal jurisdiction of a permanent nature; and it was confined to applying existing rules of international humanitarian law and not developing or creating new rules.[14] Provided it operated under its mandate, rulings and judgements of the ICTY would be difficult to ignore.

Establishment of the ICTY represented a judicial response to reports of serious violations of human rights including rape. In many cases the international community seeks to find a way of responding to such violations by means other than forcible intervention, which is more difficult to justify than humanitarian or judicial intervention. Establishing a permanent body could be seen to be intervening in

[11] Ibid.

[12] Birdsall, A, 2007, Creating a more "just" order: the ad hoc International War Crimes Tribunal for the former Yugoslavia, *Cooperation & Conflict*, 42, 4, 397–418, p 397.

[13] Quintana, JJ, 1994, Violations of international humanitarian law and measures of repression: the International Tribunal for the former Yugoslavia, *International Review of the Red Cross*, 300, p 226.

[14] Ibid, pp 227–8.

internal concerns, so it is important that the ICTY was an ad hoc judiciary.

Andrea Birdsall argued convincingly that the establishment of the ICTY 'constituted an important precedent for multi-lateral action towards institutionalising respect for the rule of law and principles of individual justice', and concluded that 'this suggests that these norms are being taken increasingly seriously and are being given priority over other fundamental principles of order such as sovereignty and non-intervention'.[15] The institutionalising of attitudes and values became an increasingly important element in the development of rejection of tactical rape and sexual violence in war, and the ICTY was a step towards such institutionalisation. Birdsall described it as constituting 'external intervention by a number of states into the internal affairs of another sovereign state in order to enforce human rights laws and to protect principles of justice'. Her definition of justice as 'enforcement of international human rights laws and norms aimed at holding perpetrators accountable and ending the culture of impunity' is consistent with the role of the ICTY in furthering the acceptance and response to the norm rejecting tactical rape.[16] There was little doubt that the ICTY would be judging behaviours and events in a sovereign state. There was also little doubt that international society was prepared to hold accountable those who contravened existing international laws. Birdsall perceived the ICTY demonstrating that human rights norms were in train to cascade from the first phase of institutionalisation of new norms into international law.[17]

However, rejection of the use of rape as a tactic for policy attack on a civilian population was still not integrated into the recognised spectrum of human rights violations. It was as the ICTY progressed that tactical rape and sexual violence in conflict achieved recognition as crimes against humanity, as war crimes and as gross violations of human rights. The fact that human rights norms had already been established in international law and included universal jurisdiction provisions that placed states under obligation to enforce them was significant in providing international society with grounds to take action. Birdsall noted that such universal jurisdiction provisions were significant because they recognised that 'some human rights are seen as fundamental to all states and have the potential to take precedence over

---

[15] Birdsall, op cit, p 397.
[16] Ibid, p 399.
[17] Ibid, p 400.

other principles.'[18] The ICTY made clear that protection of civilian populations from tactical rape and sexual violence in conflict should be included as one of these fundamental human rights.

The ICTY, established under Chapter VII of the Charter of the UN, was a response to threats to peace and security. States used the rhetoric of established human rights norms as justification for a tribunal that would, in effect, override the sovereignty of another state. The ICTY was not a permanent fixture in international judiciaries. It was ad hoc and mandated to a specific conflict at a specific time, limited in its time frame, its geographic range and acceptable as 'an exceptional step needed to deal with exceptional situations.'[19] Importantly, it was established 'for the purpose of upholding universally agreed principles firmly established in international law.'[20] It was to investigate and prosecute within an established and widely accepted legal framework.

The ICTY provided grounds for a developing norm rejecting tactical rape and sexual violence in conflict by judging that these practices fell within the established and widely accepted frameworks. There was a legal basis for challenging and at least theoretically rejecting tactical rape and sexual violence in conflict. It accepted arguments that under certain circumstances perpetrators could be and were indicted and charged for rape and sexual violence as well as other acts seen as grave breaches and violations of accepted international law.

Not surprisingly, the leadership of the former Yugoslavia opposed the ICTY. Establishing the ICTY was interpreted as overstepping the sovereignty of an independent state, and the Tribunal's authority was challenged as certain cases proceeded. However, the Security Council continued, and such appeals were dismissed in cases such as those against Duško Tadić.[21]

> The Chamber concluded that the Tribunal was properly established by the Security Council. In reaching this conclusion, the Chamber determined that it could assess the lawfulness of Security Council actions when necessary to satisfy itself that it has the authority to proceed in a case. Upon conducting this kind of assessment, the Chamber found that the Security Council's decision to establish the

[18] Ibid, p 415.
[19] UN Security Council, 1995, p 189, quoted in Birdsall, op cit, p 403.
[20] Birdsall, op cit.
[21] ICTY, *Prosecutor v Tadić*, Judgement, Case No IT-94-1-A (ICTY App. CH.15 July 1999).

Tribunal was a legitimate measure aimed at the restoration of peace and security authorised under the United Nations Charter, and that the Tribunal had been duly established according to the rule of law.[22]

The Appeals Chamber similarly concluded that the Tribunal's primacy did not constitute an improper intrusion on state sovereignty. The Chamber noted that such actions were authorised under Article 27 of the Charter of the UN, and emphasised that state sovereignty must give way in the face of offences that 'do not affect the interests of one State alone but shock the conscience of mankind'.[23] The Appeals Chamber also rejected the assertion that the Tribunal lacked jurisdiction because the Bosnian conflict was a civil war. This particular objection was countered, and case law established regarding intra- and international conflicts.

Birdsall asserted that the ICTY was only a step in the life cycle of a developing norm, and that 'further developments need to take place in international politics and law to achieve a more universal, less discriminatory enforcement of existing norms'.[24] She referred to the work of Victor Peskin, who recognised the long-term normative impact of ad hoc courts in establishing precedents for the further extension of international law.[25] The ICTY, while not establishing new norms, extended the understanding and reaction to tactical rape and sexual violence in conflict within the application of existing norms and international law.

Building a basis in international law

The ICTY contributed significantly to the legal basis for treating tactical rape and sexual violence as contraventions of accepted international humanitarian and human rights law. The extent to which a ruling or opinion is considered legitimate may originate in the perceived legitimacy of the advocate or in the extent of international support it is perceived to be receiving. The ICTY's legitimacy came

---

[22] ICTY, 1995, Press Release, Appeals Chamber judges unanimously confirm the Tribunal's jurisdiction, C/PIO/021-E, The Hague, 2 October.

[23] Ibid.

[24] Birdsall, op cit, p 406.

[25] Peskin, V, 2000, Conflicts of justice – An analysis of the role of the International Criminal Tribunal of Rwanda, *International Peacekeeping*, 6, 128-37.

from Chapter VII of the Charter of the UN and from the widespread support it received from the Security Council and member states.

The ICTY listed what it saw as its core achievements.[26] These include: expanding on the legal elements of the crime of grave breaches of the Geneva Conventions by further defining the test of overall control; identifying the existence of an international armed conflict and an extended and exact definition of protected persons under the Conventions; narrowing the differences between laws or customs of war applicable to conflicts; and identifying a general prohibition of torture in international law that cannot be derogated from by a treaty or by internal law. Other achievements include making significant advances in international humanitarian law pertaining to the legal treatment and punishment of sexual violence in war, and the identification and application of the concept of command responsibility.[27] ICTY case outcomes and rulings established the legal bases for defining and prosecuting tactical rape and sexual violence in conflict. They provided legitimacy for changed attitudes and eventual rejection of the abuses.

Findings in the case against Tadić contributed to general jurisprudence relating to crimes against humanity and thereby to judging tactical rape. A single act could qualify as a crime against humanity as long as there was a link with a widespread or systematic attack against a civilian population. Although a 'policy' to commit crimes against humanity must exist, it need not be the policy of a state, but could be instigated or directed by a non–state organisation or group.

Rochus J.P. Pronk and Brian D. Tittemore provided an overview of significant developments from the Tadić case.[28] Commission of crimes against humanity come under customary international law for which there is individual criminal responsibility. Key elements are required under Article 5 of the ICTY Statute to judge an act as a crime against humanity. Acts needed to be committed 'during', as opposed to 'in', an armed conflict, and be linked temporally and geographically to that conflict. The ICTY Appeals Chamber, in its previous jurisdiction appeal decision in the Tadić case, had held this linking was not required as a matter of customary international law, but was nevertheless expressly required under the ICTY Statute. A further requirement

---

[26] See www.icty.org/en/about/tribunal/achievements

[27] Ibid.

[28] Pronk, RJP, Tittemore, BD, 2011, ICTY issues final judgment against Duško Tadić in first international war crimes trial since World War II, *The Center for Human Rights and Humanitarian Law at Washington College of Law*, Washington, DC: American University.

was that a systematic widespread attack on a civilian population was occurring at the time of the commission of the acts. Finally, it had to be established that the accused knew or had reason to know that by his acts or omission he was participating in the attack on the population.

Certain aspects of the ICTY Statute have particular relevance to the prosecution of perpetrators of tactical rape and sexual violence in conflict. One such aspect is the clarification of just who is deemed a protected person when applying international law. The Statute included powers to prosecute persons under the laws as set out in the Geneva Conventions. Additional Protocol I to those Conventions firmly established that civilians should never be specifically targeted in war.[29] This cleared the way for the ICTY to deal with rape of civilians as part of a policy of tactical use of rape. However, Geneva Convention IV says that protected persons are 'those in the hands of a party to the conflict or Occupying Power of which they are not nationals'.[30] This might have excluded victims of the same nationality as their abusers, but that definition of protected persons was interpreted widely by the ICTY to include victims for whom 'factors such as religion or ethnicity may be more determinative of where an individual's alliance lies than formal nationality'.[31] This provided protection to Bosnian Muslims victimised by Bosnian Serbs. It set a judicial precedent for avoiding legal loopholes to enable impunity for perpetrators of tactical rape and sexual violence.

Veronica Arbreu highlighted that Article 2 of the ICTY Statute referred to persons protected under the provisions of the Geneva Conventions.[32] The Charter of the UN is committed to promoting respect for human rights and for the fundamental freedom for all people without distinction such as their sex.[33] As an entity of the UN, the ICTY must therefore recognise the same rights for men and women,

---

[29] UN, 1977, *Additional Protocol to the Geneva Conventions of August 12 1949, and relating to the Protection of Victims of International Armed Conflicts (Protocol I)*, 8 June, 1125 U, NTS 3, 16 ILM 1331 (entered into force 7 December 1978).

[30] UN, 1949, *Geneva Convention IV Concerning the Protection of Civilian Persons in Time of War*, Article 4 (1).

[31] Askin, K, 2003, Prosecuting wartime rape and other gender-related crimes under international law: extraordinary advances, enduring obstacles, *Berkeley Journal of International Law*, 21, 288–349, p.310, note 111, referencing the Celebici Appeals Chamber Judgement.

[32] Arbreu, VC, 2005, Women's bodies as battlefields in the former Yugoslavia: An argument for the prosecution of sexual terrorism as genocide and for recognition of genocidal sexual terrorism as a violation of *jus cogens* under international law, *Georgetown Journal of Gender and the Law*, p 8.

[33] Charter of the UN, Article 1, paras 1-3.

and must provide for equal protection. It determined that civilians in the former Yugoslavia had the right to protection from crimes by forces not of their ethnic group.[34] This included protection from tactical rape and sexual violence.

The ICTY distinguished between international and internal conflicts. Theodor Meron asserted that there was no moral justification and no truly persuasive legal reasons for treating perpetrators of atrocities in internal conflicts more leniently than those engaged in international wars.[35] Article 5 of the ICTY Statute enabled prosecution of crimes against humanity, listing acts and conditions under which they might be constituted 'crimes against humanity'. This had to be included in the Statute as there was no international treaty that specifically defined 'crimes against humanity'. Article 5 recognised that such acts can be committed as part of either international or internal conflicts, and forces perpetrating these acts do not have to be state-controlled but can include 'illegitimate forces that take de facto control over defined territory, including militias, terrorist groups and organisations.'[36]

It was in the ICTY Appeals Chamber Decision on Jurisdiction that armed conflict was defined as conflict existing 'whenever there is a resort to armed force between States or protracted armed violence between governmental authorities and organised armed groups or between such groups within a State.'[37] It was judged that such conflict was deemed to exist until such time as a peaceful settlement was reached, whether or not actual combat was taking place.

Both human rights law and humanitarian law 'take as their starting point the concern for human dignity, which forms the basis of a list of fundamental minimum standards of humanity.'[38] The Geneva Conventions, Common Article 2 and the Martens Clause of the early Hague Conventions assert that 'fundamental human rights do not cease to be applicable during armed conflict'.[39] By recognising that international humanitarian law and human rights law apply in conflicts – and those conflicts may be international or internal – the application and relevance of other international instruments such as

---

[34] ICTY, *Prosecutor v Tadić*, Judgement, Case No IT-94-1-A (ICTY App. CH.15 July 1999), paras 167–8.

[35] Meron, T, 1995, International criminalisation of internal atrocities, *American Journal of International Law*, 554.

[36] Arbreu, op cit, p 9.

[37] ICTY, *Prosecutor v Duško Tadić*, Decision on the Defence Motion for Interlocutory Appeal on Jurisdiction, 2 October 1995, Case No IT-94-AR72, para 70.

[38] ICTY, *Prosecutor v Delalić*, Judgement, IT-96-21-A, 20 February, 2001, para 149.

[39] Askin, op cit, p 293.

the declarations and covenants that formulate required protection of human rights, civil and political rights, protection of women and children and prohibit torture and discrimination, were all clarified.[40] The rights to protection and justice contained in these instruments can be seen to have attained the status of *jus cogens*, meaning that these are rights considered so fundamental that states are not permitted to contract out of them.[41] It is to this status that the rejection of tactical rape and sexual violence in conflict must aspire.

Tactical rape as strategy and policy

Article 5 of the ICTY Statute enabled prosecution as crimes against humanity if a series of criminal acts, including rape, were committed as part of a widespread or systematic attack against a civilian population. I define tactical rape as rape that is part of a strategy and policy of attacking civilians, that is widespread or systematic. Kelly Dawn Askin, reviewing cases heard by the international tribunals, noted that 'evidence indicates that rape crimes are increasingly committed systematically and strategically, such that sexual violence forms a central and fundamental part of the attack against an opposing group'.[42] She also concluded that while the laws of warfare have prohibited rape of combatants and non-combatants for centuries, that increasingly 'this prohibition extends to other forms of sexual violence, including sexual slavery, forced impregnation, forced maternity, forced abortion, forced sterilisation, forced marriage, forced nudity, sexual molestation, sexual mutilation, sexual humiliation and sex trafficking.'[43] Tactical rape in the former Yugoslavia was the abuse that sparked outrage and condemnation, but the other acts that constitute sexual violence also often accompanied it. That tactical rape and sexual violence were indeed widespread was supported in the ICTY Judgement in *Prosecutor v Kvočka*.[44] There was general acceptance that widespread attacks

---

[40] UN, 1948, *Universal Declaration of Human Rights*; UN, 1993, *Declaration on Elimination of Violence Against Women*; UN, 1984, *Convention Against Torture and other Cruel, Inhuman and Degrading Treatment or Punishment*; UN, 1966, *International Covenant on Civil and Political Rights*; UN, 1989, *Convention on the Rights of the Child.*

[41] Baylis, J, Smith, S, Owens, P, 2008, *The globalisation of world politics: An introduction to international relations*, Oxford: Oxford University Press, p 583.

[42] Askin, op cit, p 297.

[43] Ibid, p 305.

[44] ICTY, *Prosecutor v Kvočka*, Judgement, IT-98-30-T, 2 November 2001, para 180, note 343; Rome Statute of the ICC, 1998, UN Document A/CONF183/9, Articles 7(1)(g), 8(2)(b)(xxii), 8(2)(e)(vi).

such as tactical rape and sexual violence in any conflict are subject to international humanitarian law. A crime against humanity was defined as 'a single act by a perpetrator taken within a widespread or systematic attack against a civilian population entails individual responsibility and an individual perpetrator need not commit numerous offences to be held liable.'[45] Deciding that offences have been committed in a 'systematic or organised' fashion can be guided by examining the nature of the crimes that may have been perpetrated as a result of either a state policy or the policy of non-state forces including terrorist groups or organisations.[46]

The ICTY ruled in the case against Kunarac, one of four accused who were convicted of various crimes dealing with rape and sexual slavery:

> It is sufficient to show that the act took place in the context of an accumulation of acts of violence, which, individually, may vary greatly in nature and gravity.[47]

Each individual act of rape may be deemed an act of tactical rape when it is part of an overall, systematic attack that is widespread and strategically motivated. When judging Vukovic, one of those accused with Kunarac, the court dismissed his defence that his actions were beyond the court's jurisdiction because even if he had raped it was not out of hatred. The court ruled:

> ... all that matters in this context is his awareness of an attack against the Muslim civilian population of which his victim was a member and, for the purpose of torture, that he intended to discriminate between the group of which he is a member and the group of the victim.[48]

This clarified the essential condition for tactical rape and sexual violence being deemed war crimes, the fact that such acts were committed as part of a strategic or policy-driven plan to gain political or military ascendency over another group or to ethnically cleanse a territory. A plan or policy may be indicative of the systematic nature of the crime

---

[45] ICTY, *Prosecutor v Duško Tadić*, Decision on the Defence Motion for Interlocutory Appeal on Jurisdiction, 2 October 1995, Case No IT-94-AR72, para 649.

[46] Charlesworth, H, Chinkin, C, 2000, *The boundaries of international law: A feminist analysis*, Manchester: Manchester University Press, p 322.

[47] ICTY, *Prosecutor v Kunarac*, Judgement, IT-96-23-T, 22 February 2001, para 419.

[48] Ibid, para 816.

and thus be 'evidentially relevant', but it is not essential to produce such a plan or policy for an attack to be deemed 'systematic'.[49]

This pre-condition of being widespread or systematic also applied when ruling on tactical rape and sexual violence as crimes against humanity. 'Crimes against humanity' had not been elsewhere formally agreed despite the term being widely used since the Nuremburg Trials. Askin said that while definitions differed:

> ... in essence, a crime against humanity consists of an inhumane act (typically a series of inhumane acts such as murder, rape, and torture) committed as part of a widespread or systematic attack directed against a civilian population.[50]

It is therefore important that there be clear understanding of what is meant by 'widespread' or 'systematic'.

An article in the Slovenian newspaper *Delo* claimed that the Yugoslav National Army had a plan for widespread rapes as a weapon of psychological warfare:

> Analysis of the Muslims' behaviour showed their morale, desire for battle and will could be crushed most easily by raping women, especially minors and even children.[51]

The existence of a plan contributed to establishing that the rapes were widespread and systematic. In the ICTY case against Tadić, where the indictment included an allegation of a 'campaign of terror which included killings, torture, sexual assaults and other physical and psychological abuse', the Trial Chamber noted that treatment received by some named witnesses was not unique: 'A policy to terrorize ... is evident.'[52] By ruling about elements of systematic attacks, the ICTY contributed substantively to establishing legal grounds for understanding tactical rape and sexual violence as violations of established humanitarian law.

In the ICTY case against Furundžija, there was further development in the understanding of rape in international law.[53] Anto Furundžija

---

[49] Askin, op cit, p 315.

[50] Ibid, p 313, note 123.

[51] Kaldor, op cit, p 56.

[52] Askin, K, 1999, Sexual violence in decisions and indictments of the Yugoslav and Rwandan Tribunals: Current status, *The American Journal of International Law*, 93, 1, January, 97-123, p 103.

[53] ICTY, *Prosecutor v Furundžija*, Judgement, IT-95-17/1-T, 10 December 1998.

was found guilty of aiding and abetting outrages on personal dignity including rape. He had been a local commander of a group within the Croatian Defence Council, known as 'the Jokers', and in mid–May 1993 had been interrogating a witness. Another accused had been rubbing a knife on the woman's inner thigh and threatening to cut her. Later she was raped orally, anally and vaginally while members of the group watched and laughed. She was deemed to have suffered severe physical and mental harm and public humiliation.[54] The Trial Chamber identified the 'objective elements' of rape in international law as the sexual penetration, however slight, of the vagina or anus of the victim by the penis of the perpetrator or any other object used by the perpetrator, or penetration of the mouth of the victim by the penis of the perpetrator. The definition also included rape when such penetration was perpetrated by coercion or force or threat of force against the victim or a third person.[55]

This definition of objective elements, particularly of the possible nature of coercion and force, was important in moving from the requirement of proof of non–consent, and the judgement noted that 'any form of captivity vitiates consent'.[56] This represented a serious attempt to define and understand the reality of rape. The Trial Chamber emphasised that while force, threat of force or coercion are relevant, these factors are not exhaustive, and the emphasis must be placed on violations of sexual autonomy.[57] Sexual autonomy was ruled to be violated 'wherever the person subjected to the act has not freely agreed to it or is otherwise not a voluntary participant', and factors such as force, threat or taking advantage of a vulnerable person provide evidence as to whether consent is voluntary.[58] The Trial Chamber also ruled that no corroboration of the victim's testimony was required and prior sexual conduct of the victim was not admissible in evidence. This was a realistic obviation of legal attempts to undermine the testimony of survivors of tactical rape or sexual violence in conflict.

Numerous rulings provided a realistic understanding of tactical rape and allied sexual attacks. In the Kvočka case, the Trial Chamber pointed out that 'sexual violence covers a broad range of acts and includes such crimes as rape, molestation, sexual slavery, sexual mutilation, forced

[54] Ibid.
[55] Ibid.
[56] Ibid, para 271.
[57] Askin, 2003, op cit, p 334.
[58] ICTY, *Prosecutor v Furundžija*, Judgement, IT-95-17/1-T, 10 December 1998, paras 457, 458.

marriage, forced abortion, enforced prostitution, forced pregnancy and forced sterilization'.[59] This Čelebići case focused on four accused, with Zejnil Delalić eventually acquitted and Zdravko Mucić, Hazim Delić and Esad Landžo convicted and sentenced to terms ranging from 7 to 25 years. The indictment alleged that in 1992, forces consisting of Bosnian Muslims and Bosnian Croats took control of those villages containing predominantly Bosnian Serbs within and around the Konjic municipality in central Bosnia. Those detained during these operations were held in the Čelebići prison camp, where detainees were killed, tortured, sexually assaulted, beaten and otherwise subjected to cruel and inhumane treatment by the four accused.

This was a significant case. It was the first judgement involving multiple defendants. It deemed the conflict in Bosnia and Herzegovina to be an international conflict because of the involvement of the Federal Republic of Yugoslavia and its forces. It provided the first elucidation of the concept of command responsibility by an international judicial body since the cases decided in the wake of the Second World War, including responsibility of civilians holding posts of authority. This was the first conviction for rape as torture by the ICTY. Rape as torture was charged as a grave breach of the Geneva Conventions and a violation of the laws and customs of war, and according to the Trial Chamber, 'there can be no question that acts of rape may constitute torture under customary law.'[60]

In the case against Kunarac, the Trial Chamber noted, 'rape is one of the worst sufferings a human being can inflict on another', and took into account that the accused had frequently told his victims 'that they would give birth to Serb babies'.[61] It emphasised that suffering need not be long-lasting, stating it was not 'open to regard the fact that a victim has recovered or is overcoming the effects of such an offence as indicating it did not constitute an outrage on personal dignity.'[62] These were important acknowledgements of the immediate and long-term impacts of rape. They demonstrated an increased commitment to confronting and bringing to account the perpetrators of tactical rape and sexual violence in war, with an increased sensitivity to the real impact of these abuses.

---

[59] Askin, 2003, op cit, p 342.
[60] ICTY, *Čelebići case: The Judgement of the Trial Chamber: The most significant legal aspects.*
[61] Kunarac Indictment, para 6.1, quoted in Askin, 1999, op cit, p 121.
[62] Kunarac Trial Chamber Judgement, para 501, quoted in Askin, 2002, op cit, p 337.

Kelly Dawn Askin reviewed the judgement on Tadić and events at Omarska camp where 'both male and female prisoners were subjected to severe mistreatment, which included beatings, sexual assaults, torture and executions'.[63] It was:

> ... particularly significant that the trial chamber cited [this] testimony concerning sexual violence and reproduced testimony attesting to the enormous pain and suffering endured by women and girls and the community at large.[64]

There was recognition of the widespread negative impact of tactical rape on a group and, importantly, it was recognition that such negative impact extended from the individuals directly attacked to their communities.

In situations of conflict there may be debate regarding where responsibility lies for criminal acts: with those who actually perpetrate those acts, those who allow or condone them or those who may authorise and plan them. Edoardo Greppi wrote:

> ... the rules of humanitarian law concerning international crimes and responsibility have not always appeared sufficiently clear. One of the thorniest problems is that relating to the legal nature of international crimes committed by individuals and considered as serious violations of the rules of humanitarian law.[65]

The basic problem seemed to be that the borderline between war crimes and crimes against humanity appears blurred.[66] Greppi noted that 'beyond any doubt' crimes against humanity had become part of international law, and judgements of the ICTY 'affirmed it openly'.[67] He focused on the 'humanity' aspect of the distinctions between the two forms of crimes because 'the principle of humanity is at the core of international humanitarian law' and 'the principle of individual responsibility has clearly been established by humanitarian law'.[68]

---

[63] Tadić Judgement, ICTY, *Prosecutor v Tadić*, Judgement, Case No IT-94-1-A (ICTY App. CH.15 July 1999), para 154.

[64] Askin, 1999, op cit, p 102.

[65] Greppi, E, 1999, The evolution of individual criminal responsibility under international law, *International Review of the Red Cross*, 81, 835, p 531.

[66] Ibid, p 532.

[67] Ibid, p 549.

[68] Ibid, p 551.

Aspects of humanitarian law, particularly regarding responsibility, required attention.

Timothy McCormack pointed out regarding humanitarian law that 'acceptance of the body of rules and principles regulating the conduct of armed conflict can be perceived as condoning the resort to force', but 'when it comes to the prosecution of war crimes and other atrocities committed in armed conflict, the existence of legal principles is crucial'.[69] An article by Frits Kalshoven and Liesbeth Zegveld, written in 2001, noted that the goal of humanitarian law is 'to preserve humanity in the face of the reality of war', and opined that Security Council decisions to establish the ICTY and ICTR had been based on the notion of individual responsibility.[70] Establishing a base of jurisprudence regarding tactical rape required that issues of responsibility were clarified if impunity were ever to be reduced.

Patricia Viseur-Sellers focused on the outcomes of ICTY sexual assault cases regarding common purpose and joint responsibility.[71] As legal adviser for gender-related crimes in the Office of the Prosecutor for the ICTY, she argued, 'war, systematic attacks against civilians or the eruption of genocide entail collective criminal conduct'.[72] She explained that the ICTY Appeals Chamber 'ruled that no one who participates in a serious violation of humanitarian law escapes the Tribunal's jurisdiction'.[73] Viseur-Sellers described the two broad forms of individual liability: direct criminal responsibility, and indirect or superior responsibility. Direct responsibility implicates any accused who has planned, instigated, committed, ordered or aided or abetted the execution of crimes within the jurisdiction of the ICTY Statute. Indirect criminal responsibility attributes liability to a person in a position of superior authority, whether military, political, business or any hierarchical status, for acts directly committed by his or her subordinates.[74]

[69] McCormack, T, 1997, From Solferino to Sarajevo: A continuing role for international humanitarian law, *Melbourne University Law Review*, 21, p 625.

[70] Kalshoven, F, Zegveld, L, 2001, *Constraints on the waging of war: An introduction to international humanitarian law*, Geneva: International Commission of the Red Cross and Red Crescent, p 186.

[71] Viseur-Sellers, P, 2004, Individual('s) liability for collective sexual violence, in K Knop, *Gender and human rights*, Oxford: Oxford University Press, 153-95.

[72] Ibid, p 153.

[73] ICTY, *Prosecutor v Duško Tadić*, Decision on the Defence Motion for Interlocutory Appeal on Jurisdiction, 2 October 1995, Case No IT-94-AR72, para 92.

[74] Viseur-Sellers, op cit, p 154.

Viseur-Sellers described the approach by which a judgement was made by the Trial Chambers and Appeals Chamber regarding criminal liability, not directly expressed in Article 7(1), the relevant article of the ICTY Statute: 'Co-perpetration or joint criminal enterprise is a form of direct liability based upon a perpetrator undertaking to participate in criminal conduct with a plurality of actors.'[75] This clarification considerably extends the range of liability of participation and responsibility of perpetrators of tactical rape and sexual violence. Viseur-Sellers would 'not presume to predict, only speculate upon the munificent effect the common purpose or joint criminal enterprise doctrine might have on the development of sexual assault jurisprudence'.[76] However, I still hope that it will indeed prove to be of benefit for justice for victims of tactical rape and sexual violence.

Other rulings contributed to jurisprudence regarding responsibility. The case against four men who were involved in acts of sexual violence at the Čelebići camp referred to violence against men and women.[77] The accused were a de facto commander at the camp, a second person with alleged authority over the camp, a worker and a guard. The court judged that even when they did not commit the specific acts of sexual violence, the accused were responsible on the basis of 'their de facto as well as their de jure positions as superiors'.[78] The Appeals Chamber deemed that superior responsibility for crimes committed by subordinates could be incurred for war crimes, crimes against humanity and genocide:

> Superior responsibility may be used to hold military and civilian leaders accountable for crimes of sexual violence committed by subordinates that the superior negligently failed to prevent or punish.[79]

Kelly Dawn Askin noted this set a precedent that could be used 'to hold superiors criminally liable for failing to adequately train, monitor, supervise, control and punish subordinates who commit rape crimes', and there could be no illusions that women and girls were not at high risk of sexual violence during war, violence and occupation.[80]

---

[75] Ibid, p 155.

[76] Ibid, p 156.

[77] ICTY, *Prosecutor v Delacić*, Indictment, IT-96-21-1, 19 March 1996 (the Čelebići Indictment).

[78] Čelebići, Trial Chamber Judgement, para 354.

[79] Askin, 2003, op cit, p 326.

[80] Ibid, p 327.

This represented progress in holding accountable those responsible for permitting or even encouraging widespread and systematic rape. Responsibility can now be placed on those judged to be in control of troops.

In the Omarska case the accused included Kvočka, who was convicted of having had sufficient influence to prevent or halt some of the abuses but rarely made use of that influence.[81] The Trial Chamber ruled it was not reasonable for those who worked at the camp not to have known that abuses were being inflicted. As well as possibly witnessing the rapes and abuses, they would have known because:

> ... evidence of abuses could be seen in the bloodied, bruised and injured bodies ... heaps of dead bodies, lying in piles ... cramped conditions and bloodstained walls ... and evidence of abuse could be heard from the screams of pain and suffering ... evidence could be smelled from deteriorating corpses, the urine and faeces....[82]

Knowledge alone was not sufficient grounds for conviction, but the accused must have participated at some level, such as aiding acts of abuse or performing acts that advanced the goals of what was a criminal enterprise. Mlađo Radić was a professional police officer who had power over guards but was convicted for using that power selectively 'while ignoring the vast majority of crimes committed during his shift'.[83] However, he was also convicted of rape, participation in sexual intimidation, harassment and assaults as well as acts of sexual violence characterised as torture taking into account 'the vulnerability of the victims, the pain deliberately inflicted and the state of anxiety in which women detainees were kept at Omarska'.[84] This again broadened the range of people responsible for contravention of international humanitarian law, and may deter participation in such violations.

The indictment of Slobodan Milošević, despite his death before any concluding ruling of the Tribunal, demonstrated that heads of sovereign states could be brought to account. Milošević was President of the Federal Republic of Yugoslavia from 15 July 1997 until 6 October 2000. He was arrested on 1 April 2001, transferred to the ICTY and charged with crimes including cruel and inhumane treatment, which

[81] ICTY, *Omarska, Keraterm and Trnopolje Camps* (IT-98-30/1), ICTY Press Release.
[82] ICTY, *Prosecutor v Kvočka*, Judgement, IT-98-30-T, 2 November 2001, para 324.
[83] ICTY, *Omarska, Keraterm and Trnopolje Camps* (IT-98-30/1), ICTY Press Release.
[84] Ibid.

included the sexual assault of women in Bosnia–Herzegovina and the sexual assault of Kosovar Albanians by forces under his command. He died on 11 March 2006 before the case against him was concluded.[85] His arrest and charges signalled that command responsibility would be applied at the highest levels of government.

In 2007, the ICTY highlighted its focus on 'senior level individuals accused of the most serious crimes', and noted that the failure at that time to arrest Radovan Karadžić and Ratko Mladić remained 'of grave concern with respect to the proper administration of justice'.[86] In July 2008, Karadžić was arrested and taken to The Hague. Both Karadžić and Mladić were charged with having superior authority and that 'by their acts and omissions and in concert with others, committed a crime against humanity' for acts that included them being 'criminally responsible for (inter alia) rape and sexual assault'.[87] Holding heads of states and senior leaders accountable is the logical outcome of recognising superior responsibility and does at least send a message to those who use tactical rape and sexual violence as strategies in conflicts that they may not have impunity.

From the Čelebići case important judgements emerged referring to rape as torture. In a key ruling, the Trial and Appeals Chambers interpreted Article 3 of its Statute, which refers to violations of laws of war or customs of war, 'to include the crimes of torture and "outrages upon personal dignity", which includes acts such as rape, within its purview'.[88] In this particular case, the elements of torture for the purposes of the war crimes provisions of the ICTY Statute were held to be the elements of torture contained in the *Convention Against Torture*.[89] This includes acts: which inflict severe pain or suffering, whether physical or mental; which are committed intentionally for obtaining information or confessions from the victim or a third person; committed as punishment, intimidation or coercion for any reason based on discrimination of any kind; and committed by or as a result of instigation, consent or acquiescence of an official or person acting

---

[85] ICTY, *Kosovo, Croatia and Bosnia*, IT-02-54.

[86] *Report of the International Tribunal for the Prosecutions of Persons Responsible for Serious Violations of International Humanitarian Law in the Territory of Former Yugoslavia to the General Assembly and Security Council*, 1 August 2007.

[87] ICTY, *The Prosecutor of the Tribunal Against Radovan Karadžić and Ratko Mladić*, IT-95-5-I.

[88] ICTY, *Prosecutor v Furundžija*, Judgement, IT-95-17/1-A (ICTY App. CH. 21 July 2000).

[89] UN, 1984, *Convention Against Torture and other Cruel, Inhuman and Degrading Treatment or Punishment*, Article 1.

in an official capacity. The Trial Chamber ruled that when rape or any form of sexual violence satisfies these elements, it might constitute torture.[90] In this case it was judged that the accused:

> ... used sexual violence as an instrument of torture and subordination, since he committed the rapes with an aim of "intimidate[ing] not only the victim but also other inmates, by creating an atmosphere of fear and powerlessness".[91]

The threat of rape was recognised as a strategy for intimidation, not just the act of rape itself.

In the case against Furundžija, there was recognition that involvement in torture may include various actions: ordering, organising, providing opportunity, and processing results of information that may be obtained. All these actions carry responsibility.[92] This case also established that being forced to watch the rape of a woman he knew constituted torture of a male victim.[93] The rulings stated that there was a generally accepted prohibition of torture which has reached the status of *jus cogens* under international law, and that 'acts constituting sexual terrorism amount to torture'.[94]

It was the Kunarac case in 2001 in which the ICTY gave its first judgement of rape as a crime against humanity and as sexual slavery.[95] The accused were convicted for crimes committed in the detention centres in Foca in 1992. ICTY Statute Article 5, which referred to crimes against humanity, did not specifically refer to sexual slavery but did list rape and enslavement as two acts 'justiciable as crimes against humanity', so 'the crime of holding women and girls for sexual servitude was charged and prosecuted'.[96] The Foca municipality was a particularly horrific centre of rape of women and girls, where from and in a range of holding places, 'forces systematically raped, gang raped and publicly raped' many women and young girls, with some being taken out, raped and returned and some being held in specific locations for 'sexual access whenever captors demanded it'.[97]

---

[90] Čelebići, Trial Chamber Judgement, para 496.

[91] Askin, 2003, p 324.

[92] Furundžija, IT-95-17/1-T, 10 December 1998, para 253.

[93] Furundžija, IT-95-17/1-T, 10 December 1998, para 267.

[94] Arbreu, op cit, p 9, referring to Furundžija.

[95] Kunarac, Trial Chamber Judgement, ICTY, *Prosecutor v Kunarac*, Judgement, IT-96-23-T, 22 February.

[96] Askin, 2003, p 333, note 242.

[97] Ibid.

The Trial Chamber referred to the definition of slavery in international law, including in the Slavery Convention, as 'the status or condition of a person over whom any or all of the powers attaching to the right of ownership are exercised', and found that indicia of slavery included absence of consent or free will, exploitation, forced labour or service, sex, prostitution and control of sexuality.[98] The judgement 'forcefully concluded that neither physical restraint nor detention is a required element of slavery, and 'implicitly accepted that fear of retribution if they escaped and were recaptured as a reason that women were psychologically prevented from escaping'.[99] However, as Askin noted, while the judgement took care to emphasise that control over a person's sexual autonomy or obliging a person to provide sexual services may be indicative of enslavement, regrettably the term 'sexual slavery' was never used in the judgement.[100]

Despite this lack, the ruling was historic for linking rape and slavery, and was welcomed by many advocates. 'This decision is historic because it puts those who rape and sexually enslave women on notice that they will not get away with these heinous crimes.'[101] Many advocates shared the sense of encouragement that there had been, at least, some recognition of these crimes and some accountability demanded.

Judicial progress

By June 2010, the ICTY had indicted more than 160 people. Proceedings against 123 had been completed and a further 40 cases were still open. These included Radovan Karadžić, the Bosnian–Serb President at the time of the conflict. He was indicted for genocide and crimes against humanity related to events at Srebrenica.[102] The other accused, Ratko Mladić, also indicted for genocide and crimes against humanity, was finally arrested in May 2011. He, too, was charged with genocide and with persecution, in which charges included sexual

---

[98] Ibid, p 338.
[99] Ibid, p 339.
[100] Ibid.
[101] Human Rights Watch, 2001, *Bosnia: Landmark verdicts for rape, torture and sexual enslavement*, 22 February.
[102] ICTY, *Amended Indictment against Radovan Karadžić Unsealed*, Press Release, 14 October 2002.

violence.[103] On 24 March 2016 Karadžić was found guilty of genocide and sentenced to 40 years' imprisonment.[104]

On the 20th anniversary of the ICTY, the President noted that it had accounted for all 161 individuals it indicted, including high-level military and political leaders, had assisted in the creation of the War Crimes Chamber of the Court of Bosnia and Herzegovina, and paved the way for the establishment of a number of other international criminal tribunals, including the first permanent ICC.[105]

Other related judiciaries began contributing to legal understandings and applications of law to contraventions by rape and sexual violence. In 2002, the ICC entered into force, established by the Rome Statute and adopted in 1998.[106] Its mandate built on work by the ICTY, defining a crime against humanity and referencing the widespread or systematic attack on civilian populations and the mental state of the individual defendant.[107] In 2003, the ICTY recommended the creation of a specialised chamber to try war crimes cases within the State Court of Bosnia and Herzegovina, and the Security Council called on donors to support its creation.[108] The efforts of cantonal and district courts were hindered by lack of support from the public, under-resourcing and witness cooperation issues, but the non-availability of suspects remained the biggest impediment to accountability.[109] There had been five cases involving nine accused transferred to the War Crimes Chamber from the ICTY.[110]

As the ICTY completed its mandate, essential functions were transferred to the new Mechanism for International Criminal Tribunals tasked with:

---

[103] ICTY, *Amended Indictment against Ratko Mladić*, IT-95-5/18-1, Count 3, paras.37(b) and (f).

[104] See http://www.icty.org/x/cases/karadzic/tjug/en/160324_judgement_summary. pdf

[105] ICTY's 20th Anniversary, Statement by President Judge Theodor Meron, 27 May 2013.

[106] Rome Statute of the ICC, 1998.

[107] van Schaack, S, 1999, The definition of crimes against humanity: resolving the incoherence, Santa Clara University Legal Studies Research paper no 07-38, *Journal of Transnational law and Policy*, 37, 787.

[108] UN Security Council, *Security Council resolution 1503 (2003) [International Criminal Tribunal for the former Yugoslavia (ICTY) and International Criminal Tribunal for Rwanda (ICTR)]*, S/RES/1503, 28 August 2003

[109] Human Rights Watch, 2007, *World report: Bosnia and Herzegovina: Events of 2006*.

[110] Human Rights Watch, 2007, *Bosnia's War Crimes Chamber – Timelines and statistics*, 12 February.

> ... continuing the "jurisdiction, rights and obligations and essential functions" (UNSC Resolution 1966) of the ICTR and the ICTY; and maintaining the legacy of both institutions.[111]

Many cases were transferred to the national courts. However, in its report of 2014-15, Amnesty International stated that: 'the War Crimes Chamber of the State Court of BiH [Bosnia-Herzegovina] made slow progress in the prosecution of crimes under international law, and was undermined by repeated criticism by high-ranking politicians', and 'the Criminal Code continued to fall short of international standards relating to the prosecution of war crimes of sexual violence'.[112]

In 2006 the ICJ began hearings in genocide cases brought by Bosnia-Herzegovina against Serbia and Montenegro. In 2007, the ICJ ruled that events at Srebrenica did constitute genocide, but cleared Serbia of direct responsibility.

Measuring effectiveness

While there have been significant contributions made to jurisprudence relating to tactical rape and sexual violence by the ICTY, there remain criticisms. As of August 2015 the ICTY had indicted 161 individuals, and had completed proceedings with regard to 147 of them. Eighteen had been acquitted, 80 sentenced (18 had been transferred to serve their sentence, 7 were awaiting transfer, 52 had served their term, and 3 died while serving their sentence), and 13 had had their cases transferred to local courts.[113] While this is something of an achievement, it is slow progress. For women it has been extremely slow. While almost half the indictments had an element of sexual violence, only 28 as at 2013 were reported to have included sexual violence.[114] It is a reality that legal proceedings progress slowly, but this is a very low pace of bringing perpetrators to account. There have been some criticisms too that the ICTY puts reconciliation before justice, with claims that high-profile personnel have put pressure on judged to acquit defendants.[115]

---

[111] See www.unmict.org/en/about

[112] See www.amnesty.org/en/countries/europe-and-central-asia/bosnia-and-herzegovina/report-bosnia-and-herzegovina/

[113] ICTY, 2015, 20th anniversary of Srebenica genocide commemorated in Potočari, ICTY Digest, 152, July.

[114] Hogan, L, 2013, Seeking justice through the ICTY: Frustration, skepticism, hope, Women Under Siege, 23 September.

[115] Ibid.

Establishing case law precedents has been important, but it remains to be seen to what extent such precedents are applied in courts. The nature of courts still needs to change to ensure sensitivity and due protection to women testifying. Court personnel still need to be trained to treat women survivors and victims with respect and to work with them to ensure they receive justice.

One of the most pertinent criticisms has its source in the conditions around the very establishment of the ICTY itself. Under Article 4 of UN Security Council resolution 827, states are required to cooperate with the ICTY by handing over indictees. ICTY procedures have included the use of sealed indictments in order to obviate evasion by those accused when they realise the extent of charges. This, too, has been a source of limiting cooperation by states. Cooperation has been slow to the point of resistance, and as noted above by Amnesty International, the national courts to which cases have been handed seem to have high-level opponents.

Conclusion

Although the conflict in the former Yugoslavia occurred in the 1990s, it remains a paradigm case from which important legal precedents and clarifications of international law were made regarding tactical rape sexual violence. For this reason, it remains a key basis for developing normative rejection and confrontation of these violations. The process of establishing this ad hoc tribunal was in itself important in that it over-ruled issues of sovereignty and demonstrated that the UN could act according to its charter to bring perpetrators to account. The fact that this court could include in its mandate those with both direct and indirect responsibility for crimes against humanity, war crimes and crimes of torture and rulings around the contexts of conflict was significant.

The ICTY contributed to the legal basis for international normative rejection of tactical rape and sexual violence in conflict as essential legal requirements for such acts to be judged as war crimes, and crimes against humanity were clarified. It redefined rules around admissibility of witnesses and evidence. It demonstrated that tactical rape and sexual violence were contraventions of existing international law, and that perpetrators should therefore be brought to account. Definitions were expanded and degrees and locus of responsibility were identified within the mandate of interpretation and application of existing law and norms.

Criticisms of slow and limited progress, particularly for women, are well founded. However, it is argued that having the court almost certainly delivered more justice than would otherwise have been delivered for victims and survivors of tactical rape and sexual violence in the conflict. I agree with Lilian A. Barria and Steven D. Roper that the ICTY has provided more justice than national courts could have provided.[116] There is also the broader argument that:

> ... international justice is not the responsibility of international courts alone. All those who are committed to justice and the rule of law – in local communities, in State governments, and around the world – have a vital part to play in ensuring that violations of international law are answered not with indifference but with determination, that principles of fairness and respect for human rights inform all efforts to secure accountability, and that the success of international justice depends on sustained support and cooperation today, and every day.[117]

The responsibility of states to prevent and to prosecute perpetrators of tactical rape and sexual violence in conflict remains. This will be further considered in Chapters Seven, Eight and Nine.

---

[116] Barria, LA, Roper, SD, How effective are international criminal tribunals? An analysis of the ICTY and the ICTR, *The International Journal of Human Rights*, 9, 3, 349-68, September.

[117] Statement by President Meron on the occasion of International Justice Day, July 2015.

SIX

Tactical rape and genocide in Rwanda

As with the conflict in the former Yugoslavia, and the judicial statements and rulings of the ICTY, the Rwandan genocide and the International Criminal Tribunal for Rwanda (ICTR) advanced the understanding of the nature and use of rape and sexual violence in war. It was another example of a 'new war', where tactical rape and sexual violence received attention from public media and the international community to a degree not previously common. Civilians were again targeted as genocide erupted within national borders. Again, international intervention took place within a context of a new understanding of the limits on sovereignty.

The ICTR was another tribunal deliberately established as an ad hoc entity, limited to extending judgements on existing international humanitarian norms and laws; when it considered tactical rape and sexual violence, it had to do so as a contravention of established international humanitarian law. In many areas the ICTR failed to perform well and failed survivors and victims of tactical rape and sexual violence. However, it produced what is arguably the most significant case in international law regarding rape and genocide, despite many reservations and a lack of substantive progress since. The conflicts and genocide in the former Yugoslavia and Rwanda occurred very close together in time and in a similar context of approaches to humanitarianism. The international community reacted in both arenas with ad hoc tribunals, but Rwanda and the ICTR exemplified a different form of conflict, a different culture, a different way of using tactical rape and sexual violence, this time in an African state.

Key events in the Rwandan conflict

The genocide in Rwanda was not spontaneous. It was one phase in a long-running series of historical and political events. From the 14th century, the population of Rwanda had been a mix of majority

Hutu, minority Tutsi and a very small number of Twa.[1] Belgian colonisers introduced ethnic identity cards in 1926, which became compulsory, and so ethnic identity was fixed from birth.[2] In 1959 a violent incident set off a Hutu uprising in which hundreds of Tutsi were killed, and 130,000 displaced and forced to flee to the Belgian Congo, Burundi, Tanganyika and Uganda.[3] Rwanda was declared a republic in 1962, with a Hutu president. By 1964, around 600,000 to 700,000 Tutsi refugees had been forced to flee Rwanda.[4] In 1973, Juvenal Habyarimana, another Hutu, took over as president in a military coup, and was formally elected in 1987.

Ongoing tension and conflict between Hutu and Tutsi military and political leadership weakened the economy, and Habyarimana lost popularity.[5] In 1988, the Rwandan Patriotic Front (RPF) was founded in Uganda as a political and military movement, aiming to secure the repatriation of exiled Rwandans and to reform the Rwandan government, including political power sharing.[6] In 1990 a rebel army, mostly Tutsi, invaded from Uganda, but power remained with the Hutu. Tutsi inside Rwanda were accused of collaborating to overthrow the government and of being a threat to Rwanda generally.[7] After extended periods of violence and with urging from the Organisation of African Unity (OAU), Habyarimana signed a peace accord in Arusha with the RPF in August 1993. In October 1993, the UN Security Council established the UN Assistance Mission for Rwanda (UNAMIR) to support peacekeeping and humanitarian assistance. However:

> … the will to achieve and sustain peace was subverted by some of the Rwandan political parties participating in the Agreement. With the ensuing delays in its implementation, violations of human rights became more widespread and the security situation deteriorated. Later, evidence demonstrated irrefutably that extremist elements of the

---

[1] Prunier, G, 1995, *The Rwanda crisis: History of a genocide*, New York: Colombia University, p 5; Clark, P, 2010, *The Gacaca courts: Post genocide justice and reconciliation in Rwanda: Justice without lawyers*, Cambridge: Cambridge University Press, Introduction, pp 12-19.

[2] See http://hmd.org.uk/genocides/life-genocide-rwanda

[3] See www.un.org/en/preventgenocide/rwanda/education/rwandagenocide.shtml

[4] Prunier, op cit, p 63.

[5] Ibid, pp 84-90.

[6] See www.un.org/en/preventgenocide/rwanda/education/rwandagenocide.shtml

[7] Prunier, op cit, pp 90-2.

Hutu majority while talking peace were in fact planning a campaign to exterminate Tutsis and moderate Hutus.[8]

Habyarimana's plane was shot down in April 1994, and he and the Burundian president travelling with him were killed.

There were accusations on both sides that the Hutu leadership had ordered the assassination.[9] Whatever the case, the shooting signalled the eruption of genocide, and in the next three months an estimated 800,000 people were killed, nearly three-quarters of the Tutsi population.[10] Eventually the RPF launched a major offensive, and Hutu militias fled to neighbouring countries with around 2 million Hutu refugees who joined the flow of Tutsi, moderate Hutu and the Twa who had been targeted in the events that became defined as genocide and that showed clear signs of being well-planned and prepared.[11] The UNHCR reported 'the largest and fastest exodus UNHCR has ever seen'.[12]

I was in the refugee camps in Tanzania following the massive exodus from Rwanda in May 1994. My experience accords with Prunier that these camps were filled with refugees who were a mix of surviving Tutsi and Hutu together with Hutu who had been involved in the massacres.[13] It was a volatile mix. A description of the camp inhabitants noted on 19 May 1994 that the refugees included 'women who have been raped' as this was evident to most workers.[14] Surprisingly, Prunier made no mention of rape in an otherwise extremely detailed accounts of events. My observations in the camp were of hundreds of women sitting dazed and apparently traumatised by events. I saw one young girl travelling alone who came to help with food distribution. This young girl was crying at the end of a day giving food to long lines of refugees. She had recognised the man she had witnessed killing her brother and raping members of her family – he was wearing the shirt she had given her brother for his birthday. She had handed the man his supplies. After, as she sat with two nuns and myself who were working in the camp, she said, "It is up to God to judge that man

---

[8] See www.un.org/en/preventgenocide/rwanda/education/rwandagenocide.shtml

[9] Prunier, op cit, pp 213-29.

[10] Clark, op cit, p 12.

[11] Prunier, op cit, pp 248-65.

[12] UN High Commission for Refugees Fact Sheet 25.7.1994, referenced in Fitzpatrick, B, 1994, *The Rwandan regional crisis*, Geneva: World Council of Churches, August, p 12.

[13] Prunier, op cit, pp 265-6.

[14] World Council of Churches, Pentecostal Appeal, 19 May 1994.

– not me." Another women sat grieving for her baby. She had run from Hutu militias, hidden in reeds of a river. When she emerged, the baby on her back had drowned. The fear of death and rape had been intense. Many other stories I heard were from women who had escaped either the threat or the reality of rape. Yet, women's stories are so often missing in historical accounts of conflict. This makes the work of Binaifer Nowrojee, which is considered in detail later in this chapter, so important.[15]

While many NGOs and observers had called the events in Rwanda 'genocide' from early in the conflict, it was some time before it was formally acknowledged as such by the international community. In 1994 the UN Special Rapporteur accepted there was a clear and unambiguous intention to destroy a group in whole or in part, referring to the incitements put out by the media (particularly radio RTLM) and reproduced in leaflets.[16] He added that even without such evidence, the intention could be deduced on the basis of a variety of concordant indications including the preparations for the acts with the distribution of firearms and the training of militias, the number of Tutsi killed and the policy of destruction of the Tutsi.[17]

The killing of Habyarimana 'was the spark to the powder keg which set off the massacre of civilians'.[18] Rene Degni-Segui reported to the UN it was certain that 'the international community is watching a human tragedy which appears to be well-orchestrated.'[19] Many civilians participated: some were threatened, some received incentives such as money or food or the right to claim the land of slaughtered Tutsi.[20] The main organisers were 'a small tight group belonging to the regime's political, military and economic elite.'[21] Radio announcements urged attacks; recruits were sent rapidly all over the country to incite and carry out many of the killings. Radio Rwanda broadcast messages throughout

[15] Nowrojee, B, 1996, *Shattered lives: Sexual violence during the Rwandan genocide and its aftermath*, New York: Human Rights Watch, September; Nowrojee, B, 2005, *Your justice is too slow: Will the ICTR fail Rwanda's rape victims?*, United Nations Research Institute for Social Development, November.

[16] Degni-Segui, R, 1994, *Situation of human rights in Rwanda*, A/49/508 S/1994/1157, 13 October, para 46.

[17] Ibid, para 46.

[18] Ibid, para 19

[19] Ibid, para 24.

[20] Prunier, op cit, pp 242-50.

[21] Prunier, op cit, p 241.

the country: 'by the fifth of May, the cleansing of the Tutsi must be complete' and 'the grave is only half full, who will help us fill it?'[22]

While empirical evidence abounded as early as May 1994, it is indicative of the attitude towards tactical rape that the UN investigators who visited Rwanda from 9 to 20 June 1994, from 29 to 31 July 1994, from 14 to 25 October 1994, from 27 March to 3 April and from 25 to 28 May 1995 did not give any particular attention to rapes apart from including rape among problems and a brief reference to 'taking women as hostages and victims of rape'.[23] It was not until the report in August–September 1995 that special attention was drawn to the systematic rapes.[24] By July 1994 the RPF had captured the Rwandan capital, Kigali, the government collapsed and the RPF announced a ceasefire. With the RPF victory, an estimated 2 million Hutu fled across the borders, mostly into Zaire. In the same refugee camps there were both survivors and perpetrators of the genocide. Women who had survived rape were in the same camps as those who had raped them. The need to protect women refugees was extreme in this situation.

In this conflict, there was clear evidence of intent to destroy a particular group and to inflict great bodily and mental harm (from tactical rape as well as other attacks). There was evidence of tactical rape being used to impose measures intended to prevent births within the group. The many cases of forced incest and children born of these attacks added to the personal and social shame perceived by victims and communities. Many women suffered such damage to sexual organs that they were unable to bear children: the Special Rapporteur noted this was the case for many 'little girls who were raped'.[25] Prevailing patriarchal attitudes meant children of rapes would not be children of the targeted group but deemed children of the attackers.[26] Still the international community resisted calling this 'genocide'; doing so would have brought responsibility to intervene. UN troops withdrew after 10 soldiers were killed and UN attempts at ceasefires failed.[27] The international response was limited to humanitarian aid to those who had escaped across the borders. It was not until after 19 July 1994, when a

---

[22] Degni-Segui, R, 1994, *Situation of human rights in Rwanda*, A/49/508 S/1994/1157, 13 October, para 46, para 59.

[23] Ibid; Degni-Segui, R, 1995, *Situation of human rights in Rwanda*, E/CN.4/1996/7, 28 1995; Degni-Segui, R, 1994, *Report on the situation of human rights in Rwanda* .

[24] Degni-Segui, R, 1996, *Report on the situation of human rights in Rwanda*, United Nations Commission on Human Rights, E/CN.4/1996/68, January.

[25] Ibid, para 20.

[26] This aspect is considered in more detail in another chapter.

[27] Prunier, op cit, p 230.

new multi-ethnic government was formed, that the Security Council established the ICTR, which eventually judged that genocide had indeed occurred, and that the use of tactical rape and sexual violence had been part of that genocide.

Understanding the nature of the genocide in Rwanda

The genocide in Rwanda in 1994 did not require high technology or large budgets. Pangas made for tilling agricultural plots became weapons. Youth groups and ordinary citizens were troops. Civilians and militia attacked civilians. The entire Hutu population was expected to attack the entire Tutsi population. The extremists' aim was for the entire Hutu populace to participate so the blood of genocide stained everybody and there could be no going back.[28] Widespread participation was evident. A Kigali lawyer and survivor recalled, 'everyone was called to hunt the enemy'.[29] He explained the process:

> But let's say someone is reluctant. Say that guy comes with a stick. They tell him, "No, get a masu [weapon]." So, ok he does and he runs along with all the rest but he doesn't kill. They say, "Hey, he might denounce us later. He must kill". Everyone must help to kill at least one person. So this person who is not a killer is made to do it. And the next day it's become a game to him. You don't need to keep pushing him.[30]

This is credible, but motives may have been political or economic. This was genocide with origins in previous events and a tragic continuation of those events. Still, orders had been given and orders had been obeyed:

> In Rwandan history, everyone obeys authority. People revere power and there isn't enough education. You take a poor, ignorant population and give them arms and say, "It's yours. Kill." They'll obey.... And in Rwanda, an order can be given very quietly.[31]

[28] Omaar, R, de Waal, A, 1994, Rwanda: Death, despair and defiance, *Africa Rights*, September, p 35, quoted in Kaldor, M, 2002, *New and old wars: Organised violence in a global era*, Cambridge: Polity Press, p 84.

[29] Gourevitch, P, 2000, *We wish to inform you that tomorrow we will be killed with our families*, London: Picador, p 24.

[30] Ibid.

[31] Ibid, p 23.

Orders included the rape and humiliation of women. When identifying the 'organisers' of the events in Rwanda, 'doubts are relatively limited', and until the late stage, 'the killers were controlled and directed in their task by civil servants in the central government' who, in turn, received orders from the capital, Kigali.[32] In a record dated 6 May 1994, prefectural authorities decided to write to burgomasters about the need to stop rapes with violence.[33] Authorities were able to control mass behaviour.

This was not an impulsive conflict. It made use of available resources such as the tools found in most households as well as what appeared to be old Kalashnikovs. Small groups were armed, but most attackers used whatever was available as weapons, from pangas to tactical rape. Genocide was planned and was recognised early as being planned:

> Some mention should, I think, be made here of the fact that (a) the killings had been carefully planned beforehand (b) gangs had been provided with weapons (c) the signal to start the massacres was broadcast in pre-arranged code over the government controlled Radio Mille Collines, saying, "It is time to gather in the harvest" and later, "the baskets are only half-full: they should be filled to the brim".[34]

Using local radio, this conflict maximised available resources rather than specific expensive alternatives.

However, the use of simple agricultural tools and public radio did not mitigate the horrific nature of events:

> Although the killing was low-tech – performed largely by machete – it was carried out at a dazzling speed: of an original population of about seven and a half million, at least eight hundred thousand people were killed in just a hundred days. Rwandans often speak of a million deaths and they may be right. The dead of Rwanda accumulated at nearly three times the rate of Jewish dead during the

[32] Prunier, op cit, pp 239, 244.

[33] Des Forges, A, 1999, *Leave none to tell the story*, New York: Human Rights Watch, p 564.

[34] Salter, E, World Council of Churches' Commission of the Churches on International Affairs, quoted in Fitzpatrick, 1994, op cit, p 12.

holocaust. It was the most efficient mass killing since the atomic bombings of Hiroshima and Nagasaki.[35]

Massive participation was clear because 'great and sustained destruction' does not occur aimlessly but 'must be conceived as the means of achieving a new order ... even if killers do not enjoy killing, they must want their victims dead', and 'they have to want it so badly that they consider it a necessity'.[36] Such destruction – and the use of tactical rape and sexual violence – was deliberate, planned and systematic.

Tactical rape and sexual violence were driven by pre-established, constructed hatreds and fear. They could kill and inflict lasting damage. Patriarchy and relationships between Hutu and Tutsi meant tactical rape and sexual violence had an impact on community identities, on social relationships and economic options. HIV/AIDS added an additional physical menace. HIV/AIDS was already rife in Rwanda, and the widespread rape of women and girls is deemed to have dramatically increased the rate of infection.[37] While difficult to ascertain exact numbers, HIV/AIDS infection was aggravated considerably between April and July 1994.[38] This added to the genocidal impact on the destruction of the Tutsi as a group.

I reported from the Tanzanian refugee camp that many attackers believed they had avenged what had happened to them some years earlier, while others were avenging what those 'avengers' had just done.[39] Antagonism between Hutu and Tutsi and the particular antagonism of Hutu to Tutsi women had been developed over previous years. The deliberate generation of hatred and fear involved, but went beyond, the constructed vulnerability of women in a patriarchal society.

Constructed hatred of Tutsi women

Hatred between Hutu and Tutsi was constructed with an additional layer of hatred targeting Tutsi women. Anastase Shyake wrote of an integrated pre-colonial population of Rwandans with two clear identity groups, the Tutsi and Hutu (with a much smaller group of Twa).[40] The

[35] Gourevitch, op cit, p 3.

[36] Ibid, pp 17-18.

[37] Rwandan Rapport National, 1995, for the Fourth World Conference on Women, Beijing, p 59.

[38] Ibid, p 59.

[39] Fitzpatrick, 1994, op cit, p 8.

[40] Shyake, A, 2005/06, *The Rwandan conflict: Origin, development, exit strategies*, A study ordered by the National Unity and Reconciliation Commission of Rwanda.

two groups shared language and cultural values. However, rather than merely accepting the fact of colonisation as the sole cause of antipathy, Catherine Newbury referred to 'corporate perception of identity'. She used this term to explain the group identification of people as objects for fear or hatred where Tutsi were not considered individuals but as a total group with a corporate identity opposed to the Hutu as a group:

> The generalisation of blame was dramatically evident in the genocide against Tutsi in Rwanda in 1994 when hardliners in the Hutu-dominated government labelled all Tutsi in the country as enemies of the state. The genocide was calculated to exterminate them.[41]

Generalising that all Tutsi were responsible for all economic or political problems was a step towards believing that defence of the state required exterminating all Tutsi. As Binaifer Nowrojee noted, the propaganda of the time suggested that Tutsi were foreign conquerors, who had refused to accept their loss of power and were bent on reasserting their control over Hutu.[42] Newbury also noted that this corporate view of ethnicity was used later to label all Hutu refugees as genocidaires (people who helped perpetrate genocide) and part of a political programme of vengeance directed against Hutu.[43]

The UN Special Rapporteur described the situation as having political causes with ethnic overtones, and the political power being strongly linked with economic power in a country that was essentially poor and over-populated.[44] The Hutu government applied quotas in schools and the public service, excluded Tutsi from the army, the police and information services.[45] Successive regimes and systems for their own political ends 'gradually conditioned the population to psychological and social acceptance of ethnic discrimination'.[46]

Sustaining this perception of division and difference rested on schools and public media. In Rwanda, public radio was the primary

---

[41] Newbury, C, 2002, Ethnicity and the politics of history in Rwanda, in DE Lorey and WH Beazley (eds), *Genocide, collective violence and popular memory: The politics of remembrance in the twentieth century*, Wilmington, DE: Scholarly Resources Inc, p 67.

[42] Nowrojee, 1996, op cit, p 12.

[43] Newbury, op cit, p 68.

[44] Degni-Segui, R, 1997, *Situation of human rights in Rwanda*, E/CN.4/1997/61 20, January, para 18.

[45] Ibid, paras 17, 18.

[46] Ibid, para 23.

communications vehicle, both in preparations for and in the perpetration of the events of 1994. Kaldor noted:

> The electronic media has an authority that newspapers cannot match: in parts of Africa, radio is "magic" [and] the use of "hate" radio to incite people to genocide in Rwanda [provided] a mechanism for speeding up the pace of political mobilization.[47]

The UN Special Rapporteur reported, 'false rumours and tracts designed to inflame ethnic hatred and encourage violence are constantly circulating in Rwanda', with the Tutsi portrayed as serious threats to the Hutu.[48] He referred to the 'long-standing campaign' and the existence of the 'Hutu ten commandments' that 'advocate an ideology of apartheid'.[49]

Public media was used to establish and construct social relationships and increase the vulnerability of Tutsi women who were frequently admired for their beauty and feared for their ability to seduce and harm Hutu men.[50] 'Tutsi women were always viewed as enemies of the state', said one Tutsi woman:

> No military man could marry Tutsi women or they would have to leave the military.... Tutsi women were considered beautiful which bred hate against them.... It led to a hate that I can't describe.... I was told I couldn't work in certain places because as a Tutsi woman I would poison the others.[51]

Stereotypes portrayed Tutsi women as arrogant, despising Hutu men as weapons for use by Tutsi men against the Hutu. Of the 10 'Hutu commandments', four dealt specifically with Tutsi women. These warned Hutu women to be vigilant against Tutsi women's wiles used to attract Hutu husbands, brothers and sons, and warned Hutu men that any who married, befriended or employed a Tutsi woman would be considered a traitor because the Tutsi 'will not hesitate to transform their sisters, wives and mothers into pistols' to conquer Rwanda.[52] The

[47] Kaldor, op cit, p 86.
[48] Degni-Segui, R, 1994, *Situation of human rights in Rwanda*, A/49/508 S/1994/1157, 13 October, para 58.
[49] Ibid, para 58.
[50] Nowrojee, 1996, op cit, p 13.
[51] Ibid, p 12.
[52] Ibid, p 13.

extremist and virulently propagandist newspaper, *Kangura*, accused Tutsi women of taking Hutu jobs, of despising Hutu men and of using their sexual prowess to seduce UN peacekeepers.[53] So women targeted in the genocide suffered from an interlinked culture: targets as Tutsi, as the property of Tutsi men, as capable of bearing the children of Tutsi men.[54]

This perception of the Tutsi as a group and of Tutsi women as a particularly hated group was key to directing violence against them and to understanding why the term 'genocide' was eventually applied to events. Women raped during the attacks and later interviewed described how their rapists mentioned their ethnicity.[55] Comments included: "we want to see how sweet Tutsi women are"; "you Tutsi women think you are too good for us"; "if there were peace you would never accept me"; "you Tutsi girls are too proud". Such remarks indicated that Tutsi women were deemed special because they were Tutsi, remarks that could be interpreted as setting the stage for their degradation.[56]

The ICTR, tactical rape and genocide

On 1 July 1994 the UN Security Council established a Commission of Experts to investigate reports coming out of Rwanda.[57] This Commission first reported to the Security Council on 1 October 1994.[58] It reported 'concerted, planned, systematic and methodical' massacres 'motivated out of ethnic hatred'[59] and media propaganda campaigns inciting hatred and the killing of Tutsi.[60] It referred to 'genocidal massacres',[61] and believed there had been breaches of norms of international law, norms prohibiting crimes against humanity and norms prohibiting genocide.[62]A second report was submitted on 9 December 1994.[63] There was overwhelming evidence of acts of

53 Ibid, p 12.
54 Ibid, p 3.
55 Ibid, p 13.
56 Ibid, p 14.
57 UN Security Council, *Security Council resolution 935 (1994) [Commission of Experts to examine violations of international humanitarian law committed in Rwanda]*, S/RES/935, 1 July 1994.
58 UN Security Council, 1994, Letter dated 1 October 1994 from the Secretary-General addressed to the President of the Security Council, S/1994/1125.
59 Ibid, para 44.
60 Ibid, para 50.
61 Ibid, para 77.
62 Ibid, para 85.
63 UN Security Council, 1994, Letter dated 9 December from the Secretary-General addressed to the President of the Security Council, S/1994/1405.

genocide committed by the Hutu intending to destroy the Tutsi, with crimes against humanity and serious violations of international humanitarian law perpetrated by both sides. It referred matters for investigation to the newly established ICTR.[64] It is notable that even so many months after NGOs, humanitarian workers, medical workers and refugees were aware of the prevalence of widespread rape, there was no mention of this in either report.

It was not until the hearing of the case against Jean Paul Akayesu, a Rwandan citizen who was Bourgmestre (Mayor) of Taba commune, that charges included rape as genocide.[65] This was almost accidental. Accounts of tactical rape were widespread despite the apathy of formal bodies. The original indictments made no mention of rape, and it was not until witnesses recounted events that the indictments were amended. One observer at the trial of Akeyesu said:

> Had it not been for the [witnesses] who linked Akayesu to the Taba rapes, the interest in the case shown by the court's one female judge, pressure from human rights and women's groups and prosecutors skilled at winning over their witnesses, the former mayor might never have been tried for Taba's rape crimes.[66]

Akayesu had been indicted for genocide, crimes against humanity and violations of Common Article 3 to the Geneva Conventions relating to his role as an authority at Taba, where numerous atrocities were committed with his knowledge and under his supervision. But while murder, lines of responsibility and incitement were included, there were no charges relating to rape.

The ICTR, having investigated events with reference to the *Genocide Convention*, concluded that, 'genocide was, indeed, committed in Rwanda in 1994 against the Tutsi as a group'.[67] The nature of the genocide was described as 'organized and planned', and was 'executed essentially by civilians including the armed militia and even ordinary citizens', and above all, 'that the majority of the Tutsi victims were non-combatants, including thousands of women and children, even

---

[64] Ibid, p 1.

[65] ICTR, *The Prosecutor v Jean-Paul Akayesu*, ICTR-96-4-T, Decision of 2 September 1998 [The Akayesu decision].

[66] Neuffer, E, 2000, *The keys to my neighbour's house: Seeking justice in Bosnia and Rwanda*, Picador, p 272.

[67] ICTR, *The Prosecutor v Jean-Paul Akayesu*, ICTR-96-4-T, Decision of 2 September 1998 [The Akayesu decision], para 126.

foetuses'.[68] This ruling had the force of a legal judgement. Part of the justification for the ruling was the established reference to planned incitement to hatred, even beyond the role played by the media. Léon Mugesera, a lecturer at the National University of Rwanda, had published two pamphlets accusing the Tutsi of planning genocide of the Hutu. In November 1992 he had called for the extermination of the Tutsi and the assassination of Hutu opposed to the president. He exhorted readers to avoid the error of earlier massacres during which some Tutsi, particularly children, were spared.[69] The intent to destroy the group was established.

In statements from particular witnesses at the ICTR hearing, the court was shocked to hear the link made between acts being judged as genocide and rape of Tutsi women.[70] On 17 June 1997, the indictment of Akayesu was amended to include allegations of sexual violence and additional charges against the accused under Articles 3(g), 3(i) and 4(2)(e) of the ICTR Statute. Evidence of witnesses had prompted prosecutors 'to renew their investigation of sexual violence in connection with events which took place in Taba at the bureau communal', and acknowledging that the reason for lack of evidence linking Akayesu to acts of sexual violence 'might include the shame that accompanies acts of sexual violence as well as insensitivity in the investigation of sexual violence'.[71] The use of 'might' would seem to be an understated reality.

Later criticisms of the ICTR have constantly and credibly noted the insensitivity of investigators and judges.[72] When a witness giving testimony about Akayesu and counts of murder volunteered the story of her six-year-old daughter being raped by three men, the prosecutor failed to pursue the point. Three judges intervened. One was a woman from South Africa who recalled, 'I couldn't understand what prosecution was doing.'[73] The original indictment was amended, concluding that 'the investigation and presentation of evidence relating to sexual violence is in the interest of justice'.[74] Despite concerns, the case was a watershed for recognising the links between tactical rape and genocide. The ICTR noted that, 'the Chamber must define rape, as

---

[68]   Ibid, para 128.

[69]   Ibid, para 10.

[70]   Ibid, paras 416, 421, 422.

[71]   Ibid, para 417.

[72]   Nowrojee, 2005, op cit, p 24.

[73]   Neuffer, op cit, p. 279.

[74]   ICTR, *The Prosecutor v Jean-Paul Akayesu*, ICTR-96-4-T, Decision of 2 September 1998 [The Akayesu decision], para 417.

there is no commonly accepted definition of this term in international law'.[75] It defined rape:

> ... as a physical invasion of a sexual nature, committed on a person under circumstances which are coercive. Sexual violence, which includes rape, is considered to be any act of a sexual nature which is committed on a person under circumstances which are coercive. This act must be committed: a) as part of a widespread or systematic attack; (b) on a civilian population; (c) on certain catalogued discriminatory grounds, namely: national, ethnic, political, racial, or religious grounds.[76]

In its concluding rulings, the Tribunal added to this definition that sexual violence is not limited to physical invasion of the human body, and may include acts that do not involve penetration or even physical contact.[77]

It went on to note that coercive circumstances need not be evidenced by a show of physical force:

> ... threats, intimidation, extortion and other forms of duress which prey on fear or desperation may constitute coercion, and coercion may be inherent in certain circumstances, such as armed conflict or the military presence of Interahamwe among refugee Tutsi women at the bureau communal.[78]

The statement included recognition that sexual violence fell within the scope of 'other inhumane acts', set forth in Article 3(i) of the Tribunal's Statute, 'outrages upon personal dignity' set forth in Article 4(e) of the Statute, and 'serious bodily or mental harm' set forth in Article 2(2)(b).[79] This was particularly important, acknowledging that coercion has many forms.

Victim testimony, included in trial proceedings, established the use of tactical rape and sexual violence as severe attacks targeting Tutsi women and girls. They are distressing to read because of the reality of suffering inherent in them, but they established the widespread nature

---

[75] Ibid, para 596.
[76] Ibid, para 598.
[77] Ibid, para 688.
[78] Ibid.
[79] Ibid.

and violence of the rapes. It was an achievement that at last there was an international court documenting and considering the true extent of damage done by tactical rape.

Witness JJ testified that the Interahamwe took young girls and women from their site of refuge near the Bureau Communal into a forest and raped them.[80] Witness JJ testified that this happened to her: she was stripped of her clothing and raped in front of other people. At the request of the Prosecutor and with great embarrassment, she explicitly specified that the rapist, a young man armed with an axe and a long knife, penetrated her vagina with his penis. On this occasion she was raped twice.[81] This account highlights the trauma experienced by many women when asked to recount sexual attacks.

Understandably many women were reluctant to testify. Elizabeth Neuffer wrote that it was not surprising that Rwandan women would not talk about being raped, when 'investigators, mostly white males, roared into villages in their white UN jeeps and treated survivors with condescension as if they were stupid rather than traumatised'.[82] This sort of response indicates the lack of understanding and lack of trained personnel to deal with survivors of tactical rape and sexual violence.

Witness JJ's testimony galvanised action to have rape charges included in the indictment of Akayesu.[83] She testified that on arrival at the Bureau Communal, the cultural centre, the women hoped that the authorities would defend them. She was surprised to the contrary. She recalled lying in the cultural centre, having been raped repeatedly by the Interahamwe, and hearing the cries of young girls around her, girls as young as 12 or 13 years old. On the way to the cultural centre to be raped there the first time, Witness JJ said that she and the others were taken past the accused who was looking at them. The second time she was taken to the cultural centre to be raped, Witness JJ recalled seeing the accused standing at the entrance of the cultural centre and hearing him say loudly to the Interahamwe, 'never ask me again what a Tutsi woman tastes like', and 'tomorrow they will be killed'.[84] It was these statements indicating that Akayesu was focused on Tutsi women, that he knew they were specific targets and was cooperating in the attacks on them that were said to have been key to his eventual conviction.

---

[80]   Ibid, para 421.

[81]   Ibid.

[82]   Neuffer, op cit, p 278.

[83]   ICTR, *The Prosecutor v Jean-Paul Akayesu*, ICTR-96-4-T, Decision of 2 September 1998 [The Akayesu decision], para 421.

[84]   Ibid.

One of the judges, openly critical of the trial proceedings, asked the witness twice if investigators had asked for the names of the men who had raped her.[85] They had not done so. Neuffer wrote that the witness had only mentioned the rapes to the prosecutor the day before, and he had realised that the refugees at the Bureau Communal were all women, 'and that they were part of a plan for their rape'.[86] This late awareness was typical of the limited examination in preparation for cases and the lack of direct questioning of those testifying.

Witness JJ continued, and after describing the accused and the statement he made regarding the taste of Tutsi women, she said he was 'talking as if someone were encouraging a player' and suggested that he was the one 'supervising' the acts of rape.[87] Most of the girls and women were subsequently killed, either at the river or in their houses or at the Bureau Communal. She told of finding her sister before she died, having been raped and cut with a machete.[88] After the testimony, investigators went to Taba, finally investigated the rape attacks, and found evidence that Akayesu was complicit.

Evidence constantly emphasised the attackers' desire to humiliate as well as physically wound. The younger sister of JJ described being raped along with another sister by two men in the courtyard of their home, after it was destroyed by Hutu neighbours and her brother and father had been killed.[89] One of the men told her that the girls were spared so they could be raped: when her mother begged the men, who were armed with bludgeons and machetes, to kill her daughters rather than rape them in front of her, the man replied that the 'principle was to make them suffer'.[90] The girls were raped, and on examination, the witness said that the man who raped her penetrated her vagina with his penis, saying he did it in an 'atrocious' manner, mocking and taunting them. She said her sister was raped by the other man at the same time, near her, so that they could each see what was happening to the other. Afterwards, she begged for death.[91] These accounts support the contention that the rapes were more than sexual attacks by forces out of control: they were intended to impart lasting humiliation and to inflict serious bodily and mental harm.

[85]   Neuffer, op cit, p 282.
[86]   Ibid.
[87]   ICTR, *The Prosecutor v Jean-Paul Akayesu*, ICTR-96-4-T, Decision of 2 September 1998 [The Akayesu decision], para 421.
[88]   Ibid.
[89]   Ibid, para 430.
[90]   Ibid.
[91]   Ibid.

Building on work at the ICTY, the Akayesu decision also recognised the difficulties for rape victims to provide corroborating evidence. It concluded that Rule 96(i) of the rules of the court alone specifically dealt with the issue of corroboration of testimony required by the Chamber, and ruled that the provisions of this Rule, which applied only to cases of testimony by victims of sexual assault, stipulated that no corroboration should be required. The ICTR quoted the ICTY ruling in the Tadić judgement, and determined that this:

> … sub-rule accords to the testimony of a victim of sexual assault the same presumption of reliability as the testimony of victims of other crimes, something which had long been denied to victims of sexual assault in common law [which] certainly does not […] justify any inference that in cases of crimes other than sexual assault, corroboration is required. The proper inference is, in fact, directly to the contrary.[92]

This was important in facilitating justice for women survivors and victims of tactical rape and in reinforcing the decision made by the ICTY. Corroboration of crimes may be required in some cases, but it is unreasonable to always require it.

The final rulings in this case established case law providing support for a developing norm and understanding of tactical rape. While Akayesu was not found to have committed rapes himself, the ICTR found beyond reasonable doubt that the accused had reason to know, in fact, did know, that sexual violence was taking place on or near the premises of the Bureau Communal. There was no evidence that the accused took any measures to prevent acts of sexual violence or to punish the perpetrators of sexual violence.[93] He was found guilty of having 'specifically ordered, instigated, aided and abetted … acts of sexual violence'.[94] It was ruled he did this:

> … by allowing them to take place on or near the premises of the Bureau Communal and by facilitating the commission of such sexual violence through his words of encouragement in other acts of sexual violence which, by virtue of his authority, sent a clear signal of official tolerance for sexual

[92] Ibid, para 134, quoting ICTY, *Tadić Judgment*, 7 May 1997, paras 535-9.
[93] ICTR, *The Prosecutor v Jean-Paul Akayesu*, ICTR-96-4-T, Decision of 2 September 1998 [The Akayesu decision], para 452.
[94] Ibid, para 692.

violence, without which these acts would not have taken place.[95]

This ruling, as in similar ones by the ICTY, established responsibility by virtue of authority that could have prevented or stopped tactical rape.

Specific and significant progress in establishing that tactical rape and sexual violence could be used as genocide came when the court ruled:

> ... with regard, particularly, to the acts described in paragraphs 12(A) and 12(B) of the Indictment, that is, rape and sexual violence, the Chamber wishes to underscore the fact that in its opinion, they constitute genocide in the same way as any other act as long as they were committed with the specific intent to destroy, in whole or in part, a particular group, targeted as such. Indeed, rape and sexual violence certainly constitute infliction of serious bodily and mental harm on the victims [FN181] and are even, according to the Chamber, one of the worst ways to inflict harm on the victim as he or she suffers both bodily and mental harm.[96]

Even with many reservations about the ICTR, this was a watershed case for victims of tactical rape and sexual violence. It clearly linked these attacks with genocide, an act condemned by the international community and the naming of which should bring responsibility for states to act to protect victims. The ruling stated explicitly that these rapes:

> ... resulted in physical and psychological destruction of Tutsi women, their families and their communities. Sexual violence was an integral part of the process of destruction, specifically targeting Tutsi women and specifically contributing to their destruction and to the destruction of the Tutsi group as a whole.[97]

It stated that sexual violence was a step in the process of the destruction of the Tutsi group – destruction of the spirit, of the will to live, and

---

[95] Ibid, para 694.
[96] Ibid, para 731.
[97] Ibid, para 731.

of life itself.[98] This ruling greatly expanded the legal basis for action and for international rejection of rape used as a means of genocide.

The ruling was a final international judicial acknowledgement that:

> ... the acts of rape and sexual violence, as other acts of serious bodily and mental harm committed against the Tutsi, reflected the determination to make Tutsi women suffer and to mutilate them even before killing them, the intent being to destroy the Tutsi group while inflicting acute suffering on its members in the process.[99]

This case may have been flawed in its process and in its lack of commitment to bringing to account those who perpetrate tactical rape and sexual violence, but it did result in progress towards full comprehension of such crimes.

Limited progress

Despite the progress made by establishing a legal case for rape and sexual violence as elements of genocide, there remained much to do before real commitment to the developing norm rejecting tactical rape. The final measure of the success of the ICTR was consideration of the extent to which it achieved the aims for which it was established. The UN Security Council believed that the establishment of an international tribunal would contribute to ensuring that certain violations were halted and effectively redressed.[100] It also believed the Tribunal would contribute to the process of national reconciliation and to the restoration and maintenance of peace.[101] There has been limited progress.

In 2009, Kirsten Keith, a former legal officer for the Prosecution at the Special Court for Sierra Leone, where she spent 2008 working on the Charles Taylor case, raised three serious criticisms of the ICTR:

> First, the apparent one-sidedness of prosecutions, with critics seeing the ICTR as administering "victor's justice"; only Hutu leaders have been tried despite evidence implicating

---

[98] Ibid, para 732.

[99] Ibid, para 733.

[100] UN Security Council, *Security Council resolution 955 (1994) [on Rwanda]*, S/RES/955, 8 November 1994, Preamble.

[101] Ibid.

members of the Tutsi-led RPF in the commission of war crimes. Second, delays in the administration of justice that impact on the rights of accused. Third, the failure of the ICTR to fully address issues of sexual violence crimes.[102]

Given the late inclusion of charges relating to rape and sexual violence, the ruling in the Akayesu case could be deemed more a matter of luck than of any real commitment to bringing justice to victims. There were no additional rulings specifically linking tactical rape and sexual violence with genocide. Indeed, there have been few rulings from the ICTR on rape at all. By the 10th anniversary of the Rwandan genocide, the ICTR had handed down 21 sentences with 18 convictions and 3 acquittals, and only 10% of those contained any rape convictions, with no rape charges even presented in 70% of those adjudicated cases.[103] This was despite widespread recognition of the extent and nature of tactical rape and sexual violence in the genocide.

There continued to be resounding criticism of the style of investigations into rape cases. Binaifer Nowrojee wrote of a lack of provision of optimal care for those testifying, of a lack of information and follow-up for women who testified, and inadequate attempts to provide witnesses with anonymity and care so that they often returned home to threats and reprisals.[104] As ground-breaking as the Akayesu judgment is, 'it increasingly stands as an exception, an anomaly'.[105] Rwandan women who are rape survivors have expressed, 'almost without exception' their sense that the ICTR failed them because they want the legal record to show 'the horrific sexual violence' they experienced.[106] They wanted respect and care in legal processes, they wanted to be kept informed, and they wanted protection from 'reprisal, exposure and stigma'.[107]

Another case, the Cyangugu trial, caused considerable controversy and outrage on the part of women's groups and trial attorneys.[108] Samuel Imanishimwe (former military garrison commander), Emmanuel Bagambiki (former prefect) and André Ntagerura (former Minister of Transportation) were all accused of genocide, complicity

---

[102] Keith, K, 2009, Justice at the International Criminal Tribunal for Rwanda: are criticisms just?, *Law in Context*, 27, 1.

[103] Nowrojee, 2005, op cit, p iv.

[104] Ibid, p v.

[105] Ibid, p 3.

[106] Ibid, p 4.

[107] Ibid.

[108] Ibid, p 14.

in genocide, direct and public incitement to commit genocide, crimes against humanity and violations of Common Article 3 to the Geneva Conventions, for crimes committed in the Cyangugu region. None was accused of committing or inciting to commit crimes of sexual violence. Ntagerura and Bagambiki were acquitted. Women's groups were outraged that they had not been permitted to have additional evidence linking the two to sexual violence and rape admitted into proceedings. A trial attorney was quoted, 'we had collected strong evidence. The women of Cyangugu were begging us to tell their story.'[109] The evidence concerned in particular the convicted man, Imanishimwe, who had raped women himself and 'had killed a woman by inserting a pistol into her vagina and shooting her to death'.[110] It is quoted as a case where rape charges could have been brought but never were 'even though the prosecutor had evidence'.[111] Unlike the Akayesu case, the prosecutor was not prepared to amend the initial charges to include rape. This was one of the cases where investigations were implemented without appropriately considering whether or not rape has occurred – although given the widespread use of rape, this would be a reasonable possibility.

Criticisms of the approach and the failings of the ICTY in regard to treatment of witnesses and of processes – and lack of processes – dealing with cases of tactical rape and sexual violence in the conflict have been many and varied. However, it must be noted that in 2014, as the Tribunal wound up its proceedings, it did publish a manual on how such courts should act. It claimed that in the 20 years of its operation it had:

> ... indicted 93 persons who were among those most responsible for the 1994 Genocide in Rwanda. Reflecting the prevalence of rape and other forms of sexual violence as weapons of war in the genocide, more than half of our indictments charged rape and other forms of sexual violence as a means of perpetrating genocide and as crimes against humanity or war crimes.[112]

The manual continued:

[109] Ibid.

[110] Ibid.

[111] Ibid.

[112] See http://unictr.unmict.org/sites/unictr.org/files/legal-library/140130_prosecution_of_sexual_violence.pdf (Foreword).

In attempting to present evidence from survivors, all of those involved in the Tribunal's justice system – prosecutors, judges, defence counsel, and victim/witness advocates – needed to be sensitized to the particular security, emotional, and physical needs of this highly-traumatized population. Protective orders were needed to safeguard survivors from threats and intimidation. Counselling, medical services, and even basic necessities such as food, clothing, and accommodation had to be provided when the survivors came to present their evidence in court. Sentences needed to reflect the true gravity of the crimes and, in so doing, restore a sense of justice for the victims.[113]

Most observers at the ICTR would agree with this credible list of needs. Not all would agree that 'the Tribunal confronted all of these challenges'. However, the existence of a manual may offer hope for improved practices, and valuable lessons may well 'assist future prosecutors and others involved in the criminal justice system to successfully investigate, prosecute, and raise awareness about rape and other crimes of sexual violence at both the international and national levels'.[114]

Other reservations arising from the Akayesu case come from reservations about the *Genocide Convention* itself. George Andreopolous raised issues around prosecution referring to Fein's observation that the most fundamental problem with the Convention is 'its unenforceability, as the perpetrator of the genocide, the state, is responsible for its prosecution'.[115] States are wary of naming genocide because this brings responsibilities that many are reluctant to enact.

Another critic is Peter Stoett, who outlined difficulties in enforcing prosecutions given the scale of genocidal acts, and he questioned whether the UN could ever be effective and impartial.[116] If there are difficulties in prosecuting genocidal killings, there will be even more reticence and enumerated obstacles to prosecuting genocidal rape because of traditional and prevailing dismissals of sexual crimes.

---

[113] Ibid.

[114] Ibid.

[115] Andreopolous, GJ, 1997, *Genocide: Conceptual and historical dimensions*, Philadelphia, PA: University of Pennsylvania Press, pp 3, 18.

[116] Stoett, PJ, 1995, This age of genocide: conceptual and institutional implications, *International Journal*, 1, 3, Summer.

Samantha Power highlighted the US responses to genocide, and these certainly provide grounds for fearing that there are many ways of states avoiding responsibility. She wrote that despite graphic media coverage, US policy-makers, journalists and citizens 'assume rational actors will not inflict gratuitous violence'.[117] She believed that they 'trust in good-faith negotiations and traditional diplomacy', and then, once killings start, they 'assume civilians who keep their heads down will be left alone', at which point, 'they urge ceasefires and donate humanitarian aid'.[118]

One clear strategy to avoid the recognition of any state's responsibility to intervene in events is to avoid naming those events as 'genocide'. The state will 'render the blood-shed two-sided and inevitable, not genocidal', and by avoiding use of the word 'genocide', the state can, 'in good conscience, favor stopping genocide in the abstract, while, simultaneously, opposing American involvement in the moment'.[119]

Such perceptions seem all too credible and strengthen views of the Convention as unenforceable. Richard Falk believed the international community had shown little real capacity to 'address the supreme moral challenge of genocidal behaviour.'[120] He referred to a directive within the Clinton administration instructing officials to avoid calling events in Rwanda 'genocide' 'because that would arouse public pressures to take some action.'[121] He listed numerous reasons and complicating causes of why the prevention of genocide is not a simple matter: 'the passion of ethnic politics' having been unleashed and resistance to intervention, with memories of colonisation being invoked.[122] Overall he felt that the primary cause of non-action was a lack of real commitment by governments to intervene. His solutions lay in preventive modes such as including tolerance as an integral element in the teaching of democratic theory and practice:

> ... reactive modes of response to genocide are likely
> to be ineffectual [and are unlikely unless] it provokes a

---

[117] Power, S, 2003, *A problem from hell: America and the age of genocide*, London: Flamingo, HarperCollins, pp xvii–xviii.

[118] Power, op cit, p xvii.

[119] Ibid.

[120] Falk, R, 1999, The challenge of genocide and genocidal politics in an era of globalisation, in T Dunne and N Wheeler, *Human rights in global politics*, Cambridge: Cambridge University Press.

[121] Ibid, p 185.

[122] Ibid.

major response that reflects security priorities of strong neighbouring states ... or regional or global actors.[123]

Recognition of tactical rape as a possible form of genocide will require much more attention.

Lisa Sharlach, however, said that crimes of genocide under international law 'are a more grave matter than widespread crimes against women on the basis of sex'.[124] Her concern was with the text of the Convention. She argued that it does not explicitly state that sexual violence is a crime of genocide, and it should be expanded to include widespread rape, regardless of whether the victims are raped on the basis of racial/ethnic, national or religious identity. In an ideal world this may be the next step in the development of effective security for women – it could strengthen the legal grounds for rejecting tactical rape. Meantime, pragmatists have little option but to use the current terms and jurisprudence from the ICTR to at least increase the pressure on states to intervene when women are being raped collectively. Sharlach also said, 'the seeming disinterest around the globe in prosecution of rape as genocide may mean that in future ethnic conflicts men believe that they have license to rape.'[125] It could be counter-productive for tactical rape to be deemed genocidal if it still failed to bring perpetrators to account. While work continues to strengthen the wording of international law and new legal precedents are being set, there is a real need to pressure states to intervene when other states are culpable in not providing security for their women.

If, as Power intimated, there is a general reluctance to respond to genocide, it is possible that this reluctance could be increased if there were any doubt regarding definitions of genocide. It is possible that states could prevaricate around definitions. Despite all this, progress towards appropriate state engagement in prevention, protection and accountability can only be achieved by really understanding all the implications of the potential use of tactical rape. The Convention remains the best hope for dealing with genocide, and with tactical rape and sexual violence as methods of perpetrating genocide.

---

[123] Ibid, p 188.

[124] Sharlach, L, 2000, Rape as genocide in Bangladesh, the former Yugoslavia and Rwanda, *New Political Science*, 22, 1, p 93.

[125] Ibid, p 102.

Conclusion

The conflict in Rwanda was judged to be genocide. Constructed hatreds made the use of tactical rape and sexual violence chillingly effective. The judgements of the ICTR advanced the notion of tactical rape and sexual violence as contraventions of international law. Importantly it established rape as a method of genocide. Some analysts who believe that rape is not killing and that genocide requires killing may still contest this. I believe that the impact of rape on women, their offspring and their communities does indeed meet the requirements of the *Genocide Convention*. Death can follow rapes. Children can be removed from a group. Children can be deemed to be from another group, thus weakening a group. This has been a significant precedent – even if it is one that has not been widely used in court proceedings.

However, the ICTR is a judiciary whose processes provided little justice for many women survivors because they reflected many prevailing attitudes that resulted in a failure to acknowledge the full impact on victims and survivors of tactical rape and sexual violence. It has been a far from perfect judiciary, but with all its defects, the ICTR did go a long way to demonstrate and provide some judicial support for bringing to account those who use tactical rape to perpetrate genocide. If the best practices that the ICTR identified are shared and adopted, there may yet be further progress. Ensuring political will to do so is, of course, another matter.

SEVEN

United Nations Security Council resolution 1325

For all their limitations, the two ad hoc international criminal tribunals, the ICTY and ICTR, contributed considerable case law that clarified and established the legal bases for rejecting tactical rape. The UN Security Council began to evince interest in tactical rape from the early 1990s in ways that had not been demonstrated earlier. The establishment of the two criminal tribunals demonstrated, at least to some degree, that tactical rape was an issue that needed international legal attention. The questions are: what degree of commitment to rejecting tactical rape is reflected in Security Council resolutions? What contributed to this change? It is acknowledged that any progress at Security Council level has little or no effect on non-state actors, but it is a beginning in making changes in state policy and practice.

A new century began with Security Council resolution 1325 in 2000 breaking new ground.[1] It has warranted close scrutiny because it was hailed as reflecting a new systematic and broad-ranging approach to dealing with women's vulnerability in conflict situations: meaningful participation of women at all levels of peace and security governance, including conflict prevention and resolution, peacekeeping and peacebuilding; protection of women and girls from sexual and gender-based violence in conflict and post-conflict settings, including emergency and humanitarian contexts; prevention of violence against women through the promotion of gender equality, accountability and justice; and the incorporation of a gendered lens to all relief and recovery efforts.[2]

Security Council resolution 1325 signalled recognition that if women are vulnerable and suffer discrimination and denial of rights during peacetime, they will be even more vulnerable during conflict. It signalled serious debate about whether the use of sexual violence in conflict (including tactical rape) was a concern for the Security Council,

---

[1]　UN Security Council, *Security Council resolution 1325 (2000) [on women and peace and security]*, S/RES/1325, 31 October 2000.

[2]　Working Group on Women, Peace and Security, http://womenpeacesecurity.org/media/pdf-2013-

and it eventually led to an acknowledgement that confronting these violations was a responsibility of that international body:

> Women, peace and security has emerged as an issue that can no longer be overlooked either by the United Nations or its member states. Accordingly, it is regarded as a new norm in the making.[3]

For all its problems, especially regarding implementation and the lack of accountability measures inherent in resolution 1325, the issue at its core was now clearly on the Security Council agenda.

Changing attitudes in the 1990s

The 1990s saw changing attitudes to humanitarianism, which contributed to an international response to tactical rape and to other forms of human suffering and need. Analysts provided useful insights. Torunn L. Tryggestad identified several key factors about change by the end of the 1990s in 'how the security concept and legitimate intervention in intra-state might be defined.'[4] These included the debate about the need to broaden the security concept to human security; the ways in which the nature of conflict had shifted to intra-state conflicts; and how civilian populations were increasingly seen as the targets and means of attack, with 'an exponential growth in the use of sexualised violence as a weapon of wa'r'[5] Michael Barnett and Thomas Weiss focused on questions raised for and from humanitarian agencies about the nature, motivations and effects of humanitarianism.[6] Agencies were engaged in identity-defining questions regarding what humanitarianism aspired to accomplish, and were concluding that the answer must include establishing the rule of law and respect for human rights.[7] The impact of public media in raising awareness and consequent demands for action in the face of 'conscience-shocking suffering' contributed

---

[3] Tryggestad, TL, 2009, Trick or treat? The UN and implementation of Security Council resolution 1325 on women, peace, and security, Global Governance: A Review of Multilateralism and International Organizations, October-December, 15, 4, p 552.

[4] Ibid, p 543

[5] Ibid.

[6] Barnett, M, Weiss, TG, 2008, *Humanitarianism in question: Politics, power, ethics*, New York: Cornell University Press.

[7] Ibid, p 3.

to states recognising the need for action.[8] Of course the motivation of states is not always disinterested; they are influenced by their own national interests and their concerns regarding security. However, as Barnett and Weiss pointed out, international laws, norms and principles are also important, and pressure to respect these can be reinforced by real-time media coverage and graphic images of suffering people – real individuals, not disembodied numbers.

The 1990s was a decade of dramatic communications showing situations that outraged and mobilised calls for action. Barnett and Weiss commented that the crises of the turbulent 1990s helped catalyse new movements, intent on protecting and rescuing those in danger.[9] As journalists, NGOs and humanitarian agencies reported and detailed atrocities in conflicts in Rwanda and the former Yugoslavia, there was mounting public condemnation and consequent unwillingness to settle for expressions of dismay without any accompanying action by states or the UN.

UN member states were aware of calls to respond. In the late 1980s and into the 1990s there was a realisation that pressure for change could come from publics that rejected bureaucratic or governmental apathy. Humanitarian crises became personalised and humanised, with faces attached to statistics and analysis. Telling the stories of individuals and highlighting the human tragedies of victims of conflicts became a strategy of investigators such as myself working for humanitarian agencies, who presented stories of individuals in conflict situations and humanitarian need to UN agencies, international NGOs and peak aid agencies. Telling such stories highlighted the impact of tactical rape, and resulted in pressure on states to respond to known incidences of widespread suffering and to the flouting of accepted norms regulating behaviour of states and within states. Pressure reached the UN as links were made between rape and international law. In 1993, ECOSOC expressed outrage at rape being used as a weapon of war.[10] In 1994 the General Assembly expressed alarm at 'the continuing use of rape as a weapon of wa'r'[11] Both these resolutions recognised rape as an instrument of ethnic cleansing, and noted that the abhorrent policy of ethnic cleansing could be a form of genocide.

[8]   Ibid, p 16.
[9]   Ibid, p 26.
[10]   OHCHR, 2001, *Rape and abuse of women in the territory of the former Yugoslavia*, Commission on Human Rights resolution 1993/8, 23 February.
[11]   UN General Assembly, *Resolution 1994/205, Rape and abuse of women in the territory of the former Yugoslavia*, 6 March 1994.

This was a time when the distinction between 'ethnic cleansing', the term used to refer to events and practices in the former Yugoslavia, and 'genocide' was not always fully clarified. In 1995, the General Assembly reaffirmed 'that rape in the conduct of armed conflict constitutes a war crime and that under certain circumstances it constitutes a crime against humanity and an act of genocide.'[12] It called on states to 'take all measures for the protection of women and children from such acts and to strengthen mechanisms to investigate and punish' those responsible.[13] With media and NGO attention, the engagement of ECOSOC and the General Assembly and reports coming from Special Rapporteurs regarding tactical rape, pressure mounted for greater international engagement and eventually the Security Council responded.

Towards resolution 1325

Awareness of events in the former Yugoslavia and Rwanda meant that the 1990s was a time of increased recognition of tactical rape, of the need to prevent this form of abuse, to protect women in conflict situations, to prosecute perpetrators and to ensure that acceptable normative expectations of states precluded what was increasingly recognised as a war crime and a crime against humanity.

La Shawn Jefferson argued that it was necessary to understand the backdrop against which such gender-based violence occurs, because it is 'a continuation – and a significant worsening – of the various discriminatory and violent ways that women are treated in times of peace'.[14] Jefferson identified several critical factors that make sexual violence in conflict resistant to eradication: women's 'subordinate and unequal status in peacetime renders them predictably at risk' in wartime; 'increasing international exposure and public outrage' have failed to result in any serious accountability; and inadequate post-conflict attention to the needs of sexual violence survivors 'reflects official disregard' and suggests a 'lack of commitment to facilitating survivors' reintegration' to their communities.[15] This understanding of the complexity of causes and the need to prevent, mitigate and

---

[12] UN General Assembly, Committee 3, 1995, *Rape and abuse of women in the areas of armed conflict in the former Yugoslavia*, 99th plenary meeting, 22 December.

[13] Ibid.

[14] Jefferson, LR, 2004, *In war as in peace: Sexual violence and women's status*, New York, Human Rights Watch, January, p 3.

[15] Ibid, p 1.

prosecute perpetrators and respond to survivors' needs helped set the scene for Security Council resolution 1325.

Jefferson highlighted 'both law and practice' where women are subordinate and lack the rights of male counterparts.[16] As she argued, all too frequently the attitudes exhibited by society, including the judiciary, put the blame on victims of rape, and judge these victims according to their previous sexual experience or according to their behaviour or even how they dress. In some cultures, failure to achieve a conviction can mean further suffering, discrimination and even imprisonment for the woman making the charges. Jefferson wrote, 'many men are accustomed to enforcing gender norms and stereotypes through physical violence'.[17] She argued, 'such violence is often culturally, sometimes legally sanctioned.'[18] Changing the legal status and achieving legal rights for women can change the degree of protection that women are afforded by courts and communities.

The realisation of the relevance of women's situations before, during and after conflict gathered momentum during the 1990s. Jefferson spoke of training combatants as one essential step.[19] Education regarding rights, international human rights law and international humanitarian law may contribute to lessening the vulnerability of women in conflict. Bringing perpetrators to account, monitoring the behaviour of combatants, documenting violations of national and international law – all these can alter attitudes and behaviours. In refugee camps in Kosovar in 1999, it was noted that women were more ready to talk about their experiences of rape than Bosnian women in similar situations just a few years earlier. A young lawyer taking depositions said that he believed it was because the Kosovars had heard that the Bosnian women were being taken seriously and were less afraid of being ignored or suffering discrimination.[20] For many of these brave women, their faith was misplaced, and it was still being reported from Syria in 2013 that:

> ... there is nowadays in Syria an overwhelming lack of confidence in the utility of documenting violations, given the fact that the work conducted so far by human

---

[16] Ibid, p 2.
[17] Ibid, p 3.
[18] Ibid.
[19] Ibid, p 6.
[20] Fitzpatrick, B, 1999, *Kosovo – The women and children*, Burwood, VIC: World Vision Australia, pp 14–15.

rights organizations has barely impacted the stand of the international community (and more specifically the Security Council) despite more than two years of a violent conflict marked by repeated patterns of devastating violations and crimes under international law.[21]

However, for some women their courage in reporting has been vindicated as some perpetrators have been charged, and the international community generally has been brought to a better understanding of what was their reality.

At least some humanitarian agencies recognise the needs of survivors of tactical rape post-conflict, and that reintegration of survivors requires economic self-sufficiency and support for women recovering from physical and psychological trauma. Many humanitarian agencies, including those connected to the World Council of Churches, World Vision, the International Red Cross and Red Crescent, all had at least some programmes focused on the needs of women victims in the conflicts in both Rwanda and the former Yugoslavia. But these were often narrowly focused, and it was not until resolution 1325 that there was a more holistic approach to dealing with tactical rape.

Laura Shepherd analysed the lead-up to resolution 1325 and the role played by women's advocacy groups.[22] From NGOs there was mounting pressure for action, and the UN had taken a series of steps towards recognising women's issues. These had begun as far back as 1975 in the UN International Year of Women, and continued in the 1979 *Convention on the Elimination of All Forms of Discrimination Against Women*, in the 1993 *Declaration on the Elimination of Violence Against Women* and 'the ever strengthening linkages between feminist theorists/ activists and the UN system.'[23] Each of these steps internationally moved forward the understanding of women's realities and needs. At the Vienna Conference on Human Rights in 1993, women's advocates and activists called for recognition of women's rights as human rights. Traditional human rights frameworks tended to exclude the realities of women's experiences and lives in conflict and in peace. There were also the UN World Conferences on Women including the 1995 Beijing Conference that produced an influential Beijing Platform of

---

[21] Euro-Mediterranean Human Rights Network, 2013, *Violence against women, bleeding wound in the Syrian conflict*, Sema Nasar, November, p 8.

[22] Shepherd, L, 2008, Power and authority in the production of United Nations Security Council resolution 1325, *International Studies Quarterly*, 52, 383-404.

[23] bid, p 387.

Action (BPFA). Shepherd noted that the BPFA set comprehensive benchmarks and a vision for improving women's lives, and that it was at Beijing, with 188 states as signatories to it, that the impact of armed conflict on women was recognised as a specific emerging issue requiring attention.[24] Some feminist analysts have commented that these World Conferences 'played a crucial role – one that would pave the way for UNSC 1325'.[25] As work to achieve security for women in conflict continues, it is important to acknowledge the strategic steps in progress so far and the international conferences with declarations, while not affecting any direct action or response, certainly did provide a context and a groundswell of opinion calling for such response. The role of NGOs was a significant contribution.

NGOs involved in preparing the way for resolution 1325 were represented by the NGO Working Group on Women, Peace and Security (NGOWG). This group lobbied members of the Security Council, applying pressure for action on behalf of women in conflict, and is largely credited with a major contribution to achieving resolution 1325. Shepherd noted it was the NGOWG, 'through its continued political presence', which was, 'able to transform decades of theorising and activism into concrete achievements in the issue area of women, peace and security'.[26] The linking of women, peace and security was a foundational step towards understanding the interaction between tactical rape and security, a key understanding of which would develop in the next decade. During the 1990s interaction between the UN and NGOs had increased, with UN agencies seeking advice and information and entering into a range of joint activities.[27]

Concurrently, the UN was acknowledging its own role in dealing with tactical rape. Importantly, it was in passing resolution 1325 that the Security Council began to consider new concepts of security, a change in attitude that would eventually lead to an even stronger focus on tactical rape in the next decade. The Security Council Presidential Statement of February 1999 condemned the increasing toll of civilian casualties in conflicts, women being the majority of those increased casualties, and increasingly the targets of combatants and armed elements. The statement referred to the need for a 'comprehensive and

---

[24] Ibid.
[25] Binder, C, Lukas, K, Schweiger, R, 2008, Empty words or real achievement? The impact of Security Council resolution 1325 on women in armed conflicts, Radical History Review, 101, 22-41.
[26] Shepherd, op cit, p 391.
[27] Ibid, p 392.

coordinated approach by Member States and international organisations' to protecting civilians in situations of conflict'.[28] The Secretary-General submitted his report to the Security Council on the protection of civilians in September 1999, and it began by acknowledging the Geneva Conventions and the 'legal norms from which there can be no derogation.'[29] It reiterated that civilians were disproportionately represented among the victims of armed conflict, with women and children disproportionately represented and deliberately targeted and subjected to gender-based violence including rape. There was reference to the ICTR and ICTY, demonstrating Security Council concern for these issues. This was indicative of the cumulative effect of NGO lobbying, the work of the criminal tribunals and the global realisation that this was an issue falling within the purview of the UN and demanding some specific response. The Secretary-General called for action by states to ratify and respect existing legal instruments, for the special protection of women and children, and asked member states to be prepared to take action against those guilty of widespread violations.[30]

Two Security Council resolutions, 1265 (1999) and 1296 (2000), addressed the protection of civilians in armed conflict, and 'functioned to suggest that the UN Security Council recognises the protection of civilians as an issue that falls under its remit'.[31] This was an important step towards accepting responsibility for confronting tactical rape. It was not until 2008 that all members of the Security Council finally accepted that tactical rape and sexual violence in conflict were a direct concern of the Security Council. But this acknowledgement of responsibility for protecting civilians created a context for resolution 1325 that focused on the protection of a section of that civilian group – women and girls. Caution was needed in applauding such a statement as it could be taken as a reinforcement of the attitude that women would always need protection. However, in March 2000, the Security Council issued a statement in which members recognised 'that peace is inextricably linked with equality between men and women', referenced 'violence against women', identified obligations of the 'international community' to 'refrain from human rights abuses in conflict situations', and called

---

[28] UN Security Council, Statement by the President of the Security Council, S/PRST/1999/6, 12 February 1999.

[29] UN, 1999, *Report of the Secretary-General to the Security Council on the protection of civilians in armed conflict*, S/1999/957, 8 September.

[30] Ibid.

[31] Shepherd, op cit, p 393.

for those responsible to be prosecuted.[32] This was indicative of an attitude respecting the rights of women rather than responding to any perceived weaknesses. As such, many feminist advocates, including myself, cautiously welcomed the approach even while registering the potential of continuing patriarchal attitudes.

With obligations of the Security Council now recognised, it remained to formulate a strategic approach to meeting those obligations. In June 2000, Mary Robinson, High Commissioner for Human Rights, presented a report on *Systematic rape, sexual slavery and slavery-like practices during armed conflict.*[33] This set the scene for the international approach to confronting tactical rape. Robinson wrote of rape and sexual violence being used as a weapon of war, and said that in order to end the cycle of violence, action was needed on a broad range of fronts, arguing that:

> ... without the full equality and participation of women, the empowerment of women, the emancipation of women's image, allowing women to develop confidence and respect for themselves, and enabling them to realise their full potential and acknowledging the full value of the contribution they make to the well-being, security and progress of society, any measure taken to prevent the systematic rape of women during armed conflicts, in fact any form of gender-based violence, will fail.[34]

This recognised the complexity of issues around tactical rape, and indicated that any strategic approach aiming at preventing it needed to reduce women's constructed vulnerability in peace as well as in conflict, and to recognise women both as potential victims and as capable and positive contributors to situations of improved peace and security. This statement was to be reflected in the overall direction of resolution 1325.

In the Open Debate prior to passing resolution 1325, many representatives made links between tactical rape and the need for the involvement of women in peacekeeping.[35] The starting point was

---

[32] UN, *Peace inextricably linked with equality between men and women says Security Council in International Women's Day Statement*, SC/6816, 8 March 2000.

[33] OHCHR, 2000 *Systematic rape, sexual slavery and slavery-like practices during armed conflict*, E/CN.4/Sub.2/2000/20 (Mary Robinson).

[34] Ibid, para 8.

[35] UN, *Stronger decision-making role for women in peace processes is called for in day-long Security Council debate*, SC/6937, 24 October 2000.

awareness of the impact of conflict on women. The Netherlands called for action to prevent gender-based violence, to support the prosecution of those responsible, to increase awareness that rape, sexual slavery, enforced prostitution and pregnancy and sterilisation were war crimes when committed in conflict situations and could be crimes against humanity under certain circumstances. It demanded an end to impunity for offenders.[36] Many member states called for more women to be included in high-level positions in both peacemaking and peacekeeping, and for gender training for peacekeeping forces, decision-makers and negotiators. The connection was made between general inequality, poverty and women's vulnerability to sexual attack and rape in conflict situations.[37] While there is so often a disconnect between the rhetoric of states and the reality of practical response, these statements were both indicators of a developing norm – and a basis (albeit limited) for later holding states to account.

Finally, on 31 October 2000, a milestone was reached in states' response to violence against women in war and conflict situations. Resolution 1325 was passed unanimously and welcomed as an important advance for women in conflict situations.[38] It was hailed as 'a vital and innovative political framework' for dealing with issues, such as tactical rape, in the pre-conflict and post-conflict phases as well as during conflict.[39] Agencies such as Human Rights Watch were among those who recognised the advance, stating that:

> … the resolution is historic not only in that it constituted the first time the Council systematically addressed the manner in which conflict affects women and girls differently from men and boys, but also because it acknowledges the crucial link between peace, women's participation in decision-making, and the recognition of women's life experiences throughout the conflict cycle.[40]

---

[36] Ibid.

[37] UN, *Security Council concludes open debate on women, peace and security*, SC/6939, 25 October 2000; www.hrw.org/legacy/pub/2008/women/HRW_AIUSA_HFAC_Subcommittee_Submission_UNSC_Res1325.pdf

[38] UN Security Council, *Security Council resolution 1325 (2000) [on women and peace and security]*, S/RES/1325, 31 October 2000.

[39] Shepherd, op cit, p 383.

[40] Human Rights Watch, www.hrw.org/legacy/pub/2008/women/HRW_AIUSA_HFAC_Subcommittee_Submission_UNSC_Res1325.pdf

It was, indeed, in its systematic and comprehensive approach that resolution 1325 demonstrated a commitment to broad-ranging strategies to confront tactical rape and sexual violence in conflict. It went beyond condemnation and rhetorical outrage to action in a way not demonstrated in previous resolutions. Writing in 2009, Aisling Swaine commented that resolution 1325 had 'moved international discourse and debate on women's role in international security forward in the last decade in that it has redefined the position of women in the context of security'.[41] It was not the solution, but it was an important step in progress towards recognising constructed vulnerability both in peacetime and in conflict.

Resolution 1325 (2000)

Resolution 1325 was a major development in states' commitment to dealing with tactical rape, and has deserved close consideration. Recognised as important in confronting gender-specific aspects of women in war, it was:

> ... the first Security Council resolution to focus specifically on women's experience of armed conflict. SC Res 1325 aims to empower women at all levels of decision making in conflict prevention, conflict resolution and peace building, in addition to reducing gender-based violence. Rather than marginalizing women's experiences, it appears to bring gender specific concerns within mainstream peace and security policy considerations.[42]

While there is a perceived intent to mainstream gender-specific concerns, mainstreaming is only directly mentioned in relation to peacekeeping missions.[43] This was progress, but by no means was it a final solution, and the resolution acknowledged that a broad-ranging approach was required to confront sexual violence in conflict.

The resolution included the customary preamble and operative paragraphs. It opened with 'recalling' numerous other resolutions:

[41] Swaine, A, 2009, Assessing the potential of national action plans to advance implementation of United Nations Security Council resolution 1325, *Yearbook of International Humanitarian Law*, 12, 405.

[42] Barrow, A, 2010, United Nations Security Council resolutions 1325 and 1820: constructing gender in armed conflict and international humanitarian law, *International Review of the Red Cross*, 92, 877, March, p 229.

[43] Ibid, referring to Clause 5, p 229.

1261 (1999), 1265 (1999), 1296 (2000) and 1314 (2000). It built on resolution 1296, which condemned all violence against civilians, particularly women, children and other vulnerable groups.[44] It 'recalled' commitments of the BFPA (A/52/231) and the outcome document of the 23rd Special Session of the General Assembly, Women 2000: Gender, equality, development and peace.[45] The body of the resolution 'recalls' resolution 1208 (1998). This is an indication of how incrementally progress is made on an issue such as women's security, with many apparently small steps towards recognition of the gravity of an issue and consequent decisions to take some action.

The preamble expressed concern that women and children are the majority of those 'adversely affected' in conflicts, and recognised them as the targets of combatants and armed elements.[46] It made specific references to established principles or agreements relating to the targeting of women and children, the relevance of existing human rights and international humanitarian law, and the need to mainstream gender perspectives across a wide range of related peacekeeping operations. Importantly for later development it also referenced the role women could play in peace and security. It is important to see these references as part of understanding the development that resolution 1325 represented.[47] Rather than assuming a by-product of conflict is that women and children may accidentally be caught in the crossfire, it recognised that increasingly, armed groups are specifically targeting civilians. This is a route to escalation of violence, and has long-term effects on possibilities for peace. This was, and remains, a vital recognition about the nature of conflicts and the deliberate targeting of women and children among civilian populations. Resolution 1325 recognised that new wars are not fought solely between armies or militias. Armed elements deliberately target civilians, contrary to established international law.

Referring to women and children as one entity, however, did raise concerns among some feminist analysts. Nadine Puechguirbal reviewed some of these concerns.[48] She concluded that the linking of women

---

[44] UN Security Council, *Security Council resolution 1296 (2000) [protection of civilians in armed conflict]*, S/RES/1296, 19 April 2000.

[45] UN, 2000, Report of the Ad Hoc Committee of the Whole of the twenty-third special session of the General Assembly, Supplement No 3, A/S-23/10/Rev1.

[46] UN Security Council, *Security Council resolution 1325 (2000) [on women and peace and security]*, S/RES/1325, 31 October 2000, para 4.

[47] Ibid.

[48] Puechguirbal, N, 2010, Discourses on gender, patriarchy and resolution 1325: a textual analysis of UN documents, *International Peacekeeping*, 17, 2, 172-87.

with children resulted in, and reflected, a negative attitude to women as being victims, with little or no agency in their own lives.[49] She deplored the ongoing association with children, noting that if women were seen 'as actors within the family and community, rather than just given the status of victim, they would have more leverage in recovering from armed conflicts'.[50] She argued that because of the ongoing portrayal of women as vulnerable victims, 'women's experiences of local issues in the sphere of security remain an untapped resource'.[51] This coincides with the caution about women being seen as in need of protection. Resolution 1325 could be accused of being couched in terms of women's vulnerability without fully acknowledging that such vulnerability is not an innate attribute of women but a constructed vulnerability – and an attribute that could be minimised or avoided by equality in times of peace. However, it did at least signpost the link between vulnerability in peace with vulnerability in conflict, and there were efforts to recognise women's agency in peacemaking and peacekeeping. From feminist analysts of resolution 1325 came a 'genuinely radical understanding' of patriarchy as the 'principal cause both of the outbreak of violent societal conflicts and the international community's frequent failures in providing long term resolutions to those conflicts'.[52] The issue, 'women, peace and security', could be weakened if women were always identified as needing protection and not contributors to peacemaking and peacekeeping. While women and children all have rights and need access to those rights, women have specific capacities and strengths that must be identified, recognised and acknowledged for them to contribute meaningfully in their societies and in reconciliation and transitions from conflict to peace.

It is no surprise that by passing resolution 1325, the Security Council reaffirmed the need to implement fully international humanitarian and human rights law protecting the rights of women and girls during and after conflicts. They have the right to be protected by existing laws, particularly the Geneva Conventions and Additional Protocols, all existing norms governing behaviour of governments and their armed forces, and applying equally to armed opposition groups and any other parties to a conflict. This echoes the approach of the two international

---

[49] Ibid, p 173.
[50] Ibid, p 178.
[51] Ibid.
[52] Ibid, p 179, quoting Enloe, C, 2005, What is patriarchy? Is the big picture an afterword?, in D Mazurana, A Raven-Roberts and J Parpart (eds), *Gender, conflict and peace keeping*, Lanham, MD: Rowman & Littlefield, p 281.

tribunals in applying existing law to the experiences of women and children in conflict.

Significantly, the preamble acknowledged that protection of women required a broader understanding of the reality of women's situations in many communities, the social, cultural, economic and political realities of women. Affording women their right to protection required action beyond direct responses to conflict situations. When the preamble prefaced direct recommendations by 'recognizing the urgent need to mainstream a gender perspective into peacekeeping operations', the use of 'urgent' reflected a degree of seriousness about strategies that followed.[53]

The preamble reaffirmed 'the important role of women in the prevention and resolution of conflicts and in peacebuilding'.[54] This was recognition beyond women as victims when conflict broke out. It acknowledged women's potential for contribution, equal participation and 'full involvement in all efforts for the maintenance and promotion of peace and security'.[55] Logically, then, the preamble called for action to increase women's role in decision-making with regard to conflict prevention and resolution. It formally acknowledged that women can contribute to prevention and recovery processes, and recognised that if women were to play an equal part in security and maintaining peace, they must be empowered politically and economically. There was a growing understanding that confronting violence against women in conflict requires confronting the inequality and subordination of women.

The preamble recognised the necessity of understanding the impact of armed conflict on women and girls. Notably, it recognised that the provision of effective institutional arrangements to guarantee women's rightful protection and full participation in the peace process 'can significantly contribute to the maintenance and promotion of international peace and security'. Related to this aim was the need 'to consolidate data on the impact of armed conflict on women and girls'. Attention was drawn to the paucity of data available and the absence of any systematic processes for documentation, collation and analysis of information to inform responses. Reliable information is needed about the potential and actual role of women in peacebuilding, especially when women and women's groups are frequently engaged in support

---

[53] Security Council, *Security Council resolution 1325 (2000) [on women and peace and security]*, S/RES/1325, 31 October 2000, Preamble, para 8.

[54] Ibid, para 5.

[55] Ibid.

responses both during and after conflicts. The preamble reiterated the reference to the Security Council's own mandate, emphasising the importance of training peacekeepers.[56]

Resolution 1325 then moved to operative paragraphs and, as in any resolution, the language signalled differing levels of commitment or differing levels of application. Sometimes states were 'urged' to take action, sometimes they were 'encouraged'. The Secretary-General was 'required' to undertake certain steps. Some concerns regarding the slow implementation of the resolution link to this language. Resolution 1325 was adopted under Chapter VI; although adopted unanimously, it is non-coercive and non-binding on states. It does 'carry a normative imperative that is intended to influence behaviour (in the short and long term) at both international and national levels'.[57] Because it was not adopted under Chapter VII, which is deemed coercive, binding on states and invoked when a breach of the peace is perceived, the language is deemed to be 'soft' in comparison to 'hard' language in other resolutions.[58] For example, resolution 1373 on counter terrorism 'decides', 'declares', 'directs', while resolution 1325 'expresses', 'emphasises' and 'requests'.[59] It has been argued that 'because the language appears weak it fails to be taken seriously by the military.'[60] However, Torunn L. Tryggestad commented that since resolution 1325, 'women, peace and security has appeared as a normative issue that is increasingly difficult for states to shun'.[61] Despite reservations and criticisms of the resolution, it was 'a remarkable development'.[62]

The first four operative paragraphs urged increased participation of women at all decision-making levels. Member states were to do so 'in national, regional and international institutions and mechanisms for the prevention, management, and resolution of conflict'.[63] The Secretary-General was to implement a plan for 'an increase in the participation of women at decision-making levels in conflict resolution and peace

[56] Ibid, para 1.
[57] Tryggestad, op cit, p 544.
[58] Swaine, op cit, p 409, referring to Otto, D, 2009, The exile of exclusion: reflections on gender issues in international law over the last decade, *Melbourne Journal of International Law*, 10, p 21.
[59] Swaine, op cit, p 410, quoting Barbour, LCO, 2009, UNSCR 1325 Annual Conference of the Human Security Network, Dublin.
[60] Ibid.
[61] Tryggestad, op cit, p 542.
[62] Ibid.
[63] UN Security Council, *Security Council resolution 1325 (2000) [on women and peace and security]*, S/RES/1325, 31 October 2000, para 1.

processes'.[64] While this focus on women's participation in decision-making was admirable, the need to reiterate the call highlighted that much still needed to be done to make this a reality.

A tentative paragraph related to peacekeeping operations. The Security Council 'expresses its willingness to incorporate a gender perspective into peacekeeping operations and urges the Secretary-General to ensure that, where appropriate, field operations include a gender component'.[65] The phrase 'where appropriate' implies a judgement but no clear parameters or conditionality. A 'willingness to incorporate' carries no required specific action.

However, it needed to be read in the context of resource requirements for gender perspectives in all phases of peace support operations.[66] The Secretary-General's report had listed: political analysis; military operations; civilian police activities; electoral assistance; human rights support; humanitarian assistance; assistance for refugees and displaced persons; development and reconstruction activities; public information; training troops and civilian police on gender issues; and gender balance in interim bodies and development of capacity within interim governing bodies.[67] The report highlighted the importance of paying attention to gender perspectives 'from the very outset of peacebuilding and peacekeeping missions, including through incorporation in the initial mandates', and importantly, it recommended that all reports of any individual mission to the Security Council 'should include explicit routine reporting on progress in integrating gender perspectives as well as information on the number and levels of women involved in all aspects of the mission'.[68] Paragraph 5 was a commitment to follow through on these identified needs, with an important implied recognition that this needed to be noted in budgetary allocations.

Paragraph 6 recognised the need for 'specialized training for all peacekeeping personnel on the protection, special needs and human rights of women and children in conflict situations.'[69] Member states

[64] Ibid, para 2, referring to UN General Assembly, 1994, *Advancement of women*, A/49/587, 1 November.

[65] UN Security Council, *Security Council resolution 1325 (2000) [on women and peace and security]*, S/RES/1325, 31 October 2000, para 5.

[66] UN, 2000, *Resource requirements for implementation of the report of the Panel on United Nations peace operations: Report of the Secretary-General*, Addendum, 27 October, A/55/507/Add.1.

[67] Ibid.

[68] Ibid.

[69] UN Security Council, *Security Council resolution 1325 (2000) [on women and peace and security]*, S/RES/1325, 31 October 2000, Operative, para 6.

had to accept responsibility for their own peacekeeping forces to demonstrate commitment. Paragraphs 7 and 8 'request[ed]' provision of training in many aspects of gender sensitivity and 'urge[d]' financial allocations and commitments to enable such training. Here, again, the mention of financial allocations indicated a seriousness to act.

This degree of seriousness continued when 'all actors' were called on to adopt 'a gender perspective' when 'negotiating and implementing peace agreements'.[70] Specific aspects were deemed to require attention: the special needs of women and girls during repatriation and resettlement and for rehabilitation, reintegration and post-conflict reconstruction; support for local women's peace initiatives and indigenous processes for conflict resolution that involve women in all of the implementation mechanisms of the peace agreements; and ensuring the protection of and respect for human rights of women and girls, particularly as they relate to the constitution, the electoral system, the police and the judiciary. This emphasised involving local women and valuing local and national processes, with a requirement for involving women in peace agreements. Proposed action included agreements on power-sharing arrangements; economic reconstruction; demobilisation and reintegration of soldiers; legislation on human rights; access to land, education and health; the status of displaced people; and the empowerment of civil society. All require attention to gender, regardless of who is doing the negotiating or implementing.

By addressing reintegration, the Security Council recognised that refugee and internally displaced women, as well as female demobilised soldiers returning to their homes, require particular care and attention. For all these women, return must be voluntary, and any facilitated return must consider issues of security. Later paragraphs dealt with the special needs of women in refugee camps and women as ex-combatants with dependants.[71] There is an implicit recognition that women are not always passive victims or bystanders in conflicts – a beginning towards recognising the individuality and varying strengths of women.

Paragraph 9, mentioning the ICC, 'could be used to lobby for a referral of the Security Council to the ICC when states fail to address cases of massive sexual violence'.[72] Women had the right to judicial processes, which is reasonable even while feminist advocates recognise these are not always just or gender equitable. Paragraph 11 called on all parties to armed conflict to respect fully international law applicable

---

[70] Ibid, para 9.
[71] Ibid, paras 12, 13.
[72] Binder et al, op cit, p 34.

to the rights and protection of women and girls as civilians. This was a key point as it reaffirmed the applicability of existing norms to women in conflict. It went on to list some of the major and non-derogable international normative agreements. While it may seem odd that a specific statement was needed to ensure that women were included as civilians, and that international law applied to women, it was in reality an important step. It built on the work and judgements of the international tribunals, and made clear that while women had specific needs, they were covered by the same international law as all civilians. This led logically to the next paragraph that dealt with impunity and accountability. It emphasised:

> ... the responsibility of all States to put an end to impunity and to prosecute those responsible for genocide, crimes against humanity, war crimes including those relating to sexual violence against women and girls.[73]

This naturally developed from recognition that such crimes were not the inevitable by-products of conflict, something to be deplored but accepted as part of conflict. It recognised that these acts contravened international law, and perpetrators were to be brought to justice.

The paragraph continued to 'stress' the need to exclude these crimes, 'where feasible', from amnesty provisions. This call to put an end to impunity was welcomed, but the inclusion of the words, 'where feasible', to exclude sexual and other violence against women from amnesty agreements, was disappointing, as they implied that exceptions could be made. The work of the ICTY and ICTR had demonstrated just how difficult it was to bring perpetrators to justice. But such difficulty should not preclude the principle of refusing amnesty. There are many instances where implementation of international humanitarian law and human rights law may prove difficult. These difficulties may be recognised, but they cannot be allowed to render it acceptable to grant amnesty to those who commit the violations.

Overall, resolution 1325 demonstrated an understanding of the impact of armed conflict on women and the need for effective institutional arrangements to guarantee their rights to protection and full participation. It recognised that such understanding and arrangements could significantly contribute to the maintenance and promotion of international peace and security. It emphasised the need to respect

---

[73] UN Security Council, *Security Council resolution 1325 (2000) [on women and peace and security]*, S/RES/1325, 31 October 2000, Operative, para 11.

existing law, and called for a gender perspective in peacemaking and peace agreements, rejecting impunity for the perpetrators of violence against women and children, and urging (albeit) 'where feasible' that amnesty for such offences be avoided.

Binder et al, writing in 2008, commented: 'surprisingly, few academic papers and legal documents reference Resolution 1325'. They went on to highlight that 'the most comprehensive UN paper on post-conflict justice, the UN secretary general's report on transitional justice and the rule of law in conflict and post-conflict societies does not mention the resolution'.[74] In fact, despite its shortcomings, there has been considerable ongoing analysis and reference to resolution 1325, which provided a significant foundation for other resolutions and for institutionalised responses at international level. A High-Level Review of progress in implementation was commissioned for 2015.

National action plans

Resolution 1325 did not include any clear mechanisms for monitoring its implementation. To ensure accountability, states were asked to formulate national action plans (NAPs). NAPs represented a relatively new approach to 'the challenge' of implementation, and 'are regarded as a practical means through which states can demonstrate the steps they are taking to meet their obligations under the resolution that had been adopted unanimously.[75] Henry F. Carey, having said that norms comprise the rules and goals of governing that constitute a regime type, referred to resolution 1325 as the epitome of a new regime.[76] It represented a stated commitment to protecting women from sexual violence in conflict. However, Carey also noted that UN member states 'are able to support the new regime in principle, even if practice will not change automatically'.[77] Universal human rights and humanitarian law institutions already prohibited sexual violence against women and sought to protect their human rights.[78] This had not resulted in preventing or even seriously prohibiting sexual violence.

Member states were called on to implement resolution 1325, to develop NAPs or other national level strategies to initiate actions,

---

[74] Binder et al, op cit, p 33, referencing UN Security Council, 2004, *The rule of law and transitional justice in conflict and post-conflict societies*, S/2004/616, 23 August.

[75] Swaine, op cit, p 411.

[76] Carey, HF, 2001, Women, peace and security: the politics of implementing gender sensitivity norms in peacekeeping, *International Peacekeeping*, 8, 2, p 50.

[77] Ibid, p 53.

[78] Ibid.

identify priorities and resources, and to determine responsibilities and time frames at a national level.[79] States were to consult with women and develop the participation of women in decision-making and peace processes, with a consequent expected increase in the number of women in institutions and UN field operations. Implementing resolution 1325 required protecting women from sexual violence in conflict and ensuring gender perspectives in training and peacekeeping. It required long and short-term objectives; specific initiatives linked to objectives, with key performance indicators, deadlines and resources; time frames for the plan and for specific initiatives; monitoring and evaluation systems; and an allocated budget.[80]

Implementation meant gender mainstreaming in all relevant policy and practice. Mainstreaming a gender perspective was defined as a process of assessing the implications for women and men of any planned action, including legislation, policies or programmes, in all areas and at all levels.[81] It was a strategy for making women's as well as men's concerns and experiences an integral dimension of the design, implementation, monitoring and evaluation of policies and programmes in all political, economic and societal spheres, so that women and men would benefit equally. There was some argument that if mainstreaming were the goal, then a separate policy document or action plan could be counter-productive.[82] This was countered by fear that gender aspects would be lost or ignored without specific plans. The outcome was that some states such as Fiji incorporated gender aspects into existing policy approaches.[83]

By February 2016, 57 countries had formulated NAPs reflecting varying degrees of commitment to decrease women's vulnerability in conflict.[84] Each should include strategies that strengthen women's access to decision-making, independence and to increased hope of countering social attitudes exposing them to particular violence such as tactical rape

---

[79] See http://www.peacewomen.org/assets/file/NationalActionPlans/un_ secreatriarygeneralraportwps_2005.pdf; UN Security Council, Statement by the President of the Security Council, S/PRST/2004/40, 28 October 2004 and UN Security Council, Statement by the President of the Security Council, S/PRST/2005/52, 27 October 2005.

[80] UN International Research and Training Institute for the Advancement of Women, 2006, *Securing equality, engendering peace: A guide to policy and planning on women, peace and security (UN SCR 1325)*, Dominican Republic.

[81] UN General Assembly, 1997, *Report of the Economic and Social Council for 1997*, A/52/3, 18 September, Chapter IV, Concepts and principles.

[82] Swaine, op cit, p 411.

[83] Ibid.

[84] See http://peacewomen.org/member-states/overview-and-analysis

during conflict. NAPs are practical measures of national commitment to implement policies and principles that form the basis of normative expectations regarding the treatment of women in conflict. In effect they indicate a varied and generally limited degree of commitment, and most have lacked adequate evaluation indicators. Developing a plan should be a process of 'awareness raising and capacity-building in order to overcome gaps and challenges to the full implementation of resolution 1325'.[85]

Of course, NAPs are not the only way to develop policy on women, peace and security, and they offer no guarantee that states are seriously committed to the implementation of declared strategies. A state may claim to be mainstreaming the concerns of resolution 1325 into other policy frameworks. However, given that states also continue to be among the perpetrators of tactical rape, commitments are always open to considerable doubt as to implementation. With this reservation, NAPs can be viewed as a statement of intent to meet agreed responsibilities and to comply with what has become a normative expectation for strategies formulated and implemented to meet the needs recognised in resolution 1325.

As an indicator of the slow pace of implementation of resolution 1325, it should be noted that the UN took five years to formulate an organisation-wide action plan.[86] Although it has since been revised, the plan was initially seen as 'a compendium of activities' rather than a forward-looking 'action-oriented document' to challenge stakeholders to change their ways of doing business and to address gaps in implementation.[87] It took time before satisfactory institutional changes, definite operational time frames and loci of responsibility were really developed. Writing in 2008, Binder et al noted that 'a review of recommendations of UN human rights committees (committee on CEDAW, on the Rights of the Child, on the Convention on Civil and Political Rights, on the Convention on Torture) shows that not a single committee referenced 1325'.[88] Work on implementing and applying resolution 1325 was slow to gain momentum. The UN itself should have been leading the early implementation of resolution 1325, but it too was slow to react.

---

[85] Ibid.

[86] UN, 2005, *UN system-wide action plan for the implementation of Security Council resolution 1325 (2005-07)*, S/2005/636.

[87] Swaine, op cit, p 414.

[88] Binder et al, op cit, p 30.

There are perceived limitations inherent in even slow increases. Puechguirbal concluded, 'the relations of inequality and the imbalance of power between women and men in the UN remain uncontested, despite the existence of resolution 1325'.[89] Charlesworth and Chinkin commented on the dissonance between equality and representation that may still arise when women are accorded participation in decision-making bodies or when equality is measured by the number of women participating, because 'this account of equality ignores the presence of underlying structures and power relations that contribute to the oppression of women'.[90] Others noted that resolution 1325 did not address root causes or structural problems such as women's access to economic or financial resources and education.[91]

The European Parliament and Council of Europe formulated documents encouraging the implementation of resolution 1325 as did NATO and the Organization for Security and Co-operation in Europe (OSCE), and some UN member states formed 'The Group of Friends of 1325'.[92] By 2008, this group comprised 31 member states and was coordinated by Canada.[93] In European countries where NAPs have been formulated, it has usually been ministries responsible for foreign affairs – development, cooperation, defence and justice – which have taken the lead, while in Africa it seems to have been ministries responsible for gender equality.[94] Uganda, for example, has included an analysis of the gendered aspects of conflict.[95]

Concerns

NAPs provide one way to ensure and monitor how states act on their commitments in the resolution. In 2013, resolution 2122 called for a High-Level Review to be presented in 2015.[96] A related Global Study on Women, Peace and Security was to be prepared and published during that High-Level Review, with numerous briefings, consultations

[89] Puechguirbal, op cit, p 184.
[90] Charlesworth, H, Chinkin, C, 2000, *The boundaries of international law: A feminist analysis*, Manchester: Manchester University Press, p 229.
[91] Binder et al, op cit, p 25.
[92] Swaine, op cit, p 414.
[93] Tryggestad, op cit, p 547.
[94] Swaine, op cit, pp 416–17.
[95] Ministry of Gender, Labour and Social Development, 2008, *The Uganda Action Plan on UN Security Council Resolutions 1325 and 1820 and the Goma Declaration*.
[96] UN, *Security Council adopts resolution 2122 (2013), aiming to strengthen women's role in all stages of conflict prevention*, SC/11149, 18 October 2013.

and research papers submitted to the Global Study. A special political high-level advisory group was created to provide advice on the Global Study. This review was anticipated to focus on some general areas such as highlighting good practice examples, implementation gaps and challenges, emerging trends and priorities for action.

There have been a number of concerns voiced regarding resolution 1325. One relates to a perceived lack of attention to women's diversity, such as the range and differences in nationality, class, ethnicity, religious, sexuality, age migration or disability status. There are also concerns that a narrow focus on the terms of resolution 1325 could mean women being viewed solely through a gender lens without consideration or appreciation of other forms of marginalisation. Issues raised by feminist analysts, considered earlier in Chapter Four, are not adequately dealt with in resolution 1325 – or in later resolutions dealt with in Chapter Eight. These concerns are regarding militarised masculinities and the fundamental relationships between gender and violence and gender and war and gender and law. Implementation of resolution 1325 also raises concerns regarding transitional justice and transitional security in the form of the police, judiciaries and security forces (considered more fully in Chapter Nine). Women's rights to security in conflict are recognised, and to some extent (albeit somewhat limited) their potential for contribution to wider social peace and security is being acknowledged.

The most fundamental area of concern is, of course, the extent to which any UN resolution makes a practical and positive impact on the lives of women. There have been steps towards institutionalising response at the global level to tactical rape, and some have involved budget allocations, which is always an indicator of the seriousness with which commitments are taken. I argue again the pragmatic approach of incremental progress. Having the resolution has not been the final solution. It has, however, been a significant beginning to developing normative rejection of tactical rape and strategies to prevent and prosecute it. However, there remain serious challenges, and perpetrators, including states, continue to use rape as a tactic in conflict.

Conclusion

The ICTY and ICTR established that tactical rape and sexual violence in conflict contravened existing international law. This was accompanied by changes in attitudes towards humanitarianism during the 1990s. At the Security Council, it was initially in response to public awareness of tactical rape and cries for action that movement began towards confronting sexual violence. Resolution 1325 recognised that confronting tactical rape and sexual violence in conflict required multifaceted actions. All member states passed resolution 1325, effectively committing to the policies and practices it outlined. When reminded of these obligations, states were asked to formulate NAPs.

Yet states continue to be among the perpetrators of tactical rape, and there are serious questions regarding the detail, means of accountability, application and implementation of resolution 1325. Women continue to suffer from this violation. The pace of measurable change is slow. This is somewhat balanced by progress in having the resolution as a basis for further advocacy and response. The review in 2015 focused on how to build on learning in the 15 years since the resolution was passed. Gaps and omissions of resolution 1325 have become clear, and the international community has begun to require more action. Some of the principal elements of resolution 1325 have been developed and integrated into attitudinal and normative change reflected in later resolutions. Resolutions and law are no guarantee of benefit for women in conflict because they remain severely gender-biased as a context. But they can be utilised by advocates for change – even as those advocates also work to change the context to one that is gender-inclusive, working for frameworks that are intrinsically fair and just for women rather than always having to adjust, adapt and insist on a gender-balanced application of laws and institutions that are inherently male.

EIGHT

After Security Council resolution 1325

Although resolution 1325 was not a solution, it was an important step in the development of international recognition and response to prevent and confront the use of tactical rape and sexual violence as deliberate strategies in many conflicts. With the limitations noted in Chapter Seven, it acknowledged women's constructed vulnerability in societies that fail to recognise women's human rights and rights to political, economic and cultural equality. Resolution 1325 did provide a basis for additional resolutions strengthening, expanding and reaffirming the importance of confronting tactical rape and sexual violence in conflict. Limitations inherent in the resolution would also be associated with further resolutions – in particular, the reality that states may make resolutions and then ignore them. But, importantly, these resolutions stimulated debate, and member states accepted that sexual violence and tactical rape fell within the mandate of the Security Council because they impacted states' security – even though, as will be considered in Chapter Nine later, the precise type of security was not always clear.

The years between resolutions 1325 (2000) and 1820 (2008)

Resolution 1325 was a welcome step, but achievements were mixed, with continuing tactical rape and sexual violence in conflicts, including those perpetrated by states. One article in 2000 referred to the rape of more than 20,000 women.[1] World Vision and other NGOs reported tactical rape in Kosovo.[2] Reports of widespread rapes in Sierra Leone led to the Special Court for Sierra Leone, established in 2002 by agreement between the UN and the government of Sierra Leone 'pursuant to Security Council Resolution 1325'.[3] The statute of this Special Court allowed 'prosecution of rape as a crime against humanity and

---

[1] Smith, H, 2000, Rape victims' babies pay the price of war, *The Guardian*, 16 April.
[2] Fitzpatrick, B, 1999, *Kosovo – The women and children*, Burwood, VIC: World Vision Australia.
[3] Statute of the Special Court for Sierra Leone, Articles 2-3.

as a violation of common Article 3 to the Geneva Conventions of 12 August 1949 for Protection of War Victims and of Additional Protocol II thereto of 8 June 1977.'[4] In 2007, the Special Court convicted three accused of rape as a crime against humanity and for sexual slavery and forced marriage.[5] This was another judiciary established and operating within a context that was not gender-equitable, although demonstrating some commitment to confronting rape in conflict.

In 2004, hundreds of thousands of Congolese women in the DRC were reported to have been subjected to sexual violence, with reports that 'an estimated 40 rapes occur every day in one province alone'.[6] By 2007, widespread rape was being carried out by all sides to the conflict. A UN expert on violence against women wrote that because of the seriousness and urgency of the situation in the DRC, his visit:

> ... focused mainly on sexual violence, which is rampant and committed by non-state armed groups, the Armed Forces of the DRC, the National Congolese Police and increasingly also by civilians.[7]

His 2007 report continued that in one province alone, records indicated:

> ... 4500 sexual violence cases in the first six months of this year alone. The real number of cases is certainly many times higher as most victims live in inaccessible areas, are afraid to report or did not survive the violence.[8]

What is interesting is that in light of the strategic approaches outlined in resolution 1325, this same UN expert also cautioned against:

> ... singling out sexual violence from the continuum of violence that Congolese women experience, which manifests itself in various forms in their homes and

[4] Ibid.
[5] Special Court for Sierra Leone, 2007, *Prosecutor of the Special Court for Sierra Leone v Alex Tamba Brima, Brima Bazzy Kamara, Santigie Borbor Kanu* (the Africa accused) (judgement) SCSL-2004-16-T at 691, 19 July.
[6] Goodwin, J, 2004, Silence=rape, *The Nation*, 19 February.
[7] UN, *UN expert on violence against women expresses serious concerns following visit to Democratic Republic of Congo*, 30 July 2007.
[8] Ibid.

communities. Violence against women seems to be perceived by large sectors of society to be normal.[9]

This reaffirmed the growing understanding that confronting sexual violence in conflict needed to be approached in the context of confronting generalised violence against women in peacetime. The report recommended that:

> ... empowerment and equality of women, socio–economic development and change of mentalities on gender must be prioritized as integral components of the reconstruction process if sustainable and just peace is to be achieved in the Democratic Republic of Congo.[10]

It was a sign of progress, of course, that there was a UN expert on sexual violence at the UNHCR, and compared with early reports from Special Rapporteurs to the former Yugoslavia and Rwanda, there was an awareness of rape and sexual violence as aspects to be documented. However, while the report reflected resolution 1325, there was a growing sense that it, alone, was insufficient to deal with tactical rape and sexual violence in conflict. A further resolution was needed and was achieved, this time more as a result of state advocacy than pressure from NGOs.

In 2005, the UK began advocating for another resolution that was 'more actionable', to 'specifically address the types of gross human rights violations that were increasingly being reported in conflict-related areas' and 'advance the women, peace and security agenda'.[11] Some women's groups initially resisted a new resolution that might revert to women being seen as vulnerable victims rather than as having strengths that were frequently undermined by societal attitudes and discrimination, an attitude that had begun to change after resolution 1325.[12] A new resolution might also distract from having resolution 1325 fully implemented.[13]

In 2008, the UK and UNIFEM hosted a conference at Wilton Park in the UK, for representatives from UN permanent missions, country

[9]   Ibid.
[10] Ibid.
[11] Achuthan, M, Black, R, 2009, *United Nations resolution 1820: A preliminary assessment of the challenges and opportunities*, September, New York: International Women's Tribune Centre, p 7.
[12] Ibid.
[13] Ibid.

level ministers, military personnel, policy-makers, NGO experts from conflict zones, and practitioners and experts in tackling sexual violence. Shortly after this conference, the US expressed an interest in advancing a resolution during its presidency of the Security Council.[14] While NGOs had little input to the actual wording, the NGO Working Group on Women, Peace and Security (NGOWG) eventually agreed to minimum requirements for the proposed resolution to sustain momentum and attention to the women, peace and security agenda. This set the scene for a debate on 'women, peace and security' and resolution 1820.

The debate before resolution 1820

Preceding resolution 1820 in 2008, there was a significant all-day debate on 'women, peace and security'[15] attended by member states, Pacific Small Island Developing States, the African Union and the European Union (EU). Even with reservations regarding the disconnect between what states' representatives say and what states actually do, it is useful to track input to this debate because this presaged acceptance of sexual violence as an issue within the mandate of the Security Council using the language of 'women, peace and security'. Comments reflected specific interest in the interconnectedness of violence against women and state security, although input from some states' representatives could also be seen as apportioning blame, deflecting attention towards other players or furthering other unrelated agendas.

Considering specific statements helps measure the degree of understanding about the reality and implications of tactical rape – not always seen from the perspective of survivors and victims, but at times from the perspective of states themselves. While this may be galling to women's advocates such as myself, it did lead to some global response when a response was perceived to be in the national interest of states.

The term most frequently used was 'sexual violence', but statements frequently referred directly to rape as a weapon and as a tactic of war. Austria used the term 'tactic', highlighting sexual violence as 'not only a manifestation of war, but a deliberate wartime tactic' as well as a security threat.[16] Argentina recognised 'an increasing use of sexual

---

[14] Ibid, p 9.
[15] UN, *Security Council demands immediate and complete halt to acts of sexual violence against civilians in conflict zones, unanimously adopting resolution 1820 (2008)*, SC/9364, 19 June 2008.
[16] Ibid, p 24.

violence as a political or military tool', noting that 'rape and other heinous forms of sexual violence can be used by agents of the State as a tool to spread terror, to torture and degrade those it considers its "enemies"'.[17] Benin recognised that such violence towards women 'was in full contradiction to international standards.'[18] The Philippines stated that sexual violence was 'deeply rooted in a pervasive culture of discrimination', highlighted by the unequal power equation that denied equal status to women 'which was manifested during conflict through the social, political and cultural norms identifying women and girls as property of men as well as sexual objects.'[19] Liberia noted that sexual violence against women during conflict was embedded in cultural beliefs and practices 'that will have to go'.[20] Panama stated that systematic acts of gender-based violence threatened international peace and security.[21] Taken together, these statements indicated a clearer awareness of the nature, causes and impact of sexual violence. While still a long way from reducing the incidence of sexual violence in conflict, it did at least demonstrate progress in providing a base for understanding and recognising the issue.

Realistically, even if unfairly, if Security Council resolutions were ever to be taken seriously by states, it was essential that what had often been dismissed as 'just' an issue for women had to be accepted as a concern for the Security Council as the forum relating to global governance and state security. This debate settled agreement that tactical rape and sexual violence in conflict did, indeed, fall within the Security Council mandate, with implications that it concerned the security of states (analysed further in Chapter Nine). Condoleezza Rice, then US Secretary of State, holding the Council Presidency, noted long-standing questions about whether the use of rape and sexual violence in conflicts was an issue for the Security Council to address.[22] She declared that the broad and high-level participation and agreement in this debate meant the Security Council would 'affirm that sexual violence against women not only affected the safety of women, but the economic situation and security of their nations.'[23] Member states must hold their troops accountable for any abuse of this recognised expectation that states 'protect and provide justice for

[17]   Ibid.
[18]   Ibid, p 29.
[19]   Ibid, p 26.
[20]   Ibid, p 2.
[21]   Ibid, p 16.
[22]   Ibid, p 6.
[23]   Ibid.

its most vulnerable'.[24] There were frequent references to security of states as well as of women.

However, there was a lack of clarity and no definition of women's security, human security, state security or even international security. The terms were frequently used interchangeably. The UN Secretary-General spoke of sexual violence posing 'a grave threat to women's security in fragile post-conflict countries' and undermining 'efforts to cement peace'.[25] The President of the General Assembly referred to the Assembly's thematic debate on 'human security', demonstrating the importance ascribed to the integration of 'human security perspectives into the Organisation's peace and security work'.[26] He continued that:

> ... people-centred solutions at the crossroads of security, development and human rights must be at the heart of efforts to fight gender-based crimes in conflict situations because such violence against women was an inherent and grave threat to human security.[27]

The UN Deputy Secretary-General said that resolution 1325 demonstrated that sexual violence was not just a gender issue, but also a fundamental security concern.[28]

Other actors supplemented these inputs from UN personnel. Major General Cammaert, a soldier with 39 years' service and a former division commander of the UN's Organization Stabilization Mission in the DRC (MONUSCO), referred to what he had seen of the violence against women and girls in conflict, and said that 'even when conflict formally ended and UN peacekeepers had been deployed, women and girls continued to be targeted'.[29] He continued, 'the current climate of impunity in most post-conflict contexts allows the many forms of violence, including sexual violence to flourish', and added that often the political will to end the vicious cycle of impunity did not exist. He urged, 'sexual violence must be seen as a threat to international peace and security.'[30] Recognition of the threat to states' security was key to moving tactical rape into the scope of the Security Council.

---

[24] Ibid, p 7.
[25] Ibid.
[26] Ibid, p 9.
[27] Ibid.
[28] Ibid.
[29] Ibid, p 10.
[30] Ibid.

Member states contributed references to security of one form or another. Croatia referred to the need for 'social norms' to ensure 'women's physical and economic security', and said that Croatia was integrating a gender perspective into its national security policy.[31] There was further recognition of the links between women's security and states' economic security. The UK highlighted how widespread sexual violence damaged prospects for post-conflict recovery and posed a threat to international peace and security.[32] Belgium referred to international peace and security.[33] Costa Rica declared systematic sexual violence exacerbated conflicts and created obstacles to resolutions.[34] Similar statements were made by Ireland, the Republic of Korea, Tonga and Bosnia and Herzegovina.

These all reflected progress in recognition of an issue for women and communities, states and the international community. Japan said clearly, 'the matter should not be treated as only a women's issue'.[35] This evidenced real change from attitudes early in the 1990s. Ghana ranked rape among core security challenges not to be viewed as only a human rights or women's issue, and for security institutions to work with women's organisations.[36] Numerous calls were for action including intergovernmental oversight of resolution 1325, because responses of states had been 'woefully inadequate'.[37] This was all seemingly positive, but it had to be balanced with the knowledge that it was often states that still perpetrated tactical rape. Rhetoric can be a useful tool for developing a norm, but without any real supporting action, it remains rhetoric.

Possibly recognising this reality, there was some emphasis on response. France believed that peace could not be re-established while remaining silent about the violence done to women; with a realisation that 'law must be supported by action', it promised that the EU would make the issue a priority 'on both political and financial levels'.[38] Specific reference to financial priorities for action sent a strong message that rhetorical commitment must be accompanied by commitment, enabling practical action and providing funds. By contrast, Vietnam urged against unnecessary administrative and financial burdens for

[31]   Ibid, p 11.
[32]   Ibid, p 12.
[33]   Ibid, p 13.
[34]   Ibid, p 15.
[35]   Ibid, p 16.
[36]   Ibid, p 17.
[37]   Ibid.
[38]   Ibid, p 13.

member states.[39] Actually financing steps to achieve the goals set out in resolutions could not be taken for granted, and this was a telling indicator of the importance of budget contributions and allocations. Canada referred to Sudan, the DRC and the wider Great Lakes region requiring a 'security-based response'.[40] Ecuador urged specific Security Council action: 'sexual violence, including violence perpetrated during times of armed conflict, should be systematically and permanently examined by the Council.'[41] Of course, it is an ongoing criticism of resolutions that they usually lack 'teeth' to act to enforce compliance with stated standards and actions.

The debate included calls for normative change as, for example, Israel noted the need for 'change in societal attitudes and norms on sexual violence'.[42]. It also referenced the need to confront societal attitudes such as patriarchy. Germany supported 'a stronger normative and operative framework on gender equality and empowerment'.[43] States actively calling for normative change was a step towards achieving it

Even China and Russia were persuaded to agree to the resolution. A letter from 71 women's organisations in the DRC calling for help was instrumental in engaging them to support the resolution.[44] Russia urged addressing the issue of women, peace and security broadly, 'not just as a matter of sexual violence'.[45] It was more guarded regarding the role of the Security Council, cautioning against 'duplication of efforts in the field' as the draft resolution appeared to be a repetition of work being done by the Assembly.[46] However, the statement included a call for 'strict sanctions, especially in situations where the practice was widespread and systematic'.[47] Admittedly, the nature of such sanctions was not spelled out, but it was a significant inclusion. China condemned sexual violence, called on all governments to investigate and punish those who perpetrated it, while urging that 'sexual violence should not be treated as a stand-alone issue'.[48] There was not a clear

[39] Ibid, p 15.
[40] Ibid, p 22.
[41] Ibid, p 23.
[42] Ibid, p 20.
[43] Ibid, p 25.
[44] Achuthan and Black, op cit, p 9.
[45] UN, *Security Council demands immediate and complete halt to acts of sexual violence against civilians in conflict zones, unanimously adopting resolution 1820 (2008)*, SC/9364, 19 June 2008, p 16.
[46] Ibid.
[47] Ibid.
[48] Ibid, p 14.

commitment to the Security Council undertaking to act on sexual violence in conflict per se, but it was close enough to ensure the resolution would eventually pass. Of course, passing a resolution is only a first step to seeing it implemented, and implementation does not necessarily always follow.

China and Russia were also among the states that focused on the role of the UN itself in confronting rape by its own troops of peacekeepers. The Secretary-General had already noted a policy of zero tolerance for abuses by its peacekeepers.[49] This policy certainly needed affirmation, but one cannot help but feel that a focus on this element of action might be construed as a way of shifting focus away from specific states and ensuring that the UN took its share of responsibility.

So the debate referenced women's security, human security, security linked with development and human rights and security as a threat to international peace and stability. Progress in recognising the links between security and the need to ensure women's right to protection from tactical rape had been made. The links between women's security and the security of states and international stability was implied, but still not clear.

Many states acknowledged that any new resolution needed accountability, benchmarks and focal points in the UN system to ensure follow-up on implementation at national levels. Italy said that the time had come to 'shift gears' in implementing resolution 1325: maintenance of peace and security demanded immediate action.[50] Tanzania called for 'stern measures' to end impunity.[51] It commented on the 'escalation of systematic and brutal acts as calculated tools of war against civilians', clear violation of existing international law requiring Security Council action.[52]

However, recognising the need for accountability and monitoring compliance was a far cry from determining precisely and practically how this should be achieved. The Netherlands referred to NAPs.[53] Spain suggested a study of 'how to structure and institutionalise an efficient response'.[54] Bangladesh noted inadequate understanding of the gender dimensions of conflict, leading to gaps in institutional capacity to address it.[55] These contributions indicated a narrowing of focus, but

[49] Ibid, p 2.
[50] Ibid, p 16.
[51] Ibid, p 25.
[52] Ibid.
[53] Ibid, p 20.
[54] Ibid, p 19.
[55] Ibid.

still did not really detail with whom or where precisely responsibility should be placed.

This debate indicated progress in understanding that sexual violence was an issue of security and whether it was security for women, for humanity, for states or for the international community, it fell within the mandate of the Security Council. The Security Council is a long way from where women survivors and victims of sexual violence experience immediate and long-standing pain, and may be considered in some ways irrelevant. But it is a forum where global policy originates, where states make commitments, where norms can be developed. Even if not all those states act on those commitments and even if they cannot be forced to do so, it is important to have a norm that rejects sexual violence and tactical rape in conflict.

Resolution 1820 (2008)

Resolution 1820 reflected many of these emerging sensitivities and understanding. The first operative paragraph was a strong statement about the reality of tactical rape where the Security Council stressed that sexual violence 'can be used or commissioned as a tactic of war', and recognised that it 'can exacerbate situations of armed conflict and may impede restoration of international peace and security.'[56] It continued that the Security Council:

> ... affirms in this regard that effective steps to prevent and respond to such acts ... can significantly contribute to international peace and security, and expresses its readiness when considering situations on the agenda of the Council, to, where necessary, adopt appropriate steps to address widespread or systematic sexual abuse.[57]

The links between women, peace and security had been explicitly recognised, but the resolution fell just short of saying that acts of sexual violence represented a threat. Expressing readiness to confront sexual violence, it failed to be explicit about the authority and duty of the

---

[56] UN Security Council, *Security Council resolution 1820 (2008) [on women and peace and security]*, S/RES/1820, 19 June 2008, para 1.

[57] Ibid.

Security Council to confront it.[58] It did align sexual violence with situations on the Security Council agenda, implying that it was within the scope of responses and concerns. Some women's groups expressed concern that the resolution applied only to sexual violence and not to other forms of gender-based violence.[59] While a legitimate concern, the resolution maintained momentum on resolution 1325, and continued a strategic approach to women's constructed vulnerability in peacetime as well as in conflict. More specific focus on detailing responses to sexual violence was progress.

Paragraph 5 was a major development. It 'Affirms its intention' when 'establishing and renewing state-specific sanctions' to consider the issue and 'take into consideration the appropriateness of targeted and graduated measures'.[60] Sanctions are a key tool in the armament of the Security Council, and referring to sanctions in the same paragraph as graduated and targeted measures indicated serious concern. The wording may be considered too weak, but its inclusion was important. It is, of course, acknowledged that the likelihood of such sanctions being applied without a veto from China and Russia is slight. However, progress on the issue of women, peace and security has demonstrated that change happens slowly and incrementally rather than in great leaps.

Acceptance of responsibility cleared the way for the Security Council demanding:

> ... the immediate and complete cessation by all parties to armed conflict of acts of sexual violence against civilians with immediate effect.[61]

This was strong language, and the next paragraph continued in similar vein, demanding that all parties protect civilians, including women and girls, from all forms of sexual violence.[62] There remains a vacuum regarding just how this could be enforced, but it did at least set an optimal standard of response.

Responsible agents such as parties to conflict, states in conflict, states, regions and sub-regions were identified to act. Specific action was urged

---

[58] Achuthan and Black, op cit, p 17, referencing Chapter VII: Action with respect to threats to the peace, breaches of the peace and acts of aggression, Charter of the UN, signed in San Francisco, California, 26 June 1945.

[59] Achuthan and Black, op cit, p 22.

[60] UN Security Council, *Security Council resolution 1820 (2008) [on women and peace and security]*, S/RES/1820, 19 June 2008, para 5.

[61] Ibid, para 2.

[62] Ibid, para 3.

on the Secretary-General and UN agencies. Countries contributing forces, civil society, NGOs and police forces were identified for specific action. The role of the Peacebuilding Commission (PBC) was stressed. The PBC was established in 2006 as an intergovernmental advisory body to support peace efforts in countries emerging from conflict, and as a key addition to the broad peace agenda. It brings together relevant actors including international donors and financial institutions, national governments, and troop-contributing countries. Its role includes marshalling resources, advising on and proposing integrated strategies for post-conflict peacebuilding and recovery and, where appropriate, highlighting gaps threatening to undermine peace.[63] The resolution called on the PBC for recommendations regarding how to address sexual violence committed during and post-conflicts.[64] Direct reference to regional bodies in reconstruction and rehabilitation processes proved an astute move, contributing to the formulation of the African Union *Gender policy* of 2009 which called on members and states to use resolutions 1325 and 1820 as points of reference in working to protect women and girls.[65]

Rejection of sexual violence in conflict was to become institutionalised at international level. The Secretary-General was requested to 'systematically include in his written reports to the Council on conflict situations his observations concerning the protection of women and girls and his recommendations in this regard'.[66] This was a major change in procedures. A detailed report on implementing resolution 1820 was requested, although this seemed to be a one-off request for focused follow-up, and concerns about continued reporting needed later clarification.

Resolution 1820 specifically recognised sexual violence used as a tactic of war to deliberately target civilian populations in order to achieve political and military objectives. It referred to sexual violence including widespread or systematic attack on civilian populations and opportunistic attacks as a consequence of environments of impunity.[67] It noted that 'rape and other forms of sexual violence can constitute a war crime, a crime against humanity or a constitutive act with respect

---

[63] See www.un.org/en/peacebuilding/

[64] UN Security Council, *Security Council resolution 1820 (2008) [on women and peace and security]*, S/RES/1820, 19 June 2008, para 11.

[65] African Union, 2009, *Gender policy*, Section III.

[66] UN Security Council, *Security Council resolution 1820 (2008) [on women and peace and security]*, S/RES/1820, 19 June 2008, para 9.

[67] Achuthan and Black, op cit, p 10.

to genocide'.[68] This reflected the work of the international tribunals. The resolution highlighted specific related issues: sexual exploitation and abuse; command responsibility; and abuse arising in UN camps for refugees and internally displaced persons. The general references to sexual violence in conflict evident in resolution 1325 were made more explicit.

Importantly, sexual violence in conflict was not presumed to be inevitable, but was to be confronted. It was a violation of existing laws, to be rejected and opposed and demanding accountability. By affirming the violation of international laws and standards, the resolution presented a tool for advocates, civil society and NGOs to use for appropriate, effective, relevant national legislation. It provided a basis for excluding amnesty and for disallowing impunity for perpetrators.

Missing from resolution 1820 was mention of any specific focal point for ensuring implementation and monitoring states' or even the UN agencies' actions. The International Women's Tribune Centre (IWTC) outlined possible avenues for strengthening the impact of the resolution.[69] They advocated a Security Council Working Group on women, peace and security, similar to the existing working group on children and armed conflict, setting time frames for certain actions, more explicit monitoring and measurements of progress, and preventing widespread violence leading to cultures of impunity and strengthening effective accountability mechanisms to prosecute perpetrators.[70] Recommendations recognised that the situation of women and girls needed to be considered individually for each community or group involved or impacted by conflicts. A concern had emerged that women would be considered an homogeneous group regardless of ethnicity, religion or socioeconomic status, and that gender would be the only lens for women dealing with injustice. It was clear that further work was needed. Resolution 1888 (2009)[71] would fill some of these gaps.

Resolution 1888 (2009)

Resolution 1888 was passed in 2009 to address the lack of specificity in resolution 1820 that had, in its turn, tried to address lack of specificity

---

[68] UN Security Council, *Security Council resolution 1820 (2008) [on women and peace and security]*, S/RES/1820, 19 June 2008, para 4.

[69] Achuthan and Black, op cit, pp 33-9.

[70] Ibid, p 33.

[71] UN Security Council, *Security Council resolution 1888 (2009) [on women and peace and security]*, S/RES/1888, 30 September 2009.

in resolution 1325. Resolution 1888 reaffirmed Security Council concerns about sexual violence as a tactic of war, and reiterated its understanding of the nature, extent and impact of such violence against women. However, it went further than resolution 1820.

Resolution 1820 had demanded that all parties immediately take measures for the protection of women and children. Resolution 1888 demanded measures including 'vetting candidates for national armies and security forces to ensure the exclusion of those associated with serious violations of international humanitarian and human rights law, including sexual violence'.[72] States had to take practical steps, and there was further institutionalisation at the UN. Such institutionalisation is important because it builds on and increases attitudes that dealing with an issue actually matters. It demands more than rhetoric to be applauded but never seriously implemented. The allocation of finances and appointment of dedicated personnel underlines required attention. The Secretary-General was to identify and appoint a Special Representative to provide 'coherent and strategic leadership' in coordination and collaboration with other entities primarily through the interagency initiative UN Action Against Sexual Violence in Conflict in situations of particular concern.[73] The Special Representative was to work with UN personnel on the ground and national governments to strengthen the rule of law and to include information about the prevalence of sexual violence in reports to the Security Council by UN peacekeeping missions. Teams of experts were to be immediately deployed to situations of particular concern with respect to sexual violence in armed conflict, working through the UN, with the consent of host governments, assisting national authorities to strengthen the rule of law.[74] These specific steps provided the leadership and focal points missing in resolution 1820. Responsibilities and responses for practical confrontation of sexual violence were placed clearly within UN structures.

Resolution 1888 addressed concerns about reporting. It called for specific proposals to ensure more effective monitoring and reporting within a time frame of three months.[75] Annual reports were to provide details on perpetrators of sexual violence, and where appropriate, regular reports on individual peacekeeping operations should include information on steps taken within those operations to implement

[72] Ibid, para 3.
[73] Ibid, para 4.
[74] Ibid, para 8.
[75] Ibid, para 26.

measures to protect civilians, particularly women and children, against sexual violence.[76] States were:

> ... to increase access to health care, psychosocial support, legal assistance and socio-economic reintegration services for victims of sexual violence, in particular in rural areas.[77]

These were specific actions to be monitored. Confronting sexual violence in conflict required multifaceted responses. The Secretary-General was to report regularly on implementation of resolution 1888 with information regarding 'parties to armed conflict that are credibly suspected of committing patterns of rape or other forms of sexual violence, in situations that are on the Council's agenda'.[78] Violations of international law regarding sexual violence were being taken seriously.

An important addition was the mention of national and local level leaders, 'including traditional leaders where they exist and religious leaders', with encouragement for them:

> ... to play a more active role in sensitising communities on sexual violence to avoid marginalisation and stigmatisation of victims, to assist with their social reintegration, and to combat a culture of impunity for these crimes.[79]

This recognised roots in cultural and societal attitudes. There would be no international acceptance of cultural or religious differences as excuses for tactical rape or other sexual violence. International norms needed to be substantiated and institutionalised at local levels. For women the danger would be that such leaders would perpetuate discriminatory attitudes and perceptions of women. There also needed to be recognition of the political, social and cultural factors that made women vulnerable. Resolution 1888 omitted specific accountability and implementation mechanisms, but what was pertinent was that it followed so quickly on resolution 1820. The pace of action was increasing.

[76] Ibid, para 25.
[77] Ibid, para 14.
[78] Ibid, para 28.
[79] Ibid, para 15.

Resolution 1889

In 2009 resolution 1889 was also passed unanimously.[80] It emphasised specific elements in resolution 1325, calling for women to be recognised as participants and agents in creating sustainable peace and security. It affirmed that confronting tactical rape required broad strategies to maximise women's capacity and potential to creating their communities and contribute positively to peace and security.

Resolution 1889 was set in the context of the Security Council being:

> ... guided by the purposes and principles of the Charter of the United Nations, and bearing in mind the primary responsibility of the Security Council under the Charter for the maintenance of international peace and security.[81]

The preamble referred to the Secretary-General's report from September 2009 that noted that the breadth of resolution 1325 often meant that 'novelty and creativity' were required in the implementation of the resolution and the difficulties that arose from a 'weak implementation framework and absence of clear targets and reliable data'.[82]Resolution 1889 was a development in that it enumerated concerns and obstacles to women's involvement in 'the prevention and resolution of conflicts and participation in post-conflict public life', and recognised more diverse causes than those recognised in resolution 1325.[83] These were acknowledged as resulting from:

> ... violence and intimidation, lack of security and lack of rule of law, cultural discrimination and stigmatisation, including the rise of extremist or fanatical views on women, and socio-economic factors including the lack of access to education.[84]

This built on references to community and religious leaders in resolution 1888, and provided a balance to the recognition of those

---

[80] UN Security Council, *Security Council resolution 1889 (2009) [on women and peace and security]*, S/RES/1889, 5 October 2009.

[81] Ibid.

[82] UN Security Council, 2009, *Women and peace and security*, S/2009/465, 16 September, para 60.

[83] UN Security Council, *Security Council resolution 1889 (2009) [on women and peace and security]*, S/RES/1889, 5 October 2009, Preamble, para 8.

[84] Ibid.

leaders with the stated need to confront attitudes and practices that rendered women vulnerable. It recognised that the marginalisation of women could delay or undermine the achievement of durable peace, security and reconciliation. Women in situations of armed conflict and post-conflict situations were still 'often considered as victims and not as actors in addressing and resolving situations of armed conflict', and there was 'the need to focus not only on protection of women but also on their empowerment in peacebuilding'.[85] This answered concerns about regarding women merely as victims in issues of peace and security. Women's capacity to engage in public decision-making and economic recovery had often not received adequate recognition or financing in post-conflict situations.[86] Mention of finance often reflects seriousness in approach to issues, so practical action was expected.

A strength of resolution 1889 was that it called for increased participation of women at all levels of the peace process: as high-level mediators and on mediation teams; in peacekeeping; and as special representatives and special envoys.[87] It frequently reiterated that women had a vital place in preventing and resolving conflicts.[88] Gender advisers were to be on relevant missions.[89] Women's development donors were 'urged' to address women's empowerment and insist on transparency in tracking funds.[90] Broad-ranging strategies would confront societal status, attitudes and inequalities contributing to women's vulnerability in peace and in conflict.

Resolutions had become more specific and action-oriented. Resolution 1889 included calls for national policies and practices to collect relevant and, where appropriate, gender-aggregated data to help understand women's needs.[91] The Secretary-General was to:

> ... ensure full transparency, cooperation and coordination of efforts between the Special Representative of the Secretary General on Children and Armed Conflict and the Special Representative of the Secretary General on sexual violence and armed conflict whose appointment has been requested by its resolution 1888 (2009).[92]

[85] Ibid, para 11.
[86] Ibid, para 10.
[87] Ibid, paras 4, 15.
[88] Ibid, paras 1, 8, 15.
[89] Ibid, para 7.
[90] Ibid, para 9.
[91] Ibid, paras 5, 10.
[92] Ibid, para 16.

The Secretary-General was to recommend within six months how the Security Council should receive, analyse and act on information of violations of resolution 1325:

> ... a set of indicators for use at the global level to track implementation of its resolution 1325 (2000), which could serve as a common basis for reporting by relevant United Nations entities, other international and regional organisations, and Member States, on the implementation of resolution 1325 (2000) in 2010 and beyond.[93]

This important and practical step enabled appropriate programmatic responses, as did the request for a review and assessment of the processes by which the Security Council received, analysed and took action on information pertinent to resolution 1325, with recommendations on how to improve coordination across the UN and with member states and civil society.[94] Requesting that all country reports include information on the situation of women and girls reinforced acceptance that this was an issue for the Security Council.[95]

This resolution still failed to identify or refer to specific sanctions for violations of relevant international law and violations of the norm rejecting tactical rape. There were still no strong enforcement measures despite more detailed reporting. However, while the reality was that tactical rape and sexual violence in war continued, international efforts to confront, prevent and bring perpetrators to account were becoming more prevalent, and there was, at least, normative rejection of the violations. Advocates had grounds to require responses of states and of international agencies. The UN was better equipped to support responses – but always within the confines of a global bureaucracy. The challenge would be to ensure effective use of available commitments and resources to confront a pernicious practice that appeared to be ever present.

2010 and beyond

A decade after resolution 1325 the role of women and peace was 'now more clearly integrated into the Council's deliberations', but there remained much more to do before sexual violence was fully

[93]   Ibid, para 17.
[94]   Ibid, para 18.
[95]   Ibid, para 5.

confronted.[96] Despite increased commitment, 'significant achievements are difficult to identify and quantify'.[97] In the first half of 2010, 7 out of 15 Presidential Statements and 13 out of 28 resolutions included a reference to women and security.[98] Still, monitoring impact needed commitment from the Security Council and efficient and effective processing of information coming from UN agencies, states, civil society and NGOs.[99] Reports from experts and specific missions, assessments and commissions of enquiry could be used by the Security Council for information, and it was suggested that the Security Council issue regular media statements to stimulate discussion and momentum.[100] Section IV of the Secretary-General's report to the Security Council in 2010 was a detailed review of the first UN system-wide Action Plan 2008-09 on the implementation of resolution 1325.[101] States and involved non-state actors needed to cooperate to make information collection viable and efficient.

Organisational practices and policies were slowly being implemented. The process towards developing indicators to monitor, analyse and review progress began in April 2010.[102] Twenty-six qualitative and quantitative indicators included some financial tracking.[103] In October 2010, a Security Council Open Debate on women, peace and security considered those indicators, and adopted a non-binding political statement that expressed support for taking them forward but did not specifically endorse them.[104] The fact of this being a non-binding political statement was a sign of reluctance to commit to enforcing compliance with these measures, and reduced the impact that they might otherwise have had on state and non-state actors. However, the adopted statement did allow some relevant operationalisation.

As these organisational and institutional developments were slowly moving, public attention again brought pressure to bear for more rapid and effective response to tactical rape. The Secretary-General reported to the Security Council that widespread rapes carried out by all sides

---

[96] UN Security Council, 2010, *Report of the Secretary-General on women and peace and security*, S/2010/498, 28 September, para 6.

[97] Ibid, para 3.

[98] Ibid, para 78.

[99] Ibid, paras 74, 76.

[100] Ibid, para 89.

[101] Ibid, Section IV.

[102] Ibid, para 112.

[103] Ibid, para 118.

[104] UN Security Council, Statement by the President of the Security Council, S/PRST/2010/22, 26 October 2010.

in the ongoing conflict in the DRC late in July and in August 2010 had 'provoked unprecedented public outrage'.[105] This outrage was sustained and could not be ignored. The Secretary-General noted that sexual violence 'is not specific to any era, culture or continent'.[106] He continued that rape is not synonymous with sexual violence that covers a wider range of acts under international law, and highlighted the fact that disaggregating sexual violence into more specific actions 'permits a more focused approach'.[107] Rejection of tactical rape such as that evident in the DRC was contributing to rejection of other abuses which fell under the general definition of sexual violence. Importantly, the report continued that while sexual violence had long been approached as a matter of reproductive health or development, 'the international community has begun to embrace the concept of conflict-related sexual violence so as to address the security-related social drivers of such violence'.[108] This reinforced the strategic approach to confronting tactical rape: recognising that tactical rape is one element of sexual violence and requiring a broad base of strategies targeting root causes and outcomes.

However, there were ongoing questions about how dealing with sexual violence 'corresponds with the fundamental purpose of security institutions'.[109] The question that appeared to have been comprehensively answered in the debate around resolution 1820 was still being asked. The answer was that while some people saw 'bullets, bombs and blades as war' and rape as a 'random disciplinary infraction or private aspect of culture-based gender relations', sexual violence in conflict must be confronted under definitions found in international law.[110] Understanding of tactical rape as purposeful and political had certainly developed.

It was recognised that in the DRC, the numbers of military casualties were 'dwarfed' by the numbers of rapes, killings and destruction experienced by civilians, so that sexual violence had become a 'front line consideration', that collapse of the rule of law often enables new and more brutal forms of rape, and that the rape of boys and men was being included in the 'repertoire of armed and political violence'

---

[105] UN General Assembly Security Council, 2010, *Report of the Secretary-General on the implementation of Security Council resolutions 1820 (2008) and 1888 (2009),* S/2010/604, para 1.

[106] Ibid, para 3.

[107] Ibid, para 4.

[108] Ibid, para 6.

[109] Ibid, para 7.

[110] Ibid.

as a method of attacking 'community norms and structures'.[111] The Secretary-General reported that it was remarkable that two days after resolution 1820 had been passed and in a conflict where the ICC was investigating a case alleging that the number of rapes far outweighed the number of killings in the CAR, a peace accord between the government and three armed groups was signed with no mention of sexual violence.[112] Progress was certainly not steady but happened in bursts, with always some backwards steps. There was progress in rhetoric and responses at global level while progress at national or local levels remained poor or non-existent. The detailed report of initiatives and progress at implementing resolutions 1820 and 1888 included the reality that, 'tragically, laudable progress at the level of policy has been overshadowed by the surge of sexual violence' in the DRC and its continuing prevalence elsewhere.[113] Recommendations included specific actions. The system of monitoring, analysing and reporting on incidents of sexual violence was proposed in response to a 'gaps analysis' identified in resolution 1888[114] along with applying increased pressure on perpetrators through sanctions, and listing in annual reports the names of those parties engaged in sexual violence in situations of armed violence.[115] Such listing had the potential to publicise and shame violators of what had become a norm rejecting sexual violence. As such this was a practical step towards deterrence.

It was with some relief that advocates saw that the emphasis was generally moving in this direction – towards practical measures and resources – at least at global level. Resolution 1960 followed within weeks with another Open Debate on sexual violence in conflict.[116] It focused on institutional structures and processes to confront sexual violence in conflict, more deliberate protection of women, and rejection of impunity. Specifically, it encouraged inclusion in annual reports to the Security Council, detailed information on 'parties to armed conflict that are credibly suspected of committing or being responsible for acts of rape or other forms of sexual violence', and providing an annexed list of the parties 'that are credibly suspected of committing or being responsible for patterns of rape and other forms of sexual violence in situations of armed conflict on the Security

---

[111] Ibid, para 8.
[112] Ibid, para 15.
[113] Ibid, para 46.
[114] Ibid, para 46(e).
[115] Ibid, para 46(a) and (c).
[116] UN Security Council, *Security Council resolution 1960 (2010) [on women and peace and security]*, S/RES/1960, 16 December 2010.

Council agenda'.[117] The Security Council expressed 'its intention to use this list as a basis for more focused United Nations engagement with those parties, including, as appropriate, measures in accordance with the procedures of the relevant sanctions committees.'[118] This listing mechanism, similar to that relating to offenders against Children and Armed Conflict (CAAC), resolution 1960, obviated the divide between victims according to their age, so that lists of perpetrators include those who offend against women and girls without the cut-off at age 18. There was some concern by women's advocates that this mechanism was limited to situations on the Security Council agenda.[119] The divide between global response and real difference on the ground remained, but at least at global level there was progress. Impunity was being challenged with specific strategies. Reference to the UN Sanctions Committee and to the ICC sent clear political messages. Serious action was proposed with the resolve that 'when adopting or renewing targeted sanctions in situations of armed conflict, to consider including, where appropriate, designation criteria pertaining to acts of rape and other forms of sexual violence', and a quite detailed list of those who would be expected to share relevant information with the UN Sanctions Committee when this consideration was being undertaken.[120] The extent to which member states would eventually accede to such referrals in practice was still to be determined, but the resolve to do so was a major step. All of this progress was, of course, within a context of states resolving action to confront the offence of tactical rape while states continued to offend.

A strong message was sent to states that were called on 'to make and implement specific and time-bound commitments to combat sexual violence'.[121] Some proposed strategies included the 'issuance of clear orders through chains of command prohibiting sexual violence and the prohibition of sexual violence in Codes of Conduct, military field manuals, or equivalent.'[122] States were further called on 'to make and implement specific commitments on timely investigation of alleged

---

[117] Ibid, para 3.

[118] Ibid.

[119] See www.peacewomen.org

[120] UN Security Council, *Security Council resolution 1960 (2010) [on women and peace and security]*, S/RES/1960, 16 December 2010, para 7.

[121] Ibid, para 5.

[122] UN Security Council, *Security Council resolution 1969 (2011) [on Timor-Leste]*, S/RES/1969, 24 February 2011, para 5.

abuses in order to hold perpetrators accountable.'[123] The Secretary-General was to monitor implementation:

> ... of these commitments by parties to armed conflict on the Security Council's agenda that engage in patterns of rape and other sexual violence, and regularly update the Council in relevant reports and briefings.[124]

This time, the Security Council seemed more serious in expecting all parties to act responsibly but the ongoing criticism of the UN generally is that it has little capacity to enforce compliance with resolutions.

The Secretary-General was to establish 'monitoring, analysis and reporting arrangements on conflict-related sexual violence, including rape in situations of armed conflict and post-conflict'.[125] These were to take into account 'the specificity of each country' in order to 'ensure a coherent and coordinated approach at the field level'.[126] The Secretary-General was to:

> ... engage with United Nations actors, national institutions, civil society organizations, health-care service providers, and women's groups to enhance data collection and analysis of incidents, trends, and patterns of rape and other forms of sexual violence to assist the Council's consideration of appropriate actions, including targeted and graduated measures.[127]

The first annual report was due within 12 months.

Forty-three delegates spoke in the Open Debate based largely on the Secretary-General's report.[128] There was general accord that impunity must be ended for violators of international law who perpetrated sexual violence in conflict.[129] Developments included the appointment

---

[123] UN Security Council, *Security Council resolution 1960 (2010) [on women and peace and security]*, S/RES/1960, 16 December 2010, para 5.

[124] Ibid, para 6.

[125] Ibid, para 8.

[126] Ibid.

[127] Ibid.

[128] UN General Assembly Security Council, 2010, *Report of the Secretary-General on the implementation of Security Council resolutions 1820 (2008) and 1888 (2009)*, S/2010/604, 24 November.

[129] UN Security Council, *Security Council resolution 1960 (2010) [on women and peace and security]*, S/RES/1960, 16 December 2010.

of the Special Representative to the Secretary-General on Sexual Violence in Conflict, a new post within the UN structure. The post's wide-ranging mandate covered addressing impunity by supporting national entities to prosecute; empowering women to seek redress; mobilising political leadership; increasing recognition of rape as a tactic and consequence of conflict; and ensuring more coherence in UN response.[130] The Special Representative's priorities included facilitating a rapid response mechanism based on a matrix of indicators; identifying and promoting exemplary responses; urging media attention when there is insufficient attention and under-resourcing for situations of sexual violence in conflict; supporting national institutions; and the development of appropriate government strategies to combat sexual violence.[131] On appointment the Special Representative, Margot Wallstrom of Sweden, urged member states to 'turn the tide against impunity'.[132] She highlighted her authority to inform the Security Council on sanctions, saying, 'In this regard, the leverage that we gain from the credible threat of Council sanctions against perpetrators of sexual violence cannot be overestimated.'[133] Within the limits of its powers the UN did appear to be acting to enforce responses to tactical rape. Wallstrom was correct to emphasise the effect of including even the possibility of sanctions as a measure of the seriousness being given to the issue. Sanctions represent one of the Security Council's most powerful strategies, and it was significant that the issue of tactical rape was even in the field of consideration of using sanctions. Realistically, however, the chances of sanctions ever actually being applied for reasons relating to tactical rape and sexual violence remained remote.

Wallstrom stressed states' national interest for security. She warned that 'where sexual violence has been a way of war, it can destroy a way of life', and went on to note that children accustomed to rape and violence could grow into adults who accepted such behaviour as the norm.[134] 'International peace and security is indivisible from women's peace and security.'[135] She also made the link that survivors and victims of sexual violence are casualties of conflict. This was a way of

---

[130] UN General Assembly Security Council, 2010, *Report of the Secretary-General on the implementation of Security Council resolutions 1820 (2008) and 1888 (2009)*, S/2010/604, 24 November, para 23.

[131] Ibid, para 24.

[132] Security Council SC/10055, 14 October 2010.

[133] Ibid.

[134] Ibid.

[135] UN Security Council, *Security Council resolution 1960 (2010) [on women and peace and security]*, S/RES/1960, 16 December 2010, p 4.

asserting that those survivors and victims had the right to be accorded the same degree of consideration as other casualties. She believed that prosecution of perpetrators equalled protection for victims, noting that, 'rape victims are the only casualties of war that a nation dishonours, rather than honours'.[136] She highlighted the need for effective rule of law and strong legal structures.[137] Support for survivors needs to deal with different levels of trauma, different social impacts and different suffering – but support is still a right to be respected.

The Secretary-General reported on the preparation for a team of experts that would be multidisciplinary and available for rapid deployment to assist governments to reinforce judicial systems weakened by conflict.[138] Other developments included formulating strategies for governments to combat sexual violence in conflict; improving services for victims of sexual violence in conflict and generally strengthening protection from and prevention of sexual violence in conflict; arrangements for improved reporting; defining the roles of women's protection advisers; and dealing with sexual violence in peace and mediation processes.[139] This was serious institutionalisation, and significantly the Secretary-General concluded, 'there can be no security without women's security'.[140]

The days of failing to recognise the interconnectedness of women's human security and international security had passed. At global level, states were being confronted by their responsibilities. Mexico called for strengthening the ICC to enable effective prosecutions. There was no dissent from the resolve to publish the list of perpetrators, no question of the relevance of the issue to the Security Council and no questioning that sexual violence in conflict related to state security. A norm-rejecting behaviour does not equate to a guarantee that that behaviour will be eliminated, but it is a significant development.

Developments continued. In 2013, resolution 2106 affirmed that sexual violence:

> ... when used or commissioned as a method or tactic of war or as a part of a widespread or systematic attack against civilian populations, can significantly exacerbate and

---

[136] Ibid, p 4.
[137] SC/10122 examples: Bosnia and Herzegovina, p 12; Nigeria, p 11.
[138] UN General Assembly Security Council, 2010, *Report of the Secretary-General on the implementation of Security Council resolutions 1820 (2008) and 1888 (2009)*, S/2010/604, 24 November, paras 23, 26.
[139] Ibid, paras. 27-34, 35, 37, 38, 42.
[140] Ibid, para 47.

prolong situations of armed conflict and may impede the
restoration of international peace and security[141]

This demonstrated just how much progress had been made in linking
women's security with state security. Later, in 2013, a UN Press Release
for resolution 2122 noted that:

> International Commissions of Inquiry now routinely
> include gender crimes investigators, as seen in those
> established most recently in the context of Côte d'Ivoire,
> Libya, North Korea and Syria.[142]

However, challenges remain. Conflicts continue and tactical rape
continues. Resolution 2122 set out to design a systematic approach to
the implementation of commitments on women, peace and security
with plans for a High-Level Review of resolution 1325 in 2015, and
the Secretary-General was required to commission a global report
on the implementation gaps and challenges and emerging trends and
priorities for action.[143] Resolution 2122 addressed the rights of women
who become pregnant as a result of rape during conflict, and the need
to ensure that humanitarian aid includes support for access to the full
range of sexual and reproductive health services, including regarding
pregnancies resulting from rape.[144]

As the 2015 target date for reaching the Millennium Development
Goals (MDGs) approached, UN member states, the UN system,
civil society organisations, academia, research institutions and others
cooperated to identify what was called the post-2015 development
agenda.[145] In January 2015, a panel discussion organised by UN Women
on the centrality of gender equality and empowerment of women
and girls for the post-2015 agenda stressed that only a transformative
approach could steer the world onto a more just, equitable and

---

[141] UN Security Council, *Security Council resolution 2106 (2013) [on women and peace and security]*, 24 June 2013, para 1.

[142] UN, 2013, Press Release, referring to S/RES/2122, October 2013.

[143] UN Security Council, *Security Council resolution 2122 (2013) [on women and peace and security]*, S/RES/2122, 18 October 2013.

[144] UN, 2013, Press Release, referring to S/RES/2122, October 2013.

[145] See www.unwomen.org/en/what-we-do/post-2015

sustainable path.[146] Such an agenda can only progress rejection of tactical rape.

Conclusion

Progress between resolution 1325 in 2000 and resolution 1820 in 2008 was slow, but was followed by an acceleration of attention and institutionalisation. Greater understanding of tactical rape and sexual violence in conflict was evidenced in debates, reports and resolutions. Commitment to confront this issue has grown and, importantly, the level of institutionalisation within the Security Council system has been significant.

However, there remain many areas that require greater attention and clarification. The need to confront states that are perpetrators of tactical rape and sexual violence in conflict continues. Condemning such tactics at a global level is a start. There is, at least, an accepted standard of rejection of such violations, and no longer any dismissive attitude that rape in conflict is somehow inevitable. Finding effective mechanisms at global level will be a prolonged process, but this, too, has at least begun. Having tactical rape and sexual violence in conflict on the agenda of the major international security forum is progress. But if survivors and victims are ever to receive the justice to which they have a right, more will need to be done to prevent these violations and to bring to account those who perpetrate them. The rhetoric of states needs to be translated into practice at national, regional and local levels. The context of this progress is overwhelmingly male, and there is much work to be done to ensure gender equality in legal and political environments. When I first approached a male academic at university about a study of how tactical rape and sexual violence in conflict was moving into states' political awareness, his response was, "Well, it is dreadful and sad for women, but you cannot really believe that states or something like the Security Council would take on this issue. It's a women's issue." I would say that it is certainly a women's issue – but just as certainly it is an issue for men, communities, states and the international community. It has now been recognised as such. There has been considerable progress.

---

[146] See www.unwomen.org/en/news/stories/2015/01/ending-gender-inequality-through-the-post-2015-agenda

NINE

Women and security

The Security Council finally began to address and confront tactical rape and sexual violence in conflict as violations of international humanitarian law, and began taking practical steps to institutionalise action to prevent and to prosecute those responsible for these crimes. Significantly, it recognised them as a security threat, falling within the Security Council mandate. The nature of that threat needs to be fully understood. It is a threat that forms the basis for member states, not only the Security Council, to be required to recognise and accept their responsibility to confront tactical rape and sexual violence in conflict.

What sort of security threat?

It is significant that the Security Council has recognised tactical rape and sexual violence in conflict as falling within its mandate as issues of security concern. Writing in 2001, Judith G. Gardam and Michelle J. Jarvis noted that:

> ... for the first time, sexual violence against women during armed conflict was a distinct issue within the UN system. In particular, the sexual abuse of women during armed conflict was linked with the maintenance of international peace and security and the United Nations system as a whole was prompted to respond.[1]

Clarity is needed regarding the nature of those security concerns. Security is not just about the absence of threat and not just about uncovering and addressing sources of insecurity.[2] It is also about providing the values that make a person feel secure. The context for women's security needs to be gendered if women's needs are to fairly and appropriately met. Lee-Koo averred that the key was to reconstruct

---

[1] Gardam, JG, Jarvis, MJ, 2001, *Women, armed conflict and international law*, Netherlands: Kluwer Law International, p 148.

[2] Lee-Koo, K, 2002, Confronting a disciplinary blindness: Women, war and rape in the international politics of security, *Australian Journal of Political Science*, 37, 3, 525–36, p 535.

concepts such as 'international politics' and 'security'.[3] She noted that realists define security in political and military terms as the protection of the boundaries and integrity of the state against the dangers of an anarchical international environment. She concluded that within this discourse, women as a gendered grouping cannot be seen or heard, and are placed outside the realm of the 'international', which threatens lives and engenders gross insecurity in 'silenced and unseen space'.[4] While progress has been made at global level in the Security Council, this remains a context designed with and by male understandings of reality and largely concerned with the security of states.

Women's security – human security – is bound up with the security of states but has its own distinct areas of emphasis, especially regarding tactical rape and sexual violence in conflict. It is essential to appreciate the interconnectedness of human and international security. In 1998, Canada and Norway formed a partnership in human security that subsequently became the Human Security Network, 'an informal coalition of states that is committed to human security'.[5] Eventually, the Commission on Human Security was established and released a seminal report in 2003.[6] That report defined human security as protecting vital freedoms.[7] It means protecting people from critical and pervasive threats and situations, building on their strengths and aspirations. It means creating systems that give people 'the building blocks of survival, dignity and livelihood'.[8] Human security connects different types of freedoms – freedom from want, freedom from fear and freedom to take action on one's own behalf.[9]

When considering how human security can be delivered, the report offered two general strategies: protection and empowerment.[10] Protection shields people from dangers. It requires a concerted effort to develop norms, processes and institutions that systematically address insecurities. Empowerment enables people to develop their

[3] Ibid, p 535.

[4] Ibid, p 527.

[5] von Tigerstrom, B, 2006, International law and the concept of human security, in U Dolgopol and J Gardam, *The challenge of conflict: International law responds*, Leiden and Boston, MA: Martinus Nijhoff Publishers, p 603.

[6] Commission on Human Security, *Outline of the report of the Commission on Human Security*, http://www.cfr.org/content/publications/attachments/Human_Security. pdf

[7] Ibid

[8] Ibid, p 1.

[9] Ibid, p 1.

[10] Ibid.

potential and become full participants in decision-making. Protection and empowerment are mutually reinforcing – both strategies are required. Women have been seen as in need of protection, but this often means a failure to empower them so they can utilise their innate strengths and capacities. It also often means that women are specifically disempowered, which renders them vulnerable and therefore perceived as in need of protection – a cycle that has to be broken.

In 2006, B. von Tigerstrom noted that human security offered a way of 'identifying and prioritizing issues to be addressed in respect of international law and conflict'.[11] Recognition by policy-makers of the interdependence of women's security and international security meant recognition of the interdependence of human security and state security. This was an important step as it was a recognition long espoused and promoted by feminists, activists and some NGOs, but largely ignored by power brokers.

In March 2010, the Secretary-General presented a summary report on human security to the UN General Assembly.[12] He referred to (inter alia) the Human Security Network, the report of the Commission on Human Security and the 2005 World Summit that had considered human security, and stated that the concept 'is gaining wide support in the United Nations and other forums'.[13] In a debate in the General Assembly in May 2008:

> ... broad consensus was reached by Member States on the need for a new culture of international relations that goes beyond fragmented responses and calls for comprehensive, integrated and people-centred approaches.[14]

As part of this new awareness it was noted that:

> ... human security draws attention to a wide range of threats faced by individuals and communities and focuses on the root causes of such insecurities. In addition, by understanding how particular constellations of threats to individuals and communities translate into broader intra- and inter-State security breaches, human security seeks to prevent and mitigate the occurrence of future threats, and

[11] von Tigerstrom, op cit, p 614.
[12] UN General Assembly, 2010, *Home security*, A/64/701, 8 March.
[13] Ibid, para 1.
[14] Ibid, para 7.

in this regard can be a critical element in achieving national security and international stability.[15]

The Security Council recognised that tactical rape and sexual violence in conflict, as breaches of international humanitarian law, were threats to international stability. This was a route to securing women's protection, and was welcomed as long as it also meant women's empowerment, enabling women to use their own inherent power.

Human security is vital, but it complements state security rather than replacing it.[16] As part of states' populations, women need those states to be secure, and importantly they may need protection from those states. The concept of state security has developed from securing borders, institutions and values to greater recognition of individuals and communities in ensuring their own security.[17] Human security broadens the focus from the security of borders to the lives of people and communities inside and across those borders.[18] It puts people at the centre of focus, with a requirement for freedom from fear, from want, and to live in dignity.[19]

The 2011 *World development report* used the term 'citizen security', claiming it sharpened the focus on freedom from physical violence and from fear of violence.[20] There are reservations about the use of the term 'citizen' as women are often excluded from real citizenship with allied political and economic access. As early as 1997, Ann Tickner had argued that terms such as 'citizen', 'head of household' and 'breadwinner' are not neutral terms and are can be problematic for women.[21] She recalled that previously security had been defined in the realist paradigm, in political/military terms, as the protection of the boundaries and integrity of the state and its values against the dangers of a hostile international environment. In the 1980s there began a trend towards defining security in economic and environmental terms as well as in political and military terms.[22] Where early considerations of security focused on the causes and consequences of wars from a top-

---

[15] Ibid, para 25.
[16] Commission on Human Security, op cit.
[17] Ibid, p 5.
[18] Ibid, p 6.
[19] Ibid, p 1.
[20] World Bank, The, 2011, *World development report: Conflict, security and development*, Washington, DC: The World Bank, p 106.
[21] Tickner, A, 1997, "You just don't understand": troubled engagements between feminists and IR theorists, *International Studies Quarterly*, 41, 4, December, p 627.
[22] Ibid, p 624 (see notes 59 and 155).

down perspective, feminists were more concerned with communities or individuals, with analysis of the impact of conflict and related violence to understand the extent to which unjust social relations contribute to insecurity.[23]

Women's security, human security and state security

The 2011 *World development report* provided insights into the interdependence of women's security, state security and sexual violence in conflict.[24] It reiterated that states are part of an international system that confers certain benefits and requires certain behaviours.[25] The required behaviours include: helping to maintain interstate security by not threatening each other and by observing 'rules of warfare'; and upholding international law and treaty obligations and behaviour at home consistent with international norms such as upholding human rights.[26] Importantly, these expectations now include rejection of tactical rape and sexual violence in conflict because such violations are acknowledged as breaches of the rules of warfare, of international law and treaty obligations and contraventions of international norms regarding human rights. States that do not meet these expectations create stresses between states. Major stresses that are likely to result in violence between or within states are often a combination of security, economic and political stresses.

Conflict in one state can destabilise the security of its neighbouring states. Violence has an economic impact and disrupts development community-wide for long periods. The *World development report* estimated that it takes an average of 14 years of peace before resumption of economic growth paths.[27] The violence in Rwanda in the 1990s spread over into the DRC with the outflow of refugees and unresolved conflicts between the Hutu and Tutsi. Development consequences of violence, like its origins, spill across borders with implications for the neighbours, the region and globally.[28] Estimates suggest that countries lose 0.7% of their annual GDP for each neighbour engaged in a civil

---

[23] Tickner, A, 2001, *Gendering world politics: Issues and approaches in the post-Cold War era*, New York: Columbia University Press, p 48.

[24] The World Bank, op cit; Human Security Report Project, 2010, *Human security report 2009: The causes of peace and the shrinking costs of war*, Vancouver, BC, www.hsrgroup.org/human-security-reports/20092010/overview.aspx

[25] The World Bank, op cit, p 109.

[26] Ibid.

[27] Ibid, p 63.

[28] Ibid.

war.[29] There is a shared interest in global, regional and state peace and prosperity, and a shared interest in ensuring security for populations.

Political and economic issues can be triggers for violence and conflict within states. Injustice and exclusion can also act as stresses on security, and there has been found to be a strong correlation between past human rights abuses and current risks of conflict.[30] Most contemporary armed conflicts are 'low intensity' civil wars that avoid major military engagements but frequently target civilians with great brutality, and include the threat and perpetration of sexual and physical violence against women and children as a systematic weapon of war.[31]

For political, economic and humanitarian reasons, no country or region can afford to ignore areas where repeated cycles of violence flourish, or where men or women are disengaged from protection and participation in the workings of the state. Human security is a pre-eminent goal underpinned by justice and economic independence, and there is a need for states as well as the international community to act pre-emptively before violence recurs or escalates.[32] Survivors of tactical rape and sexual violence frequently suffer from discrimination and exclusion that renders them economically and socially isolated. Many women rear children of rape in poverty. Many also wait for some acknowledgement of their suffering and for justice. State actors as well as civil society have a responsibility to participate in the empowerment and protection of all their population, including women. Where state actors have been party to attacking or rendering women vulnerable, there should be adequate means of holding them accountable. The role of the ICC, ICJ and criminal tribunals may be part of this response. The period of transition from conflict to peace is often critical. If social protection and empowerment is delivered only through international humanitarian aid, then governments and communities have few incentives to take responsibility for the prevention of violence, and nor do national institutions have incentives to take on responsibility for protecting all vulnerable citizens.[33]

Relevant to dealing appropriately with tactical rape and sexual violence is the recognition that emerged by 2011 that it is incorrect to think of the progression from violence to sustained security as linear. Almost every civil war begun after 2003 was a resumption of a

---

[29] Ibid, p 65.
[30] Ibid, p 82.
[31] Ibid, p 60.
[32] Ibid, p 252.
[33] Ibid, p 253.

previous civil war.[34] The impact of tactical rape and sexual violence is long-lasting. If action is not taken to bring perpetrators to justice, to meet the physical, psycho-social and economic needs of survivors and victims of tactical rape and sexual violence, and to confront the root causes of women's constructed vulnerability, the potential for recurring violence increases. As was seen in the conflicts in both Rwanda and the former Yugoslavia, perpetrators of violence were often convinced that they were avenging previous injustices. Failure to offer support, to challenge societal attitudes such as rejection of the victims of rape, failure to achieve some sort of accountability and disallow impunity – all of these failures may be the foundation for the next wave of violence.

The children born of tactical rape in the conflicts in Rwanda and the former Yugoslavia became adults growing up in societies dealing with the trauma of conflicts. For the most part they will have been reared by mothers likely to be suffering extreme physical and/or emotional damage. Many of these children and their mothers will have suffered from social stigma, discrimination and ostracisation. Economic effects may have been significant. Mothers may have had additional trauma seeing their offspring rejected by their communities. Many of these children are reported to have grown up with a sense of being the children of criminal acts by men perceived as 'the enemy'. A doctor from the DRC reported the words of a 22-year-old woman made pregnant by being raped by 10 combatants who also killed her husband in front of her, providing further representation of the impact that rape has in Congolese communities:

> Today, when I walk with my baby, the people in the community say that I am the enemy's woman, and that the child belongs to the enemy.... I am alone. What I find upsetting is that nobody will come near my baby; everybody says he is cursed. And the baby is frightened because the neighbours are always shouting at him.[35]

The challenge is that for human security to be achieved, such attitudes and their consequent suffering for women and child victims of tactical rape and sexual violence must be confronted. Appropriate services in healthcare, economic support, social reintegration, emotional counselling, community education and institutional reform of justice

[34] Ibid, p 57.
[35] Amnesty International, 2004, *Democratic Republic of Congo: Mass rape – Time for remedies*, 25 October, p 35.

and security agencies and delivery of justice all need to be determined with women's participation. Then such services and programmes need to be resourced and delivered to all survivors of rape in conflict, the women who suffered directly, the children born of those rapes, and their communities. The approach to survivor care must assist all those who are survivors of the general trauma of the conflicts as well as involving men, where possible.[36]

Specific responses of states vary. Scott, Billingsley and Michaelson highlighted that the West 'ultimately acted decisively to address problems of the disintegrating Yugoslavia, but ignored the Rwandan genocide, a human rights tragedy on an even larger scale'.[37] The relationship between the Security Council and sovereign states is in ongoing tension. Scott et al recognised: 'the task is not to find alternatives to the Security Council as a source of authority but to make the Security Council work better than it has'.[38] This would include ensuring that gender bias is confronted. The outcome document of the 2005 World Summit stated that each individual state has the responsibility to protect its population from genocide, war crimes, ethnic cleansing and crimes against humanity. This may seem a statement of the obvious, but state actors are among the perpetrators of such serious crimes despite global rhetoric. Where a state does not provide such protection, other states have a responsibility to intervene – and the Security Council has established grounds for doing so when sexual violence is used against populations. Gareth Evans noted that the debated Responsibility to Protect (R2P) is relevant in specific and narrowly focused problem areas.[39] These are situations where widespread atrocity crimes are clearly being committed or where such crimes are imminent according to warning signs.

Evans acknowledged that it is more difficult to pin down countries where serious violations of international law are likely in the future, perhaps because of history of such crimes, continuation or re-emergence of relevant internal tensions and incapacity to control

---

[36] Harvard Humanitarian Initiative, with support from Oxfam International, 2010, 'Now the world is without me': An investigation of sexual violence in Eastern Democratic Republic of Congo, April, Cambridge, MA: Harvard Humanitarian Initiative, p 9.

[37] Scott, SV, Billingsley, AJ, Michaelson, C, 2010, International law and the use of force: A documentary and reference guide, Santa Barbara, CA, Denver, CO and Oxford: Praeger Security International ABC-CLIO, LLC, p 108.

[38] Ibid.

[39] Evans, G, 2010, The responsibility to protect: consolidating the norm, Paper presented at the 39th IPA Conference on the UN Security Council and the responsibility to protect, Vienna, Favorita Papers, 1/2010.

potentially explosive situations.[40] Rwanda and the former Yugoslavia are among countries that could be assessed as likely for re-emergence of tensions and renewed violence because each was a form of civil war, and as Barbara Walter asserts, 'since 2003 *every* civil war that has started has been a continuation of a previous civil war'.[41] Without credible settlement or peace processes, the cycle of violence will continue.[42] I argue that there will be potential for renewed violence in states where there is no accountability, where there is impunity, where there is no redress or reparation, no attention to children of tactical rape and no change in the societal attitudes and status of women. But intervention will be a political step, and it would appear that, 'the approach whereby policy considerations will override legal considerations in cases of emergencies is likely to dominate'.[43] It is at least now established that tactical rape and sexual violence in conflict are contraventions of international humanitarian law, and they present a threat to women's security, to human security and to international security. It remains to be seen how often international or state intervention to redress these violations follow such abuses and threats – particularly where state actors are the perpetrators.

There are ongoing discussions regarding the specific responsibilities of Security Council states with the power of veto that prevent action to provide security for at-risk populations, including women and girls. There have been increasing calls by UN member states and civil society for voluntary restraint on the use of the veto by the Permanent Members of the Security Council, known as the 'P5', in widespread atrocity situations. The government of France, alongside the 22-member Accountability, Coherence and Transparency (ACT) group at the UN, has been at the forefront in pushing this initiative calling on the P5 to 'collectively renounce their veto powers' in widespread atrocity situations, such as genocide, crimes against humanity and war crimes.[44] This proposal had more than 40 states supporting it in 2015.[45]

The international community and states concerned about human and international security have a responsibility to ensure accountability for those who fail to respect agreed international law and treaties,

---

[40] Ibid.

[41] Walter, BF, 2010, *Conflict relapse and the sustainability of post-conflict peace*, September.

[42] Ibid.

[43] Scott et al, op cit, p 110.

[44] See www.globalpolicy.org/component/content/article/200-reform/52474-reforming-the-working-methods-of-the-un-security-council-the-act-initiative.html

[45] Amnesty International, 2015, *Annual report 2014/2015*.

including other state and non-state actors. Such accountability must be evident as soon as possible after cessation of hostilities – the period of transitional justice is a key factor in the provision of security for victims and survivors of tactical rape and sexual violence, and requires state-level action. Prioritisation of basic security and justice reforms programmes has been part of successful core tools to develop resilience to violence.[46] This needs to be a priority wherever there has been ongoing violence, particularly where there has been tactical rape and sexual violence, if the cycles of violence are to be broken. Promoting democratic principles promotes human security and development. This requires building strong institutions, establishing the rule of law and empowering people.[47]

State-level institutionalisation of security

Legitimate institutions and governance serve as an immune system and defence against ongoing conflict for states.[48] The legitimacy of institutions refers to their capacity, inclusiveness and accountability.[49] Where institutions and governance are not legitimate, a state can be fragile in terms of development and political security, and more vulnerable to civil war. Of 17 fragile states (as measured by The World Bank) between 1990 and 2008, 14 experienced major civil wars.[50] Recognised institutional indices relevant to the reduction of violence (including sexual violence) include 'rule of law; levels of corruption; respect for human rights; democratic governance; bureaucratic quality; oversight of security sectors and equity for the disadvantaged.'[51] These indices can indicate the need to act to prevent conflict.

Tactical rape and sexual violence against women can also be signs of rising tensions and incipient conflict. Continuation of these violations indicates that peace has not been achieved in a state. Rosan Smits and Serena Cruz noted that 'rape is seen as strategy for undermining efforts to achieve and maintain stability in areas torn by conflict but striving to achieve peace'.[52] Ongoing rape and sexual violence after cessation of hostilities can constitute part of the long-lasting effect of

[46] The World Bank, op cit, p 255.
[47] Commission on Human Security, op cit.
[48] The World Bank, op cit, p 50.
[49] Ibid, p 84.
[50] Ibid, p 87.
[51] Ibid, p 108.
[52] Smits, R, Cruz, S, 2011, Increasing security in DR Congo: gender responsive strategies for combating sexual violence, *CRU Policy Brief*, June, p 2.

such crimes, and can spread into peacetime practice, when norms are broken down and there is a perceived impunity for perpetrators. The cyclical nature of many conflicts means that attention must be paid to indicators of potential conflict, even as peace seems to be established. Paul D. Williams noted, when writing about protection of civilians in peace operations, that when deterrence of events such as massacres is the objective, there is a need to strengthen global norms, reinforcing certain values to the point where it is well understood they must not be violated.[53] This is a principle that must be applied to deterrence of renewed tactical rape and sexual violence in conflicts because, as can be seen in the DRC, when 'norms of war are internalised into everyday male behaviour', sexual violence continues after conflict ceases.[54] The challenge is to support states to internalise normative rejection of tactical rape and sexual violence in war as an integral part of their planning and responses to protect their populations. This may act as a deterrent to further involvement in these crimes as well as appropriate transitions to justice after they have occurred.

Even when rape and sexual violence are not tactical or part of a systematic use as a weapon, they are indicative of tensions. They should be used as warning signs of armed conflict and indicate the need for prevention strategies.[55] Within a state, underlying weaknesses that increase risks of repeated cycles of violence have been identified as deficits in security, in justice and inadequate job creation.[56] As rejection of tactical rape and sexual violence in conflict moves from international to national levels to confront security risks, there are justifiable concerns of feminist analysts regarding the nature of political and institutional structures. Jacqui True's insightful review concluded that 'malestream' visions of international relations distort knowledge of both 'relations' and 'international' transformation, and concluded:

> ... if one wants to gain fresh insights into the processes of transformation of world order, averting one's gaze from the processes of state formation ... has its limits as a research strategy.[57]

[53] Williams, PD, 2010, Enhancing civilian protection in peace operations: insights from Africa, *The Africa Center for Strategic Studies*, September, 53-4.
[54] GSDRC, 2009, *Conflict and sexual and domestic violence against women*, 1 May , p 9.
[55] Ibid, p 2.
[56] The World Bank, op cit, p 248.
[57] True, J, 2001, Feminism, in S Burchill, R Devetak, A Linklater, M Paterson, C Reus-Smit and J True, *Theories of international relations*, New York: Palgrave Macmillan, p 265.

True has provided a reminder that throughout modern history:

> ... women have been told that they will receive equal human rights, equality with men, after the war, after liberation, after the national economy has been rebuilt, and so on: but after all these "outside" forces have been conquered, the commonplace demand is for things to go back to normal and women to a subordinate place.[58]

If the rejection of tactical rape and sexual violence in conflict is to be reflected in state institutions, it is imperative to avoid the tendency to delay women's security, justice and strengthening of their positions in societies. Eric Blanchard highlighted that 'feminist security theory articulates an alternative vision', which entails 'revealing gendered hierarchies, eradicating patriarchal structural violence and working towards the eventual achievement of common security'.[59] There is at least – and at last – some progress in recognising the need for women's security, but Blanchard continued:

> Ironically, the policy world of nation states has recently begun to outpace the academic discipline of International Relations in its acceptance of feminist issues, as evidenced by the rapid diffusion of "gender mainstreaming" bureaucracies and gender sensitive policies across states from a diverse range of cultures and levels of gender equality.[60]

It would be reasonable but probably optimistic to assume that security reform will follow the inclusive and restructured approach of feminist security theory. Much further research, analysis and comment to support advocacy for women's security is needed. As the policy world of states and the international community continues to evolve, some tasks are still far from completed.

However, there has been useful work done regarding how strengthening women's security, justice and equality at state level has had an impact on international stability. Mary Caprioli and Mark

[58] Ibid, p 248.
[59] Blanchard, E, 2003, Gender, international relations and the development of feminist security theory, *Signs: Journal of Women in Culture and Society*, 28, 4, p 1305.
[60] Ibid, p 1306, quoting True, J, Mintrom, M, 2001, Transnational networks and policy diffusion: the case of gender mainstreaming, *International Studies Quarterly*, 45, 1, p 29.

Boyer claimed that states exhibiting high levels of gender equality also exhibit lower levels of violence in international crises and disputes.[61] Caprioli extended this analysis to militarised interstate disputes, and found a similar relationship where 'states with the highest levels of gender equality display[ed] lower levels of aggression in these disputes and were less likely to use force first'.[62] Working with Peter Trumbore, Caprioli found:

> ... states characterized by norms of gender and ethnic inequality as well as human rights abuses are more likely to become involved in militarized interstate disputes and in violent interstate disputes, to be the aggressors during international disputes, and to rely on force when involved in an international dispute.[63]

As understanding of the full impact of tactical rape and sexual violence has grown, and so, too, has the understanding of its implications for states' development and international security. In 2006, UN Secretary-General Kofi Annan was of the opinion that:

> ... the world is starting to grasp that there is no policy more effective [in promoting development, health, and education] than the empowerment of women and girls. And I would venture that no policy is more important in preventing conflict, or in achieving reconciliation after a conflict has ended.[64]

Recognising such interdependence between women's equality, justice and security with international security is important.

[61] Caprioli, M, Boyer, MA, 2001, Gender, violence, and international crisis, *Journal of Conflict Resolution*, 45, 4, August, 503-18.
[62] Caprioli, M, 2003, Gender equality and state aggression: the impact of domestic gender equality on state first use of force, *International Interactions*, 29, 3, July/September, 195-214, quoted in Hudson, VM, Caprioli, M, Ballif-Spanvill, B, McDermott, R, Emmett, CF, 2009, The heart of the matter: the security of women and the security of states, *International Security*, 33, 3, Winter, 7-45.
[63] Caprioli, M, Trumbore, PF, 2006, Human rights rogues in interstate disputes, 1980-2001, *Journal of Peace Research*, 43, 2, March, 131-48, quoted in Hudson et al, op cit.
[64] Annan, K, 2006, No policy for progress more effective than empowerment of women, Secretary-General says in remarks to Woman's Day Observance, UN press conference, 8 March.

Basic principles for sustained violence prevention and recovery have also been identified: inclusive-enough coalitions for change; some early results to build confidence and create momentum for longer-term institutional transformation; and pragmatic best-fit options to address immediate challenges.[65] Where lack of accountability has been a source of tension, strategies need to focus on responsiveness to citizens and to act against abuses perpetrated during a conflict.[66] I argue that confronting the impact of tactical rape and sexual violence, early results in justice and accountability for these violations as well as broader democratic accountability is particularly essential as women, their children and their communities struggle to confront crimes and to end the impunity of perpetrators. It has been noted that the inclusion of populations affected and targeted by violence has been productive, and that 'including women leaders and women's groups has a good track record in creating continued pressure for change'.[67] This may seem self-evident to those who are aware of structural discrimination against women, but at least it is now being officially more widely recognised as an effective approach to rehabilitation and reconstruction activities as they pertain to building and reforming security institutions after periods of extreme sexual violence in conflict.

Security sector reform and transitional justice

After conflict the security sector of states involved usually requires reform, particularly in arenas where security forces have been implicated in tactical rape and sexual violence. Security sector reform operations need to cover a range of strategies and actions: demilitarisation and peacebuilding; establishing civilian control and oversight of the security sector; professionalising the security forces; and strengthening the rule of law.[68] Such reform typically involves defining a country's long-term security needs and vision; conducting an audit of existing security sector institutions, laws, policies and capacities; identifying structural issues, discriminatory practices and other barriers to meeting state security requirements; and developing a plan to bridge the gap between what exists and what is needed to provide effective security.[69]

[65] The World Bank, op cit, p 248.
[66] Ibid, p 249.
[67] Ibid, p 250.
[68] UN Women, Women and security sector reform, www.unwomen.org/en/what-we-do/peace-and-security
[69] Ibid.

If these actions and processes are inclusive, they can be productive in strengthening local ownership of peacebuilding processes by enabling those affected to have a role in change and building their confidence in state security agencies.

Without being enabled to participate, women in particular are unlikely to see reason to trust these agencies. I argue that it is reasonable and sensible and just for women to have a role in designing and implementing processes and systems that recognise their trauma and that provide appropriately for survivors to testify and ensure official accountability for the wrongs they have suffered. Women who have experienced tactical rape and sexual violence in conflict will have particular concerns about the trustworthiness of the police, military and security sector representatives where those sectors have been involved in perpetrating, condoning, even of ignoring those crimes. Women may also have trepidation about the role of judiciaries where they may struggle to be afforded their rightful justice. Addressing this issue and institutionalising security provision involves a broad set of reforms, such as excluding ex-combatants who are known to have committed sexual violence from security sector positions; establishing specialised police units for investigating crimes of tactical rape and sexual violence in war; recruiting more women into the security sector; strengthening the capacity of health services to collect forensic evidence; and providing legal services to victims.[70] In Rwanda, for example, the UN agency, UN Women, has provided support to strengthen female parliamentarians' oversight role, to improve women's access to justice through the National Police Gender Desk, to develop protocols and policies on sexual and gender-based violence, to improve services for victims, and partnering on gender-sensitive reform with other security sector institutions.[71]

Security sector reform is intended to transform security sectors and systems, 'which includes all the actors, their roles and responsibilities – working together to manage and operate the system in a manner which is more consistent with democratic norms'.[72] This cannot be achieved when women survivors of tactical rape and sexual violence are excluded. A UNIFEM *Workshop on gender and security sector reform* in 2003 concluded that gender-responsive security sector reform requires normative, institutional and procedural reform of security institutions

[70] Ibid.
[71] Ibid.
[72] OECD, 2005, *Security system reform and governance*, DAC Guidelines and Reference Series, Paris: OECD, p 20.

that includes a commitment to protect women, to advance their rights and practical access to services, to ensure policies are translated into instructions and incentives for implementers.[73] This must apply to women who have suffered and survived tactical rape and sexual violence, and a particular point of focus must be their first contact with security and justice systems. It is essential to work with traditional authorities to raise awareness of women's security needs.[74] The needs of women also need to be recognised in general policy-making processes that follow cessation of hostilities. These would include the development of national security policies, peace agreements, codes of conduct and the strategies of donors and international organisations.[75]

A major area of concern for survivors of tactical rape and sexual violence in conflict is the need for transitional justice. An important aspect of tactical rape and sexual violence is that impact does not necessarily cease after cessation of hostilities. Even when conflict appears to have ceased there can be an ongoing context with prevalent damage to social behaviours and behavioural norms. Sexual violence as a tool of conflict can become a way of life: once entrenched in the fabric of civilian society, it lingers long after 'the guns have fallen silent'.[76] During conflict the priority should be to protect civilians and halt tactical rape and sexual violence by armed elements. After conflict the priority should be to avoid a repetition of patterns of violence and exclusion, thus preventing the 'normalisation' of brutal and widespread sexual violence committed by security forces, combatants and non-combatants alike.[77]

In 2007, Médecins Sans Frontières (MSF) commented that the extent of sexual violence against women in the DRC was significant as an indicator of the breakdown of social relationships after so many years of conflict.[78] They argued that 'social norms' had been considerably weakened, allowing individuals to engage in acts of extreme violence with almost absolute impunity.[79] This perception of impunity was

---

[73] UNIFEM, 2009, *Workshop on gender and security sector reform*, Summary, September, p 3.

[74] Ibid, pp 7–8.

[75] Ibid.

[76] UN General Assembly Security Council, 2010, *Report of the Secretary-General on the implementation of Security Council resolutions 1820 (2008) and 1888 (2009)*, S/2010/604, para 14.

[77] Ibid, para 21.

[78] Médecins Sans Frontières, 2007, *Ituri: 'Civilians still the first victims'*: *Permanence of sexual violence and military operations*, Geneva, October, p 20.

[79] Ibid.

linked with the justice system in the DRC, described by the UN as being in a 'deplorable state' and with widespread reports of corruption and political interference.[80] This was recognition of the broad impact of tactical rape and sexual violence and the need for strategies to confront and reform a seriously flawed security sector. MSF continued:

> In rare cases where women brave all obstacles and dare to report sexual violence, it has been widely reported that senior officers shield the men under their command from prosecution and deliberately obstruct investigations. Intrinsically linked to addressing the widespread impunity within the DRC will be the task of changing society's attitude towards victims of rape and sexual violence. Changing such attitudes represents an enormously difficult and complex task as they are embedded within societal values and customary law.[81]

Changing attitudes is difficult, but an essential strategy will be the achievement of effective transitional justice.

Transitional justice refers to the set of judicial and non-judicial measures that have been implemented by different countries in order to redress the legacies of widespread human rights abuses. It has been recognised that:

> ... transitional justice mechanisms can be critical in helping societies cope with the legacies of conflict, including widespread human rights violations. Through both judicial and non-judicial means, transitional justice aims to rebuild social trust, reform justice systems and law enforcement institutions, strengthen accountability for war crimes, promote national reconciliation, support those affected by conflict, and advance democratic governance.[82]

Given the possibility of renewed conflict when issues are unresolved and there are generational impacts of tactical rape, justice needs to be

---

[80] UN, *UN expert on violence against women expresses serious concerns following visit to Democratic Republic of Congo*, 30 July 2007, quoted in Médecins Sans Frontières, op cit, p 20.

[81] Médecins Sans Frontières, op cit, p 20.

[82] UN Women, Transitional justice, www.ictj.org/about/transitional-justice

delivered during the recovery period for communities, survivors and victims.

According to the International Center for Transitional Justice (ICTJ) there are four core elements of transitional justice. The first is criminal prosecutions, particularly those that address perpetrators considered to be the most responsible.[83] The second is reparations, through which governments recognise and take steps to address the harms suffered (such initiatives often have material elements such as cash payments or health services as well as symbolic aspects such as public apologies or day of remembrance).[84] The third core element is institutional reform of abusive state institutions such as armed forces, the police and courts, to dismantle, by appropriate means, the structural machinery of abuses and to prevent the recurrence of serious human rights abuses and impunity.[85] The final core element identified is truth commissions or other means to investigate and report on systematic patterns of abuse, recommend changes and help to understand the underlying causes of serious human rights violations.[86]

Truth commissions may negotiate a degree of immunity in exchange for testimony and may grant some collective amnesties, often a compromise between justice and peace. There may be tensions arising from each of these approaches, and some may be selected according to local practices. There may also be the use of traditional courts, although in Rwanda, for example, these have a mixed degree of success, reinforcing the need to complement the use of community-based justice systems with building formal justice systems.[87]

Transitional societies emerging from serious conflict 'often adopt amnesty laws to consolidate fragile peace or fledgling democracy'.[88] For women and communities recovering from tactical rape and sexual violence, amnesty is unlikely to be acceptable as a viable alternative to accountability, even when governments might want to further other goals relating to recovery. The warnings of Jacqui True regarding promises made to women by recovering governments but which are not eventually delivered must be noted.[89] The institutions to support these elements of transitional justice, often requiring security sector

[83]   ICTJ, www.unwomen.org/en/what-we-do/peace-and-security
[84]   Ibid.
[85]   Ibid.
[86]   Ibid.
[87]   The World Bank, op cit, p 107.
[88]   ICTJ, 2009, Amnesty must not equal impunity, Focus: 2009 DRC Amnesty Law.
[89]   True, op cit, p 248.

reform, need to be in place for recognisable accountability and an end to impunity.

It is possible that transitional justice may not be given high priority by governments that have more concern for economics, and lack understanding that transitional justice is essential for effective, long-lasting recovery. The possibility of recurrence, of the spread of violence and of the ongoing lack of development, all have implications beyond the immediate post-conflict stage. The end of conflict and the recovery and rehabilitation phases provide important opportunities to call for legal and judicial reforms, which can, in turn, be factors in developing compliance with international standards and law. For women, such reforms can be critical in abolishing discriminatory laws and practices that keep them dependent on male family members and prevent them from participating fully in peacebuilding and reconstruction.[90]

During recovery periods, international donors play a significant role in setting priorities for change and development. Many development agencies focus on building national capacity but may neglect building capacity in security and criminal justice systems, missing opportunities to act for prevention.[91] Pragmatically, greater understanding of the inter-relatedness of human security, inter-state and intra-state security, with the consequent understanding of the need for security reform and transitional justice to prevent renewed conflicts, may result in the recognition of the needs of survivors of tactical rape and sexual violence. Whatever the motivation, security and justice are essential at both national and international levels.

The need to transition from international to national justice and security

The Security Council has recognised that 'when states are unwilling or unable to protect their civilians then international actors … may become engaged to remind parties of their obligations to protect civilians and may take measures to prevent abuses and protect people from harm', and has progressively identified the protection of civilians as part of the business of the Security Council.[92] If people are to move on, and if the possibility of renewed violence arising from a sense of unresolved issues is to be prevented, if there is to be security within and between states, their security institutions must be legitimate and

[90]   UN Women, Transitional justice, op cit.
[91]   The World Bank, op cit, Chapter 6.
[92]   Oxfam, 2011, *Protection of civilians in 2010*, p 3

must be seen to be legitimate. This applies to relevant criminal tribunals and other international judiciaries as well as to national courts and justice systems.

John Cencich acted as an investigator of sexual violence for the ICTY, and outlined 10 specific difficulties he encountered when investigating.[93] He included in these difficulties the need to recognise and work with differences between civil and common law; issues around who is in charge of investigations; differences in methods of interrogation; differences regarding admissibility of hearsay and circumstantial evidence; differences in ways of using intelligence and counter-intelligence; differences in perceived need for personal security; and attitudes to individual criminal responsibility and joint criminal enterprises.[94] Cencich concluded that it is imperative that investigators be properly trained in international criminal law and in dealing with the inherently different personal and legal needs of the accused and accusers associated with charges before the courts.[95] Earlier chapters highlighted the reality that the operation of the ICTY and ICTR had some serious deficits. By the 10th anniversary of its establishment, the ICTR had handed down 21 sentences, with 18 convictions and 3 acquittals.[96] Ninety per cent of those cases included no rape convictions, and no rape cases were even brought by the prosecutor's office in 70% of those cases.[97] The decade revealed a lack of political will at senior management level to integrate sexual violence crimes into a consistently followed prosecution strategy.[98] This report was titled *Your justice is too slow*, reflecting the sense of frustration of many women in Rwanda. Prosecutions were hampered by inadequate investigations, inappropriate investigating methodology and a lack of training for staff. Some cases moved forward without the inclusion of rape charges, even when the prosecutor had strong evidence of such crimes.[99] Despite statements about the need for justice for rape victims, the UN 'has managed to transpose some of the crushing limitations and biases that rape victims encounter in their national jurisdictions

---

[93] Cencich, JR, 2009, International criminal investigations of genocide and crimes against humanity, *International Criminal Justice Review*, 19, 2, June, 175-91.

[94] Ibid.

[95] Ibid, p 189.

[96] Nowrojee, B, 2005, *Your justice is too slow: Will the ICTR fail Rwanda's rape victims?*, United Nations Research Institute for Social Development, November, p iv.

[97] Ibid.

[98] Ibid.

[99] Ibid.

to the international legal system it administers', and there is concern to ensure the same does not happen at the ICC.[100]

With the ICTR proceeding slowly, and tens of thousands of cases awaiting trial, Rwanda attempted transition to local justice, 'blending local conflict-resolution traditions with modern punitive legal system to deliver justice'.[101] Cases were transferred to the community-based courts known as Gacaca in the hope that this justice system would have community support and would be able to deliver justice to the survivors of the genocide, including women who had suffered from tactical rape and sexual violence. Human Rights Watch reported in 2011 that since 2005, 12,000 courts had tried 1.2 million cases.[102] Within a few months after the genocide, jails had been bursting. By 1998, there were an estimated 130,000 prisoners in jails built for 12,000 prisoners, and conventional courts had tried approximately 1,292 suspects between December 1996 and 1998.[103] There were some achievements but many concerns relating to lack of fair trials due to untrained or corrupt judges, lack of rights to legal representation and failure of community members to denounce false testimonies because they feared reprisal.[104] Related to this fear of reprisal was the reality that rape had been used as a tactic of war, to humiliate, intimidate and traumatise whole communities. Reprisals can fuel further violence, and, as the climate descends into general lawlessness, opportunistic rape by civilians can become a normal part of life.[105] Perceived impunity for perpetrators can contribute to the generalised breakdown of security within the society. If Gacaca courts were to offer resolution and accountability, they had to be seen to be just. Security for women testifying also needed to be effective.

Genocide-related rape cases, originally deemed to be under the jurisdiction of conventional courts, were transferred to Gacaca in 2008. Women had preferred conventional courts, believing they would have a better chance of confidentiality, and many were surprised and felt betrayed when cases were suddenly transferred to the Gacaca. Human Rights Watch reported the government as saying that some women had requested a more speedy response and that many victims who had

---

[100] Ibid, p 26.
[101] Human Rights Watch, 2011, *Justice compromised: The legacy of Rwanda's community-based Gacaca courts*, p 8.
[102] Ibid.
[103] Ibid, p 9.
[104] Ibid, p 11.
[105] Care International, 2009, *Voices Against Violence: Rape as a weapon of war*, July.

contracted HIV/AIDS were dying before courts could hear cases.[106] However, rape victims uniformly expressed disappointment at having to appear in Gacaca rather than conventional courts, as Gacaca proceedings failed to protect their privacy. The government had changed relevant laws so Gacaca could be held behind closed doors, but the nature of the process meant that the whole community knew of cases, and there were some instances in which there was no witness as to whether or not trials were fair.[107] Many women noted the bias of judges where, for example, judges were related to the accused, and in one case, the judge was the brother of a man accused of rape during the genocide.[108] There were allegations of women being bribed to drop cases and of judges demanding bribes.[109] Some rape victims were offered support counsellors and some were accompanied to Gacaca when they feared attacks from relatives of the accused. However, complaints were rife. Often witnesses failed to appear and Gacaca sometimes tried cases with only the accused and accuser present, and some women found judges asked 'bad' or 'insensitive' questions, although some were satisfied with the process and outcome.[110] There were many complaints that compensation was only awarded in cases regarding property, with no compensation being offered to those who had been raped.[111] While some Rwandans felt the Gacaca process helped reconciliation, others pointed to corruption, and argued that the accused received sentences that were too lenient, or were convicted on flimsy evidence.[112] The government vehemently rejected calls for the ICTR to prosecute crimes committed by the RPF in 1994. According to Human Rights Watch, Gacaca courts did try thousands of sexual violence and other particularly serious cases, and imposed mandatory lifetime solitary confinement for those convicted.[113] Overall, there were reasons for concern that as the ICTR closed, there would be little application of the findings that emerged from its work to ensure state-level justice and appropriate security for victims of tactical rape and sexual violence. Failure to effectively resolve their issues would not auger well for future stability.

[106] Human Rights Watch, op cit, p 12.
[107] Ibid, p 119.
[108] Ibid, p 120.
[109] Ibid, p 121.
[110] Ibid, p 124.
[111] Ibid, p 130.
[112] Human Rights Watch, *Rwanda: Events of 2001*, p 1.
[113] Ibid.

The situation in the former Yugoslavia also gave reason for concern as the ICTY drew to a close, and responsibility for ongoing work passed to the national courts and judicial systems. Many perpetrators of tactical rape and sexual violence were still experiencing impunity for those crimes. The government of Bosnia and Herzegovina has failed to ensure justice and reparation for thousands of women who were raped during the 1992–95 war.[114] As in Rwanda, there is a perceived failure to comprehensively investigate and prosecute before international and national courts. In many cases, women face stigmatisation, ongoing trauma and other psychological and physical problems. They often live in poverty and cannot afford medicines. As in Rwanda, too, no reparation for victims of sexual violence has been required by international law, and this absence of reparation creates additional difficulties for victims to deal with the past and to move on with their lives.[115] In Bosnia and Herzegovina this situation is exacerbated by women survivors of war crimes of sexual violence knowing they are discriminated against even at the level of social benefits available to them in comparison with what is available to war veterans.[116] It is in such practical ways that governments and communities could and should ensure security for victims and survivors.

Conclusion

There are serious security threats inherent in acts that are now officially acknowledged as violations of international law: the threat of the spread of political and sexual violence across borders; the threat to economic development; the threat to societal norms when conflict ceases; and the threat of recurrence of violence when there is insufficient accountability and justice. There are clear links between women's security, human security and state security with international stability. States are crucial in the provision of security for their populations, including security for women. They have a responsibility to ensure a viable and functioning security sector. The international community has a responsibility to monitor and hold to account state and non-state actors who perpetrate tactical rape and sexual violence in conflict.

Timely transition to effective and appropriate justice is a basis for recovery, rehabilitation and recovery of any community or individual.

[114] Amnesty International, 2009, *Bosnia and Herzegovina: 'Whose justice?' The women of Bosnia and Herzegovina are still waiting*, pp 3-4.

[115] Ibid.

[116] Ibid, p 41.

States and the international community, including multilateral organisations, NGOs and donors, generally have a responsibility to ensure appropriate services for women survivors and victims of tactical rape and sexual violence in conflict. Needs will include health, community education, economic strategies inclusive of women, trauma counselling and policies and practices that empower women politically and socially. The international community needs to be cognisant of the balance required between aid and development if national agencies are to develop sustainable programmes to empower women, reduce socially induced vulnerability and ensure women have due access to their rights.

TEN

Significant progress and ongoing challenges

Tactical rape and sexual violence in conflict continue to be perpetrated globally by state and non-state actors. They are being used with terrifying effectiveness, creating legacies of a negative impact on women, men, girls, boys and communities. Given the extent to which these crimes continue, it may seem irrational to talk of progress in confronting them. Yet there has been progress, in many ways remarkable progress, in recognising the reality and the implications of tactical rape and sexual violence in conflict. After centuries of states and the international community appearing to ignore, accept, condone or exploit the prevalence of these crimes, formal normative rejection has emerged at an international level, and there is some hope of it spreading among states. This is a beginning, albeit limited and uneven, to what is hoped will be eventual effective prevention of such crimes.

While even the formulation of this goal can be deemed progress, there is much more to be done to track how this change was effected, to identify what further change is required in policies and practices of the security and judicial systems, to pressure for widespread national implementation of commitments made by states at international level, to understand and advocate for appropriate support needed by women survivors and victims of tactical rape and sexual violence in conflict, to pressure for timely and due accountability of perpetrators of these crimes, to ensure women's participation in changing systems, policies and practices that affect their lives, and to ensure a sound understanding of the extent and nature of these abuses experienced by women in conflict.

It is important to reflect on the signposts, strategies and actors in change from accepting tactical rape and sexual violence as an inevitable part of conflict to international normative rejection of these crimes. While this change has occurred mostly at international level and is yet to make a measurable difference to the experience of many women, understanding this progression may help future advocacy. It comes with the acknowledgement that any such action has little or no impact or relevance to non-state perpetrators of tactical rape and sexual violence in conflict.

It is useful to understand what advances have been achieved and how they were achieved. This means 'joining the dots' between legal judicial rulings, advocacy by NGOs and states, UN debates, resolutions and institutionalisation to track the pattern of actions exemplifying international normative rejection of contraventions of international law and threats to security. With considerable pressure from NGOs, the ICTY and ICTR provided legal bases for subsequent pressure on the international community to look seriously at what were established as violations of international law. The Security Council is a key player in that it has considerable influence on the norms of states as a group. NGOs worked with some states to achieve resolution 1325, which was a breakthrough in the international community recognising tactical rape and sexual violence in conflict as an issue for security. Realisation of the interconnectedness of women's security, human security and state security has been major progress with significant outcomes. The Security Council is a forum of states capable of pressuring state actors perpetrating tactical rape and sexual violence in conflict. Resolutions building on resolution 1325 were the result of action by some states that understood the implications of these crimes.

Scrutiny of the processes of the two tribunals by women's groups and analysts contributed to awareness of the need to change judicial proceedings to meet women's rights to justice – to work to change gendered law. Increased understanding of the nature and impact of tactical rape and sexual violence in conflict led to greater understanding of the need for change both pre- and post-conflict. It has led to understanding women's status, strengths and potential for participation in policies and practices of their communities. Feminist analyses accompanied these changes and brought to the fore the essential nature of gendered law and institutions that were often assumed to be gender-inclusive. The changing attitude to humanitarianism was a context conducive to questioning policies and practices of multilateral agencies, NGOs and donor agencies, civil society and state and non–state actors. Public media contributed to maintaining focus on the issue.

Recognition of tactical rape

In the early 1990s rape and sexual violence were still often dismissed as unfortunate by–products of conflict, despite ongoing efforts by advocates and activists. It has only been since the conflicts in the former Yugoslavia and Rwanda in the 1990s that any real progress can be claimed. First and central to progress was recognition and acknowledgement by the Security Council and member states that rape and sexual violence are used as military and political tactics employed in inter- and intra-state conflicts. I have defined 'tactical rape' because it is a term that encapsulates key elements in the use of widespread rape as a tactic and as a deliberate strategy in conflict. Although rape has been used for centuries, it was in the changing context of international attitudes to humanitarianism that attitudes to this particular violation of civilians began to change in the early 1990s. There was public outrage at reports of widespread tactical rape.

The conflicts being waged towards the end of the 20th century were described as 'new wars', conflicts in which attacks on civilians were employed deliberately. Attacks on civilians included attacks on women, and rape proved an effective tactic in ethnic cleansing and genocide. Media and the public called for international action to stop widespread rape reported from the former Yugoslavia and Rwanda. From the former Yugoslavia, the term 'rape as a weapon of war' began to circulate.[1] It took many years before even this term, which did not carry a full understanding of tactical rape, was accepted in general use by NGOs and states. But awareness of rape used deliberately for military and political purposes grew, and pressure to act reached the UN, which demonstrated a concern about tactical rape and a wider concern for various forms of sexual violence in conflict.

Awareness of the effect of tactical rape grew from reports of missions to conflict zones by NGOs, global media and journalists, and eventually from reports by UN Special Rapporteurs. It became impossible to ignore the suffering of individuals and communities and the evidence of a long-term negative impact on possibilities for peace and future resolution of conflicts. Gradually there was recognition that responses needed to take into account the reality of how women were rendered vulnerable in many societies. If women were rendered vulnerable in times of peace, they were even more vulnerable in conflict. Long articulated concerns of feminist analysts and NGOs were eventually, even if not entirely, registered officially in the Security Council as demanding attention. Underlying causes of the total impact of tactical rape and sexual violence in conflict had to be confronted.

Feminist analysts have argued convincingly that inequalities between men and women that contribute to all forms of insecurity can only be understood and explained within the framework of patriarchal structures

---

[1] Fitzpatrick, B, 1992, *Rape of women in war*, Geneva: World Council of Churches, December.

that extend from the household to the global economy.[2] Redressing this is integral to providing protection for women in conflict and for ensuring justice for them after conflicts. Largely because of patriarchal attitudes reflected in social relationships and cultural values, rape has long-lasting effects on communities who see 'their' women raped. Patriarchy, while variously exhibited and defined in communities, is an influential social, cultural and legal element affecting women and men. In many patriarchal communities, women are valued as 'belonging' to men, and gendered values of women emphasise chastity and fertility. Women who come to share these values may estimate their own worth through the lens of communal values. This is what makes tactical rape and sexual violence horrifyingly effective. Women survivors and victims of tactical rape suffer physically, emotionally, economically and socially. The effects can continue for generations as children born of tactical rape may be ostracised, rejected and impoverished with, and perhaps by, traumatised mothers.

Significantly there has been formal international recognition at the Security Council that confronting policies and practices that discriminate against women in peacetime is an element in confronting the use of tactical rape and sexual violence in conflict. There has also been significant recognition of the responsibility of the international community and states to respond. With perpetrators of tactical rape and sexual violence being both state and non-state actors, it is ironic that it has been the international community of states that has decried these violations – but it is a beginning. The international community as a whole has, at least, accepted the responsibility to prevent the misdeeds of some of its members. This responsibility includes attending to social attitudes and values inherent in some communities that contribute to tactical rape and sexual violence being such perniciously effective strategies to achieve military, territorial and political gains. It is a responsibility that includes formulating and implementing policies to enhance women's education, economic independence and participation in government.

The challenge is to ensure transformation of these identified responsibilities into practical and measurable action. As the international community worked in 2015 to find a political solution to the Syrian conflict, it was notable that tactical rape did not feature in any reports of agenda at the negotiation table. The reviews of progress made on specific resolutions such as 1325 and 1820 and declarations such as the

[2]   Tickner, A, 1997, "You just don't understand": troubled engagements between feminists and IR theorists, *International Studies Quarterly*, 41, 4, December, p 626.

Beijing Platform of Action provide opportunities to assess the degree of implementation and impact, and to recommend improvements in approaches and strategies to achieve stated goals. The development of a norm internationally brings with it the need for application and commitment to it at national and local levels. As with any breach of an international norm, there are limited measures to enforce compliance. State actors have continued to perpetrate tactical rape and sexual violence in conflict. Women in some states continue to be rendered vulnerable by discriminatory policies and practices. Women in some states also continue to be excluded from decision-making processes affecting their lives, and possibly denying access to their human rights.

The focus at international level has been, perhaps understandably, on prohibition and prevention of tactical rape and sexual violence in conflict. This has been unsuccessful, but it remains a desirable goal. Meanwhile, women survivors and victims need support. The international community has a responsibility to address women's needs and their right to appropriate services and resources after having survived tactical rape and sexual violence. Women need to be involved in decisions about what they want and need:

> It's time for policymakers to listen to the voices of women and girls who survive rape. Women and girls who in the midst of bloody civil wars and regional conflicts are courageously working to heal themselves and others, and stop the vicious cycle of violence.[3]

Women know the predominant social norms and institutions that constitute their social, cultural and political reality. They are aware of restrictions and limitations imposed on them that they want to resist. Women have the right to be empowered to participate in the changes they will identify as important to their lives.

Working with women to effect such change requires engaging with diverse power figures. This will likely include governments and government agencies, traditional leaders, religious leaders, and sometimes military authorities. It may mean working with rebel groups and opposition leaders. This will require becoming familiar with these entities, understanding their cultural and political agendas, and working to educate and sensitise them to the benefits of changed attitudes to women's empowerment.

[3]   Sippel, S, Musimbi, K, 2014, Changing the conversation on sexual violence in conflict, *Foreign Policy in Focus*, 18 June.

The Security Council now uses the term 'women, peace and security'. It would likely be more effective to move to 'gender, peace and security', reflecting the language of UN agencies such as World Food Programme that have replaced 'women' with 'gender' when focusing on equality in service provision. When analysing and responding to discrimination against women it would be wise to adopt holistic approaches to causes of diverse types of rape and sexual violence. Some may have been prevalent pre-conflict and continue in post-conflict phases, arising from a combination of factors such as ethnicity, religion, socioeconomic status or a specific disability. These will intersect with gender, and while adding to the complexity of identifying appropriate responses, cannot be separated.

However, the scope of support services that are likely to be needed is broad, and state response remains inadequate. In 2015 the Secretary-General reported to the Security Council:

> Despite the political momentum and visibility gained in recent years, the reality on the ground is that many Governments have not been able to create an environment in which survivors feel safe to report sexual violence. The fear of stigmatization and reprisals is almost universal, and often compounded by a sense of futility stemming from the limited services available and the painfully slow pace of justice. Even in settings where primary health care is available, further capacity-building and resources are urgently needed to help frontline staff deliver comprehensive care, including mental health and psychosocial support.[4]

Physical wounds and health issues require appropriate resourcing from sensitised, qualified personnel aware of cultural and social attitudes as well as the physical results of rape and sexual abuse. Many women experience additional emotional trauma when reporting and seeking medical help for conditions and suffering incurred as a result of tactical rape and sexual violence in conflict. This barrier to reporting makes it difficult to fully document the extent and gravity of violations. Health issues may range from inability to bear or raise children to HIV/AIDS and many others.

Counselling that understands the social and cultural context in which the woman has been raised and in which she is living can be a viable

---

[4] UN Security Council, 2015, *Conflict-related sexual violence*, S2015/203, 23 March, para 5.

option. A range of support disciplines could be involved. Victoria Canning pointed out that a sociological approach that has been 'slow to engage in discourses around human rights' and even slower 'in developing sociological understandings of gender and human rights', largely ignored gendered inequalities, which 'leaves the violation of women at the bottom of a priority list regarding international humanitarian law.'[5] She argued that sociological approaches highlighting and challenging women's subordination may support prevention and conviction at localised and international levels.[6] Appropriate counselling might confront women's possible loss of self-esteem as well as loss of community regard. Women's attitudes to abortion where and when this is even an option will be influenced by community values – requiring consideration with great care and sensitivity. Many women may face economic need where communities are based on dependence on a male for economic survival. With possible complications around inheritance laws when a child born of rape is deemed a child of the enemy or an outsider to the community, such economic hardship may be generational. Programmes that empower women economically may be essential.

In states where tactical rape and sexual violence in conflict are ongoing, the situation of survivors and victims is further exacerbated, as was also reported in 2015:

> In situations of live conflict, such as the Central African Republic, Iraq, Somalia, South Sudan, the Sudan and the Syrian Arab Republic, service provision is further impeded by access restrictions and a climate of fear.[7]

Remembering that state actors, despite international commitments, remain among the perpetrators of tactical rape and sexual violence in conflict, the international community has an ongoing responsibility to enact effective strategies to urge – to compel – compliance with the established norm of rejection of these violations. The Secretary-General's report (2015) highlighted:

---

[5] Canning, V, 2010, Who's human? Developing sociological understandings of the rights of women raped in conflict, *The International Journal of Human Rights*, 14, 6.

[6] Ibid.

[7] UN Security Council, 2015, *Conflict-related sexual violence*, S2015/203, 23 March, para 5.

... 45 parties in the list of parties credibly suspected of committing or being responsible for patterns of rape and other forms of sexual violence in situations of armed conflict on the agenda of the Security Council (annex), 13 of which appear for the first time.[8]

These included both state and non-state actors.[9]

Confirming that tactical rape contravenes international humanitarian law

Establishing tactical rape and sexual violence in conflict as contraventions of international humanitarian law has been essential to the normative condemnation of these crimes. The ICTY and ICTR, as they investigated breaches of international humanitarian law and examined cases of rape and sexual violence, provided the legal bases for international concern. The two ad hoc tribunals were mandated to investigate and bring to account perpetrators of violence in the former Yugoslavia and Rwanda. They were to apply existing international law, not establish new law, and it proved possible to prosecute tactical rape within the existing legal framework. The term 'rape' was finally defined comprehensively in international law.

At the ICTY, judgments found rape under certain circumstances to be a crime against humanity, a war crime, slavery and torture. Specific clarifications and definitions were valuable in setting legal precedence and ensuring recognition that tactical rape and sexual violence in war contravene international law. There was clarification of terms within international law such as 'protected persons'; of international law applied to conflicts within as well as across borders; and of tactical rape as a method of ethnic cleansing. The ICTR contributed to the eventual acknowledgement that rape and sexual violence could be methods of genocide under the terms of the international 1948 *Convention on the Prevention and Punishment of the Crime of Genocide*. Part of this acknowledgment was that rape had become increasingly not only a weapon of war, but also a policy-determined, tactical weapon of genocide. The international community of states had formally rejected genocide and accepted responsibility to prevent and respond to genocide, so there was consequent responsibility to respond to tactical rape and sexual violence where used to perpetrate

---

[8] Ibid, para 3.
[9] Ibid, Annex.

genocide. However, it is recognised that the reluctance sometimes demonstrated by states to respond to events deemed genocide by other means may also apply to genocide perpetrated through tactical rape and sexual violence in conflict. Despite the acknowledged shortcomings of processes, including the additional and unacceptable suffering of women testifying, the outcomes of these two judiciaries contributed positively to case law, to legal definitions, and to recognition of the need for accountability of perpetrators. They underpinned progress in understanding and acceptance by the Security Council that these violations constitute threats to human security and to the security of states.

The experiences of many women testifying in the ICTY and ICTR exposed underlying social attitudes. This included attitudes demonstrated in the operation of the tribunals themselves, with judges and prosecutors at times reflecting levels of insensitivity and lack of care that shocked most observers. The extent and intrinsic cruelty of the rapes and sexual violence documented in survivor and witness accounts in both conflict arenas demonstrated the deliberate, planned and authorised nature of attacks on women. They also demonstrated the multifaceted and long-term suffering of victims. Analysis of court proceedings at the ICTY and ICTR results in the conclusion that serious reservations regarding adversarial male court constructs, expressed by feminist analysts, are indeed justified. The negative impact on women who suffered tactical rape and sexual violence being required to testify is clear. Testimonies regarding the insensitivity of courts, judges and investigators, the risks and indignities encountered by witnesses, and the limited attention paid to tactical rape and sexual violence all demonstrated the need for greater understanding and more effective responses, for lessons to be learned about the operation of courts and judiciaries dealing with witnesses. The manual of best practice produced by the ICTR outlines many of the lessons learned by this judiciary when dealing with crimes of tactical rape and sexual violence in conflict.[10] It is to be hoped that this will inform other judiciaries.

The issue of concern now is how justice will be delivered to those who have not received justice from the tribunals and for who it may seem that suffering goes unacknowledged and perpetrators go unpunished. For these women and their communities justice will be delivered at local, national level after the conclusion of work by

---

[10] http://unictr.unmict.org/sites/unictr.org/files/legal-library/140130_prosecution_of_sexual_violence.pdf

the international courts. States that have made Security Council commitments to confronting tactical rape and sexual violence in conflict have clear responsibilities to act at a national level. These responsibilities include criminalising rape and sexual violence, and defining them in accordance with internationally established standards.

One clear challenge is ensuring support for the ICC – practical support through funding and resourcing, through states cooperating and submitting those indicted for trial, and through facilitating investigation and prosecution. All courts need personnel trained in issues relating to tactical rape and sexual violence, including the now established legal bases for investigating and prosecuting perpetrators. National and local courts need the capacity to assume responsibilities from international tribunals. Continued and sustained action at a number of levels and by a number of stakeholders will be required to cement progress achieved in tribunals. National and international monitors will be responsible to watch tribunals pass over responsibilities to national and domestic judiciaries. They need to observe and evaluate how community courts deal with backlogs of cases, and see if impunity for perpetrators of tactical rape and sexual violence in conflict is in any way deferred if there are competing calls for priority in caseloads.

The list of obstacles still to be overcome before the justice system functions appropriately in cases of sexual violence is long and varied. Legal frameworks are often inadequate, with cases prosecuted and adjudicated based on legal frameworks not in line with international standards for prosecuting war crimes. There may not be adequate protection and support for survivors and witnesses, and many women can be re-traumatised. Progress in case law and in establishing tactical rape and sexual violence in conflict as contraventions of international law will be marred if these practical challenges are not met.

Establishing a security issue

The acceptance that tactical rape and sexual violence against women in conflict fall within the mandate of the Security Council has been a significant achievement. This is despite acknowledgement that there are clear limitations on the degree of impact of Security Council resolutions and normative rejection on state actors that perpetrate these crimes, and even less impact on the non-state actors perpetrating them. There was, however, acceptance that deliberate, policy-based, widespread violation of international law contributed to international instability. Resolution 1325 (2000) seemed to recognise the responsibility of the Security Council and alignment with security.

Resolution 1325 was passed unanimously in 2000. This demanded action be taken to confront and prevent sexual violence in all its forms (including tactical rape), and to prosecute perpetrators. The resolution was remarkable for the breadth of understanding of the nature, causes and effect of sexual violence in conflict, and for recognition of it as a violation of international law. Perhaps even more remarkable was the explicit acknowledgement that confronting sexual violence in conflict required confronting social attitudes, community structures and value systems that render women vulnerable to violence in peacetime. There was recognition of women's potential to play constructive roles in peacemaking and reconciliation.

In 2008, preceding the passage of resolution 1820, member states formally acknowledged the links between tactical rape, sexual violence in war and security. This was a significant step, bringing what had long been seen as 'just' an issue for women into the most important security organ of the international community. This resolution and others that followed represented further steps in institutionalising confrontation of sexual violence in the UN. Once it had been recognised in resolution 1325, that approaches to prevention and protection required diverse strategies, appropriate programming and action for implementation was more likely to be effected.

Significantly there is now greater understanding of the extent to which the interests of women's security, human security and international stability intersect and contribute to a normative rejection of tactical rape and sexual violence in conflict. It is established that unresolved tactical rape and sexual violence in war, with insufficient or unsatisfactory accountability and justice, leads to recurring conflict. When perpetrators escape accountability and are granted impunity, the cycles of enmity can continue. Conflict in one state can spill over into neighbouring states. Economic development is impeded when neighbouring states are in conflict. There is evidence that tactical rape can erode social norms and without accountability for perpetrators, violations occurring in conflict carry over into peacetime. There can be a cycle of violence against women in peacetime leading to violence against women in conflict, then a lack of accountability, leading to renewed conflict and more violence against women in conflict. Women's security as part of human security is closely interlinked with the security of states.

Building on legal decisions that these abuses were violations of existing international law, steps were taken towards confronting what was increasingly recognised as a security threat falling within the mandate of the Security Council. Resolutions have increasingly acknowledged the responsibility to prevent, monitor and hold to account the perpetrators of tactical rape and sexual violence in conflict.

The challenge lies in changing the gendered concept of security and security structures. Eric Blanchard argued that 'feminist security theory articulates an alternative vision', which entails 'revealing gendered hierarchies, eradicating patriarchal structural violence and working towards the eventual achievement of common security'.[11] Feminist analysts need to provide convincing grounds for advocates working with them to influence policy-makers and high-profile leadership at international and national levels. True and Mintrom were quoted in 2001:

> Ironically, the policy world of nation states has recently begun to outpace the academic discipline of International Relations in its acceptance of feminist issues, as evidenced by the rapid diffusion of "gender mainstreaming" bureaucracies and gender sensitive policies across states from a diverse range of cultures and levels of gender equality.[12]

Hopefully this has improved, and while it would be a reasonable expectation, it is probably optimistic to assume that security reform would inevitably follow the inclusive and restructured approach of feminist security theory. However, it remains essential that academia continues a serious focus on feminist security policies and practices, with additional research and analysis from interconnected disciplines contributing understanding of state crime. Green and Ward proposed seemingly disparate approaches such as criminology, political science, history, human rights and international humanitarian law.[13]

Institutionalising rejection of tactical rape

A measure of commitment to rejecting tactical rape and sexual violence in conflict is the degree to which statements are institutionalised by resourcing policies and practices. Resolutions have been valuable in moving forward normative rejection of tactical rape and sexual violence

---

[11] Blanchard, E, 2003, Gender, international relations and the development of feminist security theory, *Signs: Journal of Women in Culture and Society*, 28, 4, p 1305.

[12] Ibid, p 1306, quoting True, J, Mintrom, M, 2001, Transnational networks and policy diffusion: the case of gender mainstreaming, *International Studies Quarterly*, 45, 1, p 29.

[13] Green, P, Ward, T, 2004, *State crime: Governments, violence and corruption*, London: Pluto Press, reviewed by KE Fernandez, 2007.

in conflict, but practical action at the UN has been needed to see those resolutions implemented.

Earlier analysis showed that senior appointments have been made, ongoing procedures for regular reporting set in train, and budget allocations agreed by states at the Security Council. A policy of zero tolerance for sexual violation and exploitation by peacekeepers was declared, although it remains an ongoing challenge to see this fully implemented with appropriate accountability and enforcement. Resolution 1888 included a requirement regarding peacekeeping and encouragement for states 'to increase access to health care, psychological support, legal assistance and socio-economic reintegration services for victims of sexual violence in particular in rural areas'.[14] Training programmes for all personnel involved in the aftermath of conflicts are to include gender-related issues, and women are to be actively recruited and involved in all UN activities relating to peacekeeping, peacemaking and reconstruction and recovery initiatives. Resolution 1888 reinforced the decisions that teams of experts were to be immediately deployed to situations of concern regarding sexual violence in armed conflict, working through the UN and the host government assisting national authorities strengthening the rule of law.[15] Support for the Special Representative of the Secretary-General on Sexual Violence in Conflict has been positive. Resolution 2106 (2013) outlined a comprehensive approach and framework to prevent conflict-related sexual violence, and more than 140 member states of the General Assembly endorsed the 2013 *Declaration of Commitment to End Sexual Violence in Conflict.*

In 2007, 13 UN agencies were put under the UN initiative UN Action Against Sexual Violence in Conflict,[16] for better coordination and accountability, programming, advocacy and support for national efforts to prevent sexual violence and to respond effectively to the needs of survivors. In 2008, the Secretary-General launched UNiTE to End Violence against Women,[17] a campaign to prevent and eliminate violence against women and girls in all parts of the world, in times of war and peace. It brought together UN agencies, individuals, civil society and governments.

---

[14] UN Security Council, *Security Council resolution 1888 (2009) [on women and peace and security]*, S/RES/1888, 30 September 2009, para 14.

[15] Ibid, para 18.

[16] See www.stoprapenow.org/

[17] www.un.org/en/women/endviolence/

Increasing pressure on states to formulate national policies and practices has been a progressive step that could result in accompanying or eventual moral consciousness-raising. Normative rejection, which may have been adopted at global level but given only rhetorical support by some leaders, may eventually become internalised as new leaders, used to hearing the rhetoric, come to believe and accept what has become collective expectations. Consequently, 'the goal of socialisation is for the actors to internalise norms, so that external pressure is no longer needed to ensure compliance'.[18] This is indeed a challenge.

In recent times there have been some heartening signs of states accepting responsibility to act on commitments. In 2014, the UN and African Union affirmed their common commitment 'to put an end to history's oldest and least condemned crime', with a landmark agreement on preventing and responding to conflict-related sexual violence in Africa. The agreement focuses on combating impunity for perpetrators, capacity-building and training of peacekeepers and security actors. It strengthens national policies, legislation and institutions, and emphasises the importance of services for survivors, empowering women and girls, and countering the stigma of survivors.[19] A spokesperson said, 'national ownership, leadership and responsibility are absolutely essential if we are to protect women and girls, but also men and boys, from these barbaric crimes.'[20] The real test is the degree to which such commitments are enacted and the degree of cooperation with such bodies as the ICC.

In 2013 state members of the G8 issued a *Declaration on Preventing Sexual Violence in Conflict*.[21] They declared that despite international efforts:

> ... sexual violence in armed conflict continues to occur. In some conflicts it is systematic or widespread, reaching appalling levels of brutality. Sexual violence in armed conflict represents one of the most serious forms of violation or abuse of international humanitarian law and international human rights law. Preventing sexual violence in armed conflict is therefore both a matter of upholding universal human rights and of maintaining international security.[22]

[18] Risse, T, Ropp, SC, Sikkink, K, 1999, *The power of human rights: International norms and domestic change*, Cambridge: Cambridge University Press, p 11.

[19] UN News Centre, *UN, African Union sign landmark agreement to curb sexual violence in African countries*, 6 February 2014.

[20] Ibid.

[21] HM Government, 2013, *Declaration on Preventing Sexual Violence in Conflict*.

[22] Ibid.

Ministers of these powerful states recognised the need for further action:

> ... to end sexual violence in armed conflict, to tackle the
> lack of accountability that exists for these crimes and to
> provide comprehensive support services to victims, be they
> women, girls, men or boys.[23]

Proposed action included funding, training for peacekeepers, support services for survivors and increased efforts to reduce impunity. While it remains to be seen just how much sustained action follows this Declaration, it does represent a significant step from attitudes at the beginning of the 1990s.

In June 2014, a Global Summit to End Sexual Violence in Conflict brought together representatives of 123 states including senior ministers and 1,700 delegates. The Summit agreed practical steps to tackle impunity for the use of rape as a weapon of war, and to begin changing global attitudes to these crimes. It issued a Statement of Action and an agreed protocol, declaring preparedness 'to end the use of rape and sexual violence in conflict', described as 'one of the greatest injustices of our time', and making clear 'that prevention of sexual violence in conflict is critical to peace, security and sustainable development'.[24] The foreword stated:

> For decades – if not centuries – there has been a near-total
> absence of justice for survivors of rape and sexual violence
> in conflict. We hope this Protocol will be part of a new
> global effort to shatter this culture of impunity, helping
> survivors and deterring people from committing these
> crimes in the first place.[25]

Other regional alliances have also responded. In 2012, the Organization for Security and Co-operation in Europe (OSCE) declared ongoing regional institutionalisation, noting that it would 'continue to examine ways to integrate into the activities of the Organization, the relevant parts of UNSCR1325 and related resolutions', and its decision to

[23] Ibid.
[24] HM Government, 2014, *Statement of Action – Global Summit to End Sexual Violence in Conflict*.
[25] HM Government, 2014, *International protocol on the documentation and investigation of sexual violence in conflict*, Appendix.

appoint an OSCE Special Representative on Gender Issues.[26] Such initiatives by states and regional groups are indicative of a broadening concern and a further sign of progress.

While there has been significant progress, there are many ongoing challenges to effectively confront tactical rape and sexual violence in conflict. Normative rejection of sexual violence in conflict warrants mainstreaming in all aspects of humanitarian response for sustained, strengthened implementation of the many resolutions and declarations. These are significant, but they are only the first steps requiring monitoring and accountability to maintain pressure on states to fulfil responsibilities they have now acknowledged. In 2014 the Secretary-General stated:

> These are notable and important advances, but it is crucial that we now focus our collective efforts on converting these political commitments into concrete actions aimed at prevention and the provision of services on the ground.[27]

The practical need is appropriate funding. It will be important that responses to prevent and confront sexual violence is coordinated so that concerns for women, girls, men and boys are not competing for funds and practical institutional support. There is a further issue regarding just how funds are shared.

> To ensure women and girls, boys and men have equal access to and benefit from humanitarian assistance – we must "follow the money". We need to know how we spend money and who benefits. This is why we are instituting a system of tracking funding – called a gender marker. Only in this way can we be sure we target all the population equally and make sure they receive the resources needed to help them to build back better after emergencies.[28]

Purposeful education programmes for UN personnel, NGOs, donors and civil society regarding tactical rape and sexual violence in conflict

---

[26] OSCE, 2012, Promoting gender equality and women's rights must be a priority for all OSCE states, says chairperson on International Women's Day, Press Release, 8 March.

[27] UN Security Council, 2014, *Conflict-related sexual violence*, S/2014/181, 13 March.

[28] V Amos, Under-Secretary-General for Humanitarian Affairs and Emergency Relief Coordinator on Gender Markers.

enable relevant understanding of knowledge gained and commitments made. These require incorporation into all policy and practice of these entities. Recognising women's constructed vulnerability in peace and consequent vulnerability in conflict should underpin development and humanitarian programming and capacity building. Currently, many international groups speak of 'people-directed' approaches to development and humanitarian operations. This is praiseworthy provided women's needs do not become subsumed.

The Security Council itself faces many challenges to fulfil its responsibilities. In future resolutions it would be advised to further strengthen its responses to parties using tactical rape and sexual violence in conflict. Sanctions have been only tentatively referenced. Applying sanctions is one of the most serious international responses to threats to state security. Tactical rape and sexual violence in conflict are recognised as a threat, and there is now a reporting mechanism for listing known perpetrators. Since 2012, in the report, *Conflict-related sexual violence*,[29] the Secretary-General named military forces, militia and other armed groups suspected of being among the worst offenders, so theoretically at least, it is not unreasonable to expect sanctions being applied.

However, there remains veto power by the Permanent Members (P5). There has been a resurgence of interest in convincing these states to refrain from using their veto power when dealing with widespread atrocity crimes. This is probably unlikely given that Russia, for example, has used its veto four times relating to the Syrian conflict where such crimes are at least strongly assumed. However, by February 2015, 68 countries had supported this option, and it is believed:

> The moral argument that the veto should not be used in cases of mass-atrocity crimes is overwhelming. The P5 have obligations under the UN Charter, as well as international humanitarian and human rights law, not to undermine the effectiveness of the UN or that body of law. And there is a political argument against using the veto in these situations – that it jeopardizes the credibility and legitimacy of the Security Council.[30]

---

[29] UN Security Council, 2012, Conflict-related sexual violence, S/2012/33, 13 January.

[30] Evans, G, 2015, Limiting the Security Council veto, *Project Syndicate*, 4 February.

While certainly challenging, this is a logical progression from normative rejection and commitment to confront threats to international stability and security, such as tactical rape and sexual violence in conflict.

Transitional justice and security sectors

It is imperative that states develop legal and normative frameworks for women's security. International and national stakeholders, the UN, donors, government organisations and NGOs, could helpfully prioritise strengthening state-level institutions such as security sectors and judiciaries. Sustained international assistance focused on security sector reform and strengthening national justice systems and courts are practical and important steps. Together they can design demobilisation and rehabilitation strategies to take women's roles and experiences into account. Inclusive approaches to women in recovery and development, building security policies and institutions post-conflict, are essential.

The challenge is to ensure that in transitions from conflict to peace, tactical rape and sexual violence are dealt with to the same extent as other breaches of international humanitarian law. International donors and agencies need to be prepared to support such reforms. Transitional justice is an essential element of providing security, and responses are essential at both state and international levels. Courts require the skill and capacity to tackle accountability for perpetrators of tactical rape and sexual violence during conflict and in the aftermath of such violence. In 2015 Navi Pillay, UN High Commissioner for Human Rights from 2008 to 2014, spoke about the ongoing violations in South Sudan:

> If the government of South Sudan is not willing or able to put a stop to this insidious form of violence that targets women and girls, the international community has a responsibility to step in. One of the main reasons we see such extreme sexual violence in South Sudan is the country's pervasive culture of impunity. The perpetrators, which includes members of the police, army and armed militias, know that there is no rigorous justice system and almost no risk of consequences. Unless this changes, the frequency and brutality of sexual violence will rise, as one cycle of violence fuels the next.[31]

---

[31] OHCHR, 2014, South Sudan on verge of catastrophe – Pillay, UN News.

This references a state actor violating the norm accepted at international level in the Security Council and other commitments. The violations continue during and post-conflict, and there is international responsibility to prevent them and to prosecute perpetrators. Reform and capacity building of security sectors are part of providing transitional justice for women and meeting responsibilities accepted by the international community to bring perpetrators to account. Despite progress in declarations and statements, tactical rape and sexual violence still present major challenges in many countries.

Understanding women's status

While efforts continue to prevent tactical rape and sexual violence in conflicts – perpetrated by both state and non-state actors – a key challenge is ensuring that states in the aftermath of conflict recognise their roles in pre-conflict rendering of women vulnerable. It is important that policies and practices are based on acknowledgement that while men and women civilians share some of the same needs, women also suffer gender-related violence, often linked to and exacerbated by their pre-conflict status. Effective peacebuilding gives due attention to the pre-conflict status of women. Confronting and dealing with the issue of women's status is essential for peacebuilding. Durch and Giffen found that the pre-conflict status of women significantly affects the probability of successful peacebuilding when a peacekeeping operation is present:

> The higher the pre-conflict status of women, the greater was the probability of peace building within five years of the end of conflict. In other words protecting and empowering women in post war settings, often cast as a moral imperative, can also be seen as an operational necessity for building sustainable peace.[32]

Guidance and direction can support the implementation of many decisions regarding women's role in peacebuilding. Strategies include setting up advisory groups, appointing gender focal points in government departments and generally ensuring that civil society organisations and women's groups are supported practically to

[32] Durch, WJ, Giffen, AC, 2010, Challenges of strengthening the protection of civilians in multi-dimensional peace operations, Background paper prepared for the 3rd International Forum for the Challenges of Peace-Keeping Operations, Australia, 27-29 April.

participate in policy and practice decisions. Women have the right to be part of developing their own security with space to participate, and in any rehabilitation and reconstruction programme.

An ongoing but significant challenge is changing social values and attitudes towards women who are sexually abused. 'Right now, the woman who gets raped is the one who is stigmatized and excluded for it,' says Dr Denis Mukwege Mukengere, Director of Panzi Hospital in Bukavu in the DRC.

> Beyond laws, we have to get social sanction on the side of the woman. We need to get to a point where the victim receives the support of the community, and the man who rapes is the one who is stigmatized and excluded and penalized by the whole community.[33]

Women's suffering can extend beyond the immediate pain of rape and sexual attack. Patriarchal attitudes held by both women and men exacerbate women's sense of shame for actions over which they have had no power:

> Irrespective of the laws on the books, if prevailing social norms and attitudes attack, blame, and shame the survivors rather than the perpetrators, the quality of their lives will not improve.[34]

Education is essential for both men and women. The Executive Director of the UN Population Fund (UNFPA) underlined the importance of holistic approaches including work with men and boys:

> Education is the basis. If you bring up boys in the context of gender neutrality and parity, what you will get is a young man who will respect not just fellow boys but girls. Men have an important a role to play in this quest for a world without gender-based violence and discrimination as women do. Laws and justice can accomplish a great deal

---

[33] See www.un.org/en/preventgenocide/rwanda/about/bgsexualviolence.shtml

[34] UN-APPG meeting on protecting women and girls in emergencies, *Tackling violence against women and girls: A joined-up response*, London, 13 November 2013.

but society has to change because it is society that breaks the laws.[35]

Zainab Hawa Bangura added, 'a country that does not respect its women in peacetime will not respect them in conflict', highlighting that sexual violence does not occur accidentally in conflict situations. 'It is planned and deliberate,' she stressed, given that state militaries and police forces were often part of it. 'The lower the status of women in society – the less education, the lower the economic opportunities – the more vulnerable they are to sexual violence when conflict breaks out,' she added, calling for a change to the system to ensure better protection of women and the prosecution of violators.[36]

This must involve ensuring women's participation in all areas of their lives:

> ... as much as it is about the security of half of the world's population, not only do women's concerns tend to be overlooked but also their voices, experiences and leadership continue to not be recognized or valued.[37]

An important development could be the Sustainable Development Goals (SDGs) and the post-2015 agenda that replaced the Millennium Development Goals (MDGs) in late 2015. There is some concern that the SDGs, like the MDGs, will have no binding force but will be a statement of aspiration. However, a High Level Global Review of progress on resolution 1325 will probably highlight best practices as well as challenges. The Commission on the Status of Women acknowledged the need for the post-2015 agenda to deal substantively and directly with gender issues.[38] It pledged to strengthen gender equality, and hope was expressed that the Commission itself would be 'further energised' in its role of championing gender equality.[39] There is a desire for a stand-alone SDG on Gender Equality and Women's Empowerment, and stringent gender indicators across all of the 17 proposed goals.

---

[35] UN News Centre, *Society's attitudes must change worldwide to stop gender-based violence, say UN officials*, 11 March 2015.

[36] Ibid.

[37] UN Women, 2015, Gender consideration in security management: a speech by Lakshmi Puri.

[38] UN News Centre, *"As women thrive, so will we all," says Secretary-General as Women's Commission opens session, pointing to "unacceptably slow" progress since Beijing*, 9 March 2015.

[39] Ibid.

Data collation and research

A further challenge is to ensure data collation and provision of resources for research into the extent, impact and confrontation of tactical rape and sexual violence in conflict. Data collection by a range of stakeholders including states, UN agencies, governments, NGOs and development funders is vital for planning post-conflict strategies. The *International protocol on the documentation and investigation of sexual violence in conflict* represented 'Basic standards of best practice on the documentation of sexual violence as a crime under international law.'[40] Importantly, having grounds for 'the distinction between whether rape occurs as a practice or a strategy matters because it might mean different policy measures are needed to effectively combat it.'[41]

Data is essential for understanding and planning for needs post-conflict, as well as for ensuring accountability with no impunity for perpetrators. It is needed to ensure programmes and services for consequences such as pregnancies and health issues, including HIV/AIDS. Data supports understanding of whether or not survivors and victims are still able to bear children and to care for children, emotionally and economically. Knowing the extent and nature of crimes supports recovery and rebuilding strategies such as truth commissions that proceed from an acknowledgement of crimes. The aim is to 'deconstruct the social reality in which the crimes were committed', so knowing the extent and nature of suffering matters.[42] It is important to have reliable data regarding current or past conflicts in which sexual violence has been used as a tactic if there is to be adequate and appropriate response to protection of civilians and accountability of perpetrators in the future.

Research and academic analyses of causes and strategies is essential. UN agencies, which are now required to mainstream women's issues, can include resources to ensure such research and analysis is available, incorporated into policy and monitored in all areas relating to post-conflict activity and crises that involve women likely to have experienced tactical rape and sexual violence. This will be an ongoing concern and challenge for the Special Representative appointed by

---

[40] HM Government, 2014, *International protocol on the documentation and investigation of sexual violence in conflict*, Appendix 4.

[41] Aljazeera, 2014, Is rape inevitable in war?, 25 February.

[42] Bijleveld, C, Morssinkhofe, A, Smeulers, A, 2009, Counting the countless: rape victimisation during the Rwandan genocide, *International Criminal Justice Review*, 19, 2, June, pp 209-10.

the Secretary-General as a foundation for provision of 'coherent and strategic leadership' in coordination and collaboration with other UN and NGO entities.[43]

A related challenge is that further field research and active scholarly debate on UN policies are still urgently needed.[44] The collation and dissemination of best practices are valuable for policy-makers. Programmes and initiatives are emerging for assessment and sharing where appropriate. UN Action has supported the design and implementation of the first-ever Comprehensive Strategy on Combating Sexual Violence in the DRC, as well as the Joint Government–UN Programme on Sexual Violence in Liberia. Funded by the Australian Government's Aid Agency (AusAID), UN Action, together with the Department of Peacekeeping Operations and the Special Representative of the Secretary-General on Sexual Violence in Conflict, has also documented best peacekeeping practices in addressing conflict-related sexual violence. From initiating firewood patrols in Darfur to establishing market escorts, night patrols and early-warning systems in the DRC, the Analytical Inventory of Peacekeeping Practice catalogues direct and indirect efforts to combat sexual violence during and in the wake of war.[45] The UN Multidimensional Integrated Stabilization Mission in the Central African Republic (MINUSCA) partnered with civil society, including women's associations, and supported efforts to strengthen capacity to monitor and investigate allegations of sexual and gender-based violence and included awareness-raising campaigns. They launched an initiative to strengthen the joint evaluation of centres for victims and survivors of sexual and gender-based violence, which support victims' reintegration into the community and continue to support the national police and gendarmerie establishing specialised units to address sexual and gender-based violence committed against women and children.[46] There are many more encouraging initiatives for monitoring and sharing.

More academic support is needed for feminist analysis, commentary and evaluation of information, processes and programmes. NGOs can

[43] UN Security Council, *Security Council resolution 1888 (2009) [on women and peace and security]*, S/RES/1888, 30 September 2009, para 4.

[44] Nduka-Agwu, A, 2009, "Doing gender": After the war: dealing with gender mainstreaming and sexual exploitation and abuse in peace support operations in Liberia and Sierra Leone, *Civil Wars*, 11, 2, June, pp 179-99.

[45] UN Women, 2010, *Addressing conflict-related sexual violence – An analytical inventory of peacekeeping practice*.

[46] UN Security Council, 2014, *Report of the Secretary-General on the situation in the Central African Republic*, S/2014/857, 28 November.

investigate and record early reports of widespread rapes, sustaining pressure on the UN and states to respond. NGOs such as Human Rights Watch and writers such as Binaifer Nowrojee have demonstrated the power of advocacy groups when they alert the international community to violations of international humanitarian and human rights law.[47]

Risse, Ropp and Sikkink recognised the role of transnational advocacy networks.[48] So, too, did Jacqui True, who described the transnational networks of women's NGOs as conduits of information and best practice models, and as having 'knowledge concerning alternative political strategies and how they may be applied to further promote gender policy change.'[49] Analysis of the development of normative rejection of tactical rape and sexual violence in war confirms the value of such networks in sharing information to pressure for change.

Conclusion

Tactical rape and sexual violence have been, and continue to be, serious and unacceptable violations of international law, of human rights and threats to security. The practices continue at a dire level and intensity, with extreme suffering and negative consequences for women and girls and, in different ways, for men, boys, societies, states and the international community. They are violations of international law perpetrated by state and non-state actors, deliberate practices and the result of deliberate policies. They could logically therefore be prevented – particularly for state actors participating in the international community. There are different aspects for non-state actors outside this international community. Wood noted 'the relative absence of sexual violence on the part of many armed groups', and argued that:

> ... if some groups do not engage in sexual violence, then rape is not inevitable in war as is sometimes claimed, and there are stronger grounds for holding responsible those groups that do engage in sexual violence.[50]

[47] Nowrojee, B, 1996, *Shattered lives: Sexual violence during the Rwandan genocide and its aftermath*, New York: Human Rights Watch, September.
[48] Risse et al, op cit, p 18.
[49] True, J, 2003, Mainstreaming gender in global public policy, *International Feminist Journal of Politics*, 5, 3, November, p 377.
[50] Wood, EJ, 2009, Variation in sexual violence during war, *Politics & Society*, 34, 3, 307–42.

This may well be the case for non-state actors and state actors. Behaviour that is deliberate has the potential to be stopped or changed. Tactical rape and sexual violence in conflict are not inevitable. Clearly articulated normative rejection and condemnation is now a reality at international level and at some national levels. This was once deemed unlikely or impossible. There is increased recognition of the reality and prevalence of tactical rape and sexual violence in conflict. Accompanying international condemnation has been growing acknowledgement that women rendered vulnerable in their societies during peacetime will be further vulnerable during conflict, and that confronting tactical rape and sexual violence in conflict requires confronting societal and cultural practices and policies that render women vulnerable.

There have been specific attempts to provide justice for women and to ensure accountability of perpetrators at relevant judiciaries such as international criminal tribunals and the ICC. There have been clear lessons learned from these attempts. There is growing awareness that many current security sectors fail women by the male context of those sectoral institutions and structures. It is acknowledged that women survivors and victims have the right to appropriate support services and supportive mechanisms – and that women have the right and capacity to be empowered to participate in decisions regarding the nature and extent of those services and support. Women's participation in community decision-making regarding peacemaking, reconciliation and more equitable social functioning is also recognised.

Some commitments have been institutionalised internationally and to some degree at national levels. Practical measures such as reporting requirements, budgetary allocations and appointment of personnel have been initiated. States prepared to meet their responsibilities have formulated NAPs and are aligning national policies and practices with international standards of law. State collectives have made joint declarations reinforcing Security Council resolutions.

Progress is being made in confronting this violation, but so much more is needed before women are safe and future generations are safeguarded physically, socially, emotionally, politically and economically. Rhetoric and goals need to be translated into action with monitoring and effective sanctions – which is no easy task.

The real measure of success will be when and how women are freed from tactical rape and sexual violence in conflicts. The reality is that these crimes continue in many countries and communities, and survivors and victims continue to experience their painful, negative effects. While states have been part of international progress in developing the norm rejecting tactical rape and sexual violence in conflict, some states remain represented among the list of perpetrators. The international community in the form of the Security Council remains limited in its capacity to confront these actors even while it has condemned the crimes. Non-state actors largely continue to be outside any form of influence, condemnation or sanction, and international norms and international law have limited effect on non-state actors likely to perpetrate tactical rape and sexual violence in conflict – although there may be some possibility for influence.

The ongoing suffering of women survivors and victims of tactical rape and sexual violence in conflict is unacceptable, deplored and normatively rejected as violations of international law. There are ways to prevent these practices, to protect women made vulnerable to them, and to bring perpetrators to account as some form of deterrence. There are ways to change the male constructs that are part of rendering women vulnerable and to empower women to participate fully in just, equitable, political and social policies and practices. The political will to do so is perhaps the missing element in achieving eradication of this particular source of suffering.

References

Acharya, A, 2007, Human security, in J Baylis and S Smith (eds), *The globalisation of world politics: An introduction to international relations*, 4th edn, Oxford: Oxford University Press, Chapter 28

Achuthan, M, Black, R, 2009, *United Nations resolution 1820: A preliminary assessment of the challenges and opportunities*, September, New York: International Women's Tribune Centre

African Union, 2009, *Gender policy*, Section III, www.usip.org/files/Gender/African_Union_Gender_Policy_2009.pdf

Aljazeera, 2014, Is rape inevitable in war?, 25 February, www.aljazeera.com/indepth/opinion/2014/02/rape-inevitable-war-2014214161229710290.html

Allen, B, 2002, Towards a new feminist theory of rape: a response from the field, *Signs*, 27, 3, Spring, 777-81

Amnesty International, 2004, *Democratic Republic of Congo: Mass rape – Time for remedies*, 25 October, www.amnesty.org/en/documents/afr62/018/2004/en/

Amnesty International, 2009, *Bosnia and Herzegovina: 'Whose justice?' The women of Bosnia and Herzegovina are still waiting*, www.amnesty.org/en/documents/EUR63/006/2009/en/

Amnesty International, 2015, *Annual report 2014/2015*, www.amnesty.org/en/annual-report-201415

Amos, V, Under-Secretary-General for Humanitarian Affairs and Emergency Relief Coordinator on Gender Markers, www.humanitarianresponse.info/topics/gender/page/iasc-gender-marker

Andreopolous, GJ, 1997, *Genocide: Conceptual and historical dimensions*, Philadelphia, PA: University of Pennsylvania Press

Annan, K, 2006, No policy for progress more effective than empowerment of women, Secretary-General says in remarks to Woman's Day Observance, UN press conference, 8 March, www.un.org/News/Press/docs/2006/sgsm10370.doc.htm

Arbreu, VC, 2005, Women's bodies as battlefields in the former Yugoslavia: An argument for the prosecution of sexual terrorism as genocide and for recognition of genocidal sexual terrorism as a violation of *jus cogens* under international law, *Georgetown Journal of Gender and the Law*, 2

Arieff, A, 2009, Sexual violence in African conflicts, Congressional Research Service, 25 November, www.fas.org/sgp/crs/row/R40956.pdf

Ashworth, G, 1999, The silencing of women, in T Dunne and N Wheeler (eds), *Human rights in global politics*, Cambridge: Cambridge University Press, 259-76

Askin, K, 1999, Sexual violence in decisions and indictments of the Yugoslav and Rwandan Tribunals: Current status, *The American Journal of International Law*, 93, 1, January, 97-123

Askin, K, 2003, Prosecuting wartime rape and other gender-related crimes under international law: extraordinary advances, enduring obstacles, *Berkeley Journal of International Law*, 21, 288-349

Baaz, ME and Stern, M, 2010, *The complexity of violence: A critical analysis of sexual violence in Democratic Republic of Congo*, Uppsala: The Nordic Africa Institute, http://nai.diva-portal.org/smash/get/diva2:319527/FULLTEXT02.pdf

Bangura, Z, 2014, The "unimaginable pain" of South Sudan's crisis, *Voice of America* , 15 December, www.voanews.com/content/south-sudan-unrest-ethnic/2555488.html

Barbour, LCO, 2009, UNSCR 1325 Annual Conference of the Human Security Network, Dublin

Barnett, M, Finnemore, M, 2008, Political approaches, in TG Weiss and S Daws (eds), *The Oxford handbook on the United Nations*, Oxford: Oxford University Press, 41-57

Barnett, M, Weiss, TG, 2008, *Humanitarianism in question: Politics, power, ethics*, New York: Cornell University Press

Barria, LA, Roper, SD, How effective are international criminal tribunals? An analysis of the ICTY and the ICTR, *The International Journal of Human Rights*, 9, 3, September, 349-68, http://stevendroper.com/ICTY.pdf

Barrow, A, 2010, United Nations Security Council resolutions 1325 and 1820: constructing gender in armed conflict and international humanitarian law, *International Review of the Red Cross*, 92, 877, March

Baylis, J, Smith, S, Owens, P, 2008, *The globalisation of world politics: An introduction to international relations*, Oxford: Oxford University Press

BBC News, 2015, Bosnia-Herzegovina country profile – Overview, 18 March, news.bbc.co.uk/2/hi/europe/country_profiles/1066886.stm

Bijleveld, C, Morssinkhofe, A, Smeulers, A, 2009, Counting the countless: rape victimisation during the Rwandan genocide, *International Criminal Justice Review*, 19, 2, June, 208-24

Binder, C, Lukas, K, Schweiger, R, 2008, Empty words or real achievement? The impact of Security Council resolution 1325 on women in armed conflicts, Radical History Review, 101, 22-41

Birdsall, A, 2007, Creating a more "just" order: the ad hoc International War Crimes Tribunal for the former Yugoslavia, *Cooperation & Conflict*, 42, 4, 397-418

Blair, A, 1999, *Doctrine of the international community*, Address to the Chicago Economic Club, Hilton Hotel, Chicago, IL, 22 April

Blanchard, E, 2003, Gender, international relations and the development of feminist security theory, *Signs: Journal of Women in Culture and Society*, 28, 4,1289-312

Boose, LE, 2002, Crossing the River Drina: Bosnian rape camps, Turkish impalement and Serb cultural memory, *Signs*, 28, 1, Gender and Cultural Memory, Autumn, 71-96

Booth, K, Smith, S, 1995, *International relations today*, University Park, PA: Pennsylvania State University Press

Border & Immigration Agency, 2007, *Democratic Republic of the Congo*, 31 July, www.unhcr.org/refworld/pdfid/46c1b9562.pdf

Brown, C, 2002, *Sovereignty, rights and justice: International political theory today*, Cambridge: Polity Press

Brownmiller, S, 1975, *Against our will: Men, women and rape*, New York: Simon & Schuster

Bufkin, J, 2005, Book review of *State crime: Governments, violence and corruption*, *Western Criminology Review*, 6, 1, 161-2

Bull, H, 1995, *The anarchical society: A study of order in world politics*, Basingstoke: Macmillan

Buzan, B, Hansen, L, 2009, *The evolution of international security studies*, Cambridge: Cambridge University Press

Canning, V, 2010, Who's human? Developing sociological understandings of the rights of women raped in conflict, *The International Journal of Human Rights*, 14, 6, 849-64

Caprioli, M, 2003, Gender equality and state aggression: the impact of domestic gender equality on state first use of force, *International Interactions*, 29, 3, July/September, 195-214

Caprioli, M, Boyer, MA, 2001, Gender, violence, and international crisis, *Journal of Conflict Resolution*, 45, 4, August, 503-18

Caprioli, M, Trumbore, PF, 2006, Human rights rogues in interstate disputes, 1980-2001, *Journal of Peace Research*, 43, 2, March, 131-48

Card, C, 1996, Rape as a weapon of war, *Special issue: Women and Violence*, Bloomington, IN: Indiana University Press

Care International, 2009, *Voices Against Violence: Rape as a weapon of war*, July, http://insights.careinternational.org.uk/publications/voices-against-violence-rape-as-a-weapon-of-war

Carey, HF, 2001, Women and peace and security: the politics of implementing gender sensitivity norms in peacekeeping, *International Peacekeeping*, 8, 2, 49-68

Cencich, JR, 2009, International criminal investigations of genocide and crimes against humanity, *International Criminal Justice Review*, 19, 2, June, 175-91

Charlesworth, H, 2010, Feminist reflections on the responsibility to protect, *Global Responsibility to Protect*, 2, 232-49

Charlesworth, H, Chinkin, C, 2000, *The boundaries of international law: A feminist analysis*, Manchester: Manchester University Press

Charlesworth, H, Chinkin, C, Wright, S, 1991, Feminist approaches to international law, *The American Journal of International Law*, 85, 4, October, 613-45

Charter of the United Nations, www.un.org/en/documents/charter

Checkel, JT, 1997, International norms and domestic politics: bridging the rationalist-constructivist divide, *European Journal of International Relations*, 3, 473-95

Checkel, JT, 1998, The constructivist turn in international relations theory, *World Politics*, 50, 324-48

Checkel, JT, 2001, Why comply? Social learning and European identity change, *International Organisation*, 553-88

Chinkin, C, 1994, Rape and abuse of women in international law, Symposium – The Yugoslav crisis: New international law issues, *European Journal of International Law*, 5, 326-41, www.ejil.org/pdfs/5/1/1246.pdf

Clark, P, 2010, *The Gacaca courts: Post-genocide justice and reconciliation in Rwanda: Justice without lawyers*, Cambridge: Cambridge University Press

Cojean, A, 2014, Syria's silent war crime: Systematic rape, *Le Monde*, 12 March [reprinted in *The New York Times*, 31 August 2015]

Commission on Human Rights, 1993, *Report of the Special Rapporteur on the situation of human rights in the territory of the former Yugoslavia*, E/CN.4/1993/50

Commission on Human Security, 2003, *Human security now 2002-2003*, http://reliefweb.int/sites/reliefweb.int/files/resources/91BAEEDBA 50C6907C1256D19006A9353-chs-security-may03.pdf

Commission on Human Security, 2003, *Outline of the report of the Commission on Human Security*, www.cfr.org/content/publications/attachments/Human_Security.pdf

Connors, J, 2000, Using general human rights instruments to advance the human rights of women, in K Adams and A Byrnes (eds), *Gender equality and the judiciary: Using international human rights standards to promote the human rights of women and the girl-child at the national level*, London: Commonwealth Secretariat

Csete, J, Kippenberg, J, 2002, *The war within the war: Sexual violence against women and girls in Eastern Congo*, New York: Human Rights Watch, www.hrw.org/sites/default/files/reports/congo0602.pdf

Degni-Segui, R, 1994, *Report on the situation of human rights in Rwanda*, E/CN.4/1995/7, 28 June

Degni-Segui, R, 1994, *Report on the situation of human rights in Rwanda*, Submitted by Special Rapporteur of the Commission on Human Rights, under para 20 of resolution S-3/1 of 25 May 1994

Degni-Segui, R, 1994, *Situation of human rights in Rwanda*, A/49/508 S/1994/1157, 13 October

Degni-Segui, R, 1995, *Situation of human rights in Rwanda*, E/CN.4/1996/7, 28 June

Degni-Segui, R, 1996, *Report on the situation of human rights in Rwanda*, E/CN.4/1996/68, January

Degni-Segui, R, 1997, *Situation of human rights in Rwanda*, E/CN.4/1997/61 20, January

Deng, E, Amnesty International, 2014, in The "unimaginable pain" of South Sudan's crisis, 15 December, *Voice of America*, www.voanews.com/content/south-sudan-unrest-ethnic/2555488.html

Des Forges, A, 1999, *Leave none to tell the story*, New York: Human Rights Watch

Dicker, R, 2015, Throwing justice under the bus is not the way to go, *Open Democracy*, 11 December, www.opendemocracy.net/openglobalrights/richard-dicker/throwing-justice-under-bus-is-not-way-to-go

Diken, B, Laustsen, CB, 2005, Becoming abject: rape as a weapon of war, *Body and Society*, 11, 1, 111–28

Dixon, R, 2002, Rape as crime in international law: Where to from here?, *European Journal of International Law*, 13, 3, 697–719

Dolgopol, U, Gardam, J, 2006, *The challenge of conflict: International law responds*, Boston, MA: Martinus Nijhoff Publishers

Draper, GIAD, 1985, Humanitarianism in the modern law of armed conflict, *International Relations*, viii, 4, 240

Dryzek, JS, 2006, *Deliberative global politics: Discourse and democracy in a divided world*, Cambridge: Polity Press

Durch, WJ, Giffen, AC, 2010, Challenges of strengthening the protection of civilians in multi-dimensional peace operations, Background paper prepared for the 3rd International Forum for the Challenges of Peace-Keeping Operations, Australia, 27-29 April

Ellis, L, 1989, *Theories of rape – Inquiries into the causes of sexual aggression*, Washington, DC: Hemisphere Publishing Corporation

Ellis, M, 2004, Breaking the silence – Rape as an international crime, Talk given to the United Nations Conference on Gender Justice, 16 September, New York

Engle, K, 1993, After the collapse of the public/private distinction: strategising women's rights, in DG Dallmeyer (ed), *Reconceiving reality: Women and international law*, New York: American Society of International Law, 143-55

Engle, K, 2005, Feminism and its (dis)content: Criminalizing wartime rape in Bosnia and Herzegovina, *American Journal of International Law*, 99, 4, October, 778-816

Enloe, C, 2000, *Maneuvers: The international politics of militarizing women's lives*, Berkeley, CA: University of California Press

Enloe, C, 2005, What is patriarchy? Is the big picture an afterword?, in D Mazurana, A Raven-Roberts and J Parpart (eds), *Gender, conflict and peace keeping*, Lanham, MD: Rowman & Littlefield, p 281

Euro-Mediterranean Human Rights Network, 2013, *Violence against women, bleeding wound in the Syrian conflict*, Sema Nasar, November

Evans, G, 2010, The responsibility to protect: consolidating the norm, Paper presented at the 39th IPA Conference on the United Nations Security Council and the responsibility to protect, Vienna, *Favorita Papers*, 1/2010

Evans, G, 2015, Limiting the Security Council veto, *Project Syndicate*, 4 February

Evenson, E, 2015, ICC success depends on its impact locally, *Open Democracy*, 26 August, www.opendemocracy.net/openglobalrights/elizabeth-evenson/icc-success-depends-on-its-impact-locally

Falk, R, 1999, The challenge of genocide and genocidal politics in an era of globalisation, in T Dunne and N Wheeler, *Human rights in global politics*, Cambridge: Cambridge University Press, 177-94

Farwell, N, 2004, War rape: new conceptualisations and responses, *AFFILIA: Journal of Women and Social Work*, 19, 4, Winter, 389-403

Fein, H, 1994, Genocide, terror, life integrity, and war crimes, in GJ Andreopolous, *Genocide: Conceptual and historical dimensions*, Philadelphia, PA: University of Pennsylvania Press, 95-108

Finnemore, M, Sikkink, K, 2001, Taking stock: The constructivist research program in international relations and comparative politics, *Annual Review of Political Science*, 4, 391–416

Fitzpatrick, B, 1992, *Rape of women in war*, Geneva: World Council of Churches, December

Fitzpatrick, B, 1994, *The Rwandan regional crisis*, Geneva: World Council of Churches, August

Fitzpatrick, B, 1999, *Kosovo – The women and children*, Burwood, VIC: World Vision Australia

Frost, M, 1996, *Ethics in international relations*, Cambridge: Cambridge University Press

Gallagher, A, 1997, Ending the marginalisation: strategies for incorporating women into the United Nations Human Rights system, *Human Rights Quarterly*, February, 283–333

Gardam, JG, 1998, Women, human rights and international law, *International Review of the Red Cross*, 324, 421–32

Gardam, JG, Jarvis, MJ, 2001, *Women, armed conflict and international law*, Netherlands: Kluwer Law International

Gibson, S, 1993, The discourse of sex/war: thoughts on C MacKinnon's 1993 Oxford Amnesty lecture, 1, *Feminist Legal Studies Journal*, 179–88

Gilbert, G, What price justice? Prosecuting crime post-conflict, in U Dolgopol and J Gardam, 2006, *The challenge of conflict: International law responds*, Boston, MA and Leiden: Martinus Nijhoff Publishers, Chapter 22

Goertz, A-M, Anderson, L, 2008, *Women targeted or affected by armed conflict: What role for military peacekeepers?*, Conference summary, 27–29 May, New York: United Nations Development Fund for Women

Goldstone, R, 2007, International Criminal Court and ad hoc tribunals, in TG Weiss and S Daws (eds), *The Oxford handbook on the United Nations*, Oxford: Oxford University Press

Goodwin, J, 2004, Silence=rape, *The Nation*, 19 February, www.thenation.com/article/silencerape/

Gourevitch, P, 2000, *We wish to inform you that tomorrow we will be killed with our families*, London: Picador

Government of Rwanda, 1995, *Rapport national du Rwanda pour le Quatrième Conférence Mondiale sur les Femmes*, Beijing, September

Green, P, Ward, T, 2004, *State crime: Governments, violence and corruption*, London: Pluto Press

Greppi, E, 1999, The evolution of individual criminal responsibility under international law, *International Review of the Red Cross*, 81, 835

Griffiths, M, O'Callaghan, T, 2002, *International relations: The key concepts*, London: Routledge

Grossman, A, 1995, A question of silence: the rape of German women by occupation soldiers, *October Magazine*, 72, Spring

Grosz, E, 1994, *Volatile bodies: Towards a corporeal feminism*, Sydney, NSW: Allen & Unwin

GSDRC (Governance and Social Development Resource Centre), 2009, *Conflict and sexual and domestic violence against women*, 1 May, www.gsdrc.org/docs/open/HD589.pdf

Haarken, J, 2002, Towards a new feminist theory of rape: the seduction of theory, *Signs*, 27, 3, Spring, 781-6

Hall, J, lawyer with Human Rights Watch, in an interview reported by A Poolos, 1999, Human rights advocates say rape is war crime, Radio Free Europe, 25 May

Hall, PA, 1989, Conclusion: the politics of Keynesian ideas, in P Hall (ed), *The political power of economic ideas*, Princeton, NJ: Princeton University Press, 351-91

Hansen, L, 2001, Gender, nation, rape: Bosnia and the construction of security, *International Feminist Journal of Politics*, 3, 1, April

Hansen, L, 2006, *Security as practice: Discourse analysis and the Bosnian war*, Oxford: Routledge

Harvard Humanitarian Initiative, with support from Oxfam International, 2010, '*Now the world is without me': An investigation of sexual violence in Eastern Democratic Republic of Congo*, April, Cambridge, MA: Harvard Humanitarian Initiative, www.oxfam.org/sites/www.oxfam.org/files/DRC-sexual-violence-2010-04.pdf

HM Government National Action Plan on UNSCR 1325, Women, Peace and Security, Department for International Development, 2010, www.peacewomen.org/assets/file/NationalActionPlans/uk_nationalactionplan_november2010.pdf

HM Government, 2013, *Declaration on Preventing Sexual Violence in Conflict*, www.gov.uk/government/publications/g8-declaration-on-preventing-sexual-violence-in-conflict

HM Government, 2014, *Statement of Action – Global Summit to End Sexual Violence in Conflict*, www.gov.uk/government/publications/statement-of-action-global-summit-to-end-sexual-violence-in-conflict

HM Government, 2014, *International protocol on the documentation and investigation of sexual violence in conflict*, Appendix 4, www.gov.uk/government/policies/preventing-sexual-violence-in-conflict/supporting-pages/international-protocol-on-the-documentation-and-investigation-of-sexual-violence-in-conflict

Hogan, L, 2013, Seeking justice through the ICTY: Frustration, skepticism, hope, Women Under Siege, 23 September, www.womenundersiegeproject.org/blog/entry/seeking-justice-through-the-icty-frustration-skepticism-hope

Hudson, VM, Caprioli, M, Ballif-Spanvill, B, McDermott, R, Emmett, CF, 2009, The heart of the matter: The security of women and the security of states, *International Security*, 33, 3, Winter, 7-45, belfercenter.ksg.harvard.edu/files/IS3303_pp007-045.pdf

Hughes, CW, Yew, ML, 2011, *Security studies: A reader*, Oxford: Routledge

Human Rights Council, 2013, *Report of the Independent International Commission of Inquiry on the Syrian Arab Republic*, A/HRC/23/58, 4 June, www.ohchr.org/Documents/HRBodies/HRCouncil/CoISyria/A-HRC-23-58_en.pdf

Human Rights Council, 2013, *Report of the Independent International Commission of Inquiry on the Syrian Arab Republic*, A/HRC/24/46, 16 August

Human Rights Watch, 1998, *Summary of the Foca report*, www.hrw.org/legacy/reports/reports98/foca/#_1_2

Human Rights Watch, 1998, *Bosnia and Herzegovina. 'A closed dark place': Past and present human rights abuses in Foca*, 10, 6 (D), July, www.hrw.org/legacy/reports/reports98/foca

Human Rights Watch, 2000, Gender-based violence against Kosovar Albanian women, 3 March, www.hrw.org/reports/2000/fry/Kosov003-02.htm

Human Rights Watch, 2001, *Bosnia: Landmark verdicts for rape, torture and sexual enslavement*, 22 February, www.hrw.org/news/2001/02/22/bosnia-landmark-verdicts-rape-torture-and-sexual-enslavement

Human Rights Watch, 2002, *World report: Rwanda: Events of 2001*, https://www.hrw.org/legacy/wr2k2/africa9.html

Human Rights Watch, 2004, *Foca confronts its past*, www.hrw.org/en/news/2004/10/14/foca-confronts-its-past

Human Rights Watch, 2007, *World report: Bosnia and Herzegovina: Events of 2006*, https://www.hrw.org/sites/default/files/reports/wr2007master.pdf

Human Rights Watch, 2007, *Bosnia's War Crimes Chamber – Timelines and statistics*, 12 February

Human Rights Watch, 2011, *Justice compromised: The legacy of Rwanda's community-based Gacaca courts*, www.hrw.org/sites/default/files/reports/rwanda0511webwcover.pdf

Human Rights Watch, 2015, *AU: ICC members should lead on justice*, 9 June, www.hrw.org/news/2015/06/09/au-icc-members-should-lead-justice

Human Rights Watch, 2015, *Iraq: ISIS escapees describe systematic rape*, 14 April, www.hrw.org/news/2015/04/14/iraq-isis-escapees-describe-systematic-rape

Human Rights Watch, 2015, *UN: Sexual violence a "tactic of war"*, Nisha Varia, 14 April, www.hrw.org/news/2015/04/14/un-sexual-violence-tactic-war

Human Rights Watch, 2015, *Mass rape in North Darfur*, 11 February, www.hrw.org/node/132709/section/3

Human Rights Watch, 2015, *'We'll kill you if you cry': Sexual violence in the Sierra Leone conflict*, 16 January, www.hrw.org/reports/2003/01/15/well-kill-you-if-you-cry

Human Security Report Project, 2010, *Human security report 2009: The causes of peace and the shrinking costs of war*, Vancouver, BC, www.hsrgroup.org/human-security-reports/20092010/overview.aspx

Iceland Ministry of Foreign Affairs, 2008, *Women, peace and security: Iceland's plan of action for the implementation of UNSCR 1325 (2000)*, 8 March, www.peacewomen.org/assets/file/NationalActionPlans/iceland_nationalactionplan_march2008.pdf

ICTY, 1995, Press Release, Appeals Chamber judges unanimously confirm the Tribunal's jurisdiction, C/PIO/021-E, The Hague, 2 October

ICTY, 2007, *Report of the International Tribunal for the Prosecutions of Persons Responsible for Serious Violations of International Humanitarian Law in the Territory of Former Yugoslavia to the General Assembly and Security Council*, 1 August 2007.

ICTY, 2015, 20th anniversary of Srebrenica genocide commemorated in Potočari, *ICTY Digest*, 152, July, http://icty.org/x/file/About/Reports%20and%20Publications/ICTYDigest/2015/icty_digest_152_en.pdf

ICRC (International Committee of the Red Cross), 1995, 26th International Conference of the Red Cross and Red Crescent Movement, 07-12-1995 Resolution, 2(B), 3-7 December, Geneva, www.icrc.org/eng/resources/documents/resolution/26-international-conference-resolution-2-1995.htm

ICTJ (International Center for Transitional Justice), 2009, Amnesty must not equal impunity, Focus: 2009 DRC Amnesty Law, ictj.org/sites/default/files/ICTJ-DRC-Amnesty-Facts-2009-English.pdf

Independent, The, 2015, 15 March, www.independent.co.uk/news/ world/why-rape-is-as-deadly-a-threat-as-the-world-has-faced-congos-cheap-weapon-of-mass-destruction-9950642.html

International Human Rights Law Group, 1993, *Token gestures: Women's human rights and UN reporting: The UN Special Rapporteur on torture*, Series of reports, Washington, DC: International Human Rights Law Group

International Law Commission, 1996, *Report of the International Law Commission on the work of its Forty-Eighth Session* (6 May-26 July 1996), Official Records of the General Assembly, Fifty-first Session, Supplement No 10, United Nations Doc A/51/10, New York, http://legal.un.org/ilc/documentation/english/reports/a_51_10.pdf

IRC (International Rescue Committee), 2013, *Syria: A regional crisis*, January, www.rescue.org/sites/default/ files/resource-file/ IRCReportMidEast20130114.pdf

Jefferson, LR, 2004, *In war as in peace: Sexual violence and women's status*, New York, Human Rights Watch, January

Jepperson, RL, Wendt, A, Katzenstein, PJ, 1996, Norms, identity, and culture in national security, in PJ Katzenstein (ed), *Culture and national security*, New York: Colombia University Press

Kaldor, M, 2002, *New and old wars: Organised violence in a global era*, Cambridge: Polity Press

Kalshoven, F, Zegveld, L, 2001, *Constraints on the waging of war: An introduction to international humanitarian law*, Geneva: International Commission of the Red Cross and Red Crescent, www.loc.gov/rr/ frd/Military_Law/pdf/Constraints-waging-war.pdf

Keith, K, 2009, Justice at the International Criminal Tribunal for Rwanda: Are criticisms just?, *Law in Context*, 27, 1, www. federationpress.com.au/journals/abstract.asp?id=334

Knop, K, 2004, *Gender and human rights*, Oxford: Oxford University Press

Koppell, C, 2015, To fight extremism, the world needs to learn how to talk to women, 12 August, *Foreign Policy*, https://foreignpolicy. com/2015/08/12/to-fight-extremism-the-world-needs-to-learn-how-to-talk-to-women-boko-haram-isis/

Leatherman, JL, 2011, *Sexual violence and armed conflict*, Cambridge: Polity Press

Lee-Koo, K, 2002, Confronting a disciplinary blindness: Women, war and rape in the international politics of security, *Australian Journal of Political Science*, 37, 3, 525-36

Lerner, S, 1998, Haitian women demand justice, *MS Magazine*, July-August, 10-11

Lindsey, C. 2001, *Women facing war: ICRC study on the impact of armed conflict on women*, Geneva: International Committee of the Red Cross, www.icrc.org/eng/assets/files/other/icrc_002_0798_women_facing_war.pdf

Maas, P, 1996, *Love thy neighbour: A story of war*, London: Papermac, Macmillan

MacKinnon, C, 1993, Crimes of war, crimes of peace, in S Shute and S Hurley (eds), *On human rights: The Oxford Amnesty lectures 1993*, New York: Basic Books

McCormack, T, 1997, From Solferino to Sarajevo: A continuing role for international humanitarian law, *Melbourne University Law Review*, 21

Malone, DM, 2007, Security Council, in TG Weiss and S Daws (eds), *The Oxford handbook on the United Nations*, Oxford: Oxford University Press

Mardorossian, CM, 1985, Theory, experience and disciplinary contentions: A response to J Haarken and B Reardon, *Sexism and the war system*, New York: Teachers College Press

Mardorossian, CM, 2002, Theory, experience and disciplinary contentions: A response to Janice Haarken and Beverley Allen, *Signs*, 27, 3, Spring, pp 787-91

Mazowiecki, T, 1993, Special Rapporteur of the Commission on Human Rights, Report pursuant to Commission resolution 1992/S-1/1 of 14 August 1992, UN Doc E/CN. 4199/50, 10 February

Médecins Sans Frontières, 2007, *Ituri: 'Civilians still the first victims': Permanence of sexual violence and military operations*, Geneva, October, www.msf.or.jp/library/pressreport/pdf/200710Ituri_GB.pdf

Meron, T, 1995, International criminalisation of internal atrocities, *American Journal of International Law*, 554

Mertus, J, 2000, *War's offensive on women*, Bloomfield, CT: Kumarian Press

Mertus, J, 2004, Shouting from the bottom of the well: the impact of international trials on wartime rape on women's agency, *International Feminist Journal of Politics*, 6, 1, March, 110-28

Milillo, D, 2006, Rape as a tactic of war – social and psychological perspectives, *AFFILIA: Journal of Women and Social Work*, 21, 2

Ministry of Foreign Affairs of Finland, 2008, *Finland's national action plan 2008-2011*, www.peacewomen.org/assets/file/NationalActionPlans/finland_nationalactionplan_september2008.pdf

Ministry of Gender, Labour and Social Development, 2008, *The Uganda Action Plan on UN Security Council Resolutions 1325 and 1820 and the Goma Declaration*, www.peacewomen.org/assets/file/NationalActionPlans/uganda_nationalactionplan_december2008.pdf

Moreno-Ocampo, L, 2009, *Sexual violence as international crime: Interdisciplinary approaches to evidence*, The Hague: International Criminal Court, 16 June

Moreno-Ocampo, L, 2010, *OTP-NGO Roundtable: Introductory remarks*, The Hague, 19 October

Mosler, H, 1995, General principles of law, in *Encyclopaedia of Public International Law*, 2, 511-27

Munkler, H, 2003, The wars of the 21st century, *International Review of the Red Cross*, 85, 849, March

Nduka-Agwu, A, 2009, "Doing gender": After the war: Dealing with gender mainstreaming and sexual exploitation and abuse in peace support operations in Liberia and Sierra Leone, *Civil Wars*, 11, 2, June

Netherlands Ministry of Foreign Affairs, 2007, *The Dutch national action plan: Taking a stand for women, peace and security*, December, www.peacewomen.org/assets/file/NationalActionPlans/dutch_nationalactionplan_december2007.pdf

Neuffer, E, 2000, *The keys to my neighbour's house: Seeking justice in Bosnia and Rwanda*, Picador, USA

Newbury, C, 2002, Ethnicity and the politics of history in Rwanda, in DE Lorey and WH Beazley (eds), *Genocide, collective violence and popular memory: The politics of remembrance in the twentieth century*, Wilmington, DE: Scholarly Resources Inc

Newman, E, 2004, The "new wars" debate: A historical perspective is needed, *Security Dialogue*, 35, 2, 173-89

Nossiter, A, 2009, In a Guinea seized by violence, women are prey, *The New York Times*, 5 October, www.nytimes.com/2009/10/06/world/africa/06guinea.html?pagewanted=all

Nowrojee, B, 1996, *Shattered lives: Sexual violence during the Rwandan genocide and its aftermath*, New York: Human Rights Watch, September

Nowrojee, B, 2005, *Your justice is too slow: Will the ICTR fail Rwanda's rape victims?*, United Nations Research Institute for Social Development, November

OECD (Organisation for Economic Co-operation and Development), 2005, *Security system reform and governance*, DAC Guidelines and Reference Series, Paris: OECD, www.oecd.org/dac/governance-peace/conflictfragilityandresilience/docs/31785288.pdf

OHCHR (Office of the High Commissioner for Human Rights), 2000 *Systematic rape, sexual slavery and slavery-like practices during armed conflicts*, E/CN.4/Sub.2/2000/20 (Mary Robinson).

OHCHR, 2001, *Rape and abuse of women in the territory of the former Yugoslavia*, Commission on Human Rights resolution 1993/8, 23 February

OHCHR, 2014, South Sudan on verge of catastrophe – Pillay, UN News, www.ohchr.org/EN/NewsEvents/Pages/DisplayNews. aspx?NewsID=14550&LangID=E

Omaar, R, de Waal, A, 1994, Rwanda: Death, despair and defiance, *Africa Rights*, September

Oosterveld, V, 2009, Lessons from the Special Court for Sierra Leone on the prosecution of gender-based crimes, *Journal of Gender, Social Policy & the Law*, 17, 2, 407-28

OSCE (Organization for Security and Co-operation in Europe), 2012, Promoting gender equality and women's rights must be a priority for all OSCE states, says chairperson on International Women's Day, Press Release, 8 March, www.osce.org/cio/887778

Osotimehin, B, Bangura, Z, 2013, OP-ED: Act now, act big to end sexual violence in DRC, Inter Press Service, 6 November, www. ipsnews.net/2013/11/op-ed-act-now-act-big-to-end-sexual-violence-in-drc/

Otto, D, 2009, The exile of exclusion: Reflections on gender issues in international law over the last decade, *Melbourne Journal of International Law*, 10

Oxfam, 2011, *Protection of civilians in 2010*, www.oxfam.org/en/policy/ protection-civilians-2010

Page, M, Whitman, T, Anderson, C, 2009, *UNSC 1325: Strategies to bring women into peace negotiations*, International Women's Democracy Network, October

Peskin, V, 2000, Conflicts of justice – An analysis of the role of the International Criminal Tribunal of Rwanda, *International Peacekeeping*, 6, 128-37

Pettman, JJ, 1996, *Worlding women: A feminist international politics*, London: Routledge

Power, S, 2003, *A problem from hell: America and the age of genocide*, London: Flamingo, HarperCollins

Pratt, M, Werchick, L, 2004, *Sexual terrorism: Rape as a weapon of war in Eastern Democratic Republic of Congo – An assessment of programmatic responses to sexual violence in North Kivu, South Kivu, Maniema, and Oriental Provinces*, United States Agency for International Development/Bureau for Democracy, Conflict and Humanitarian Assistance (DCHA) Assessment Report, 9-16 January

Pronk, RJP, Tittemore, BD, 2011, ICTY issues final judgment against Dusan Tadić in first international war crimes trial since World War II, *The Center for Human Rights and Humanitarian Law at Washington College of Law*, Washington, DC: American University, www.wcl.american.edu/hrbrief/v4i3/icty43.htm

Prunier, G, 1995, *The Rwanda crisis: History of a genocide*, New York: Colombia University Press

Puechguirbal, N, 2010, Discourses on gender, patriarchy and resolution 1325: a textual analysis of UN documents, *International Peacekeeping*, 17, 2, 172-87

Quintana, JJ, 1994, Violations of international humanitarian law and measures of repression: the International Tribunal for the former Yugoslavia, *International Review of the Red Cross*, 300

Raiser, E, 1992, *Women build bridges to the former Yugoslavia*, Geneva: World Council of Churches

Ramet, S, Rebel, PB, 2002, *The disintegration of Yugoslavia from the death of Tito to the fall of Milosevic*, Boulder, CO: Westview Press

Reardon, B, 1985, *Sexism and the war system*, New York: Teachers College Press

Rich, A, 1986, *Of woman born: Motherhood as experience and institution*, New York: Norton

Risse, T, Sikkink, K, 1999, The socialisation of international human rights norms into domestic practices, in T Risse, SC Ropp and K Sikkink (eds), *The power of human rights: International norms and domestic change*, Cambridge: Cambridge University Press, 1-38

Risse, T, Ropp, SC, Sikkink, K, 1999, *The power of human rights: International norms and domestic change*, Cambridge: Cambridge University Press

Roberts, A, Guelff, R, 1996, *Documents on the laws of war*, 3rd edn, New York: Oxford University Press

Robertson, G, 2008, *Crimes against humanity: The struggle for global justice*, New York: Allen Lane

Rome Statute of the International Criminal Court, 1998, UN Document A/CONF.183/9, www.icc-cpi.int/nr/rdonlyres/ea9aeff7-5752-4f84-be94-0a655eb30e16/0/rome_statute_english.pdf

Rwandan Rapport National, 1995, for the Fourth World Conference on Women, Beijing

Sandoz, Y, Swinarski, C, Zimmerman, B (eds), 1987, *ICRC commentary on the additional protocols of 8 June 1977 to the Geneva Conventions of 12 August 1949*, Geneva: Martinus Nijhoff Publishers

Schiessl, C, 2000, An element of genocide: rape, total war, and international law in the twentieth century, *Journal of Genocide Research*, 4, 2, 197–210

Schindler, D, 1999, Significance of the Geneva Conventions for the contemporary world, *International Review of the Red Cross*, 81, 836, December, 715–28

Scott, SV, 2004, *International law in world politics*, Boulder, CO: Lynne Rienner Publishers

Scott, SV, Billingsley, AJ, Michaelson, C, 2010, *International law and the use of force: A documentary and reference guide*, Santa Barbara, CA, Denver, CO and Oxford: Praeger Security International ABC-CLIO, LLC

Seifert, R, 1994, War and rape: a preliminary analysis, in A Stigelmayer (ed), *Mass rape: The war against women in Bosnia-Herzegovina*, Lincoln, NE: University of Nebraska Press

Sharlach, L, 2000, Rape as genocide in Bangladesh, the former Yugoslavia and Rwanda, *New Political Science*, 22, 1

Shepherd, L, 2008, Power and authority in the production of United Nations Security Council resolution 1325, *International Studies Quarterly*, 52, 383–404

Shyake, A, 2005/06, *The Rwandan conflict: Origin, development, exit strategies*, A study ordered by the National Unity and Reconciliation Commission of Rwanda

Sippel, S, Musimbi, K, 2014, Changing the conversation on sexual violence in conflict, *Foreign Policy in Focus*, 18 June, www.truth-out.org/news/item/24429-changing-the-conversation-on-sexual-violence-in-conflict

Smith, H, 2000, Rape victims' babies pay the price of war, *The Guardian*, 16 April, www.guardian.co.uk/world/2000/apr/16/balkans

Smits, R, Cruz, S, 2011, Increasing security in DR Congo: Gender responsive strategies for combating sexual violence, *CRU Policy Brief*, June

Solhjell, R, Karlsrud, J, Lie, JHS, 2010, *Protecting civilians against sexual and gender based violence in Chad*, Oslo: Norwegian Institute of International Affairs, http://brage.bibsys.no/xmlui/bitstream/handle/11250/277140/SIP-07-Report-Solhjell-Karlsrud-Sande+Lie.pdf?sequence=3

Statute of the Special Court for Sierra Leone, Article 2-3, www.rscsl.org/Documents/scsl-statute.pdf

Steans, J, 1998, *Gender and international relations*, New Brunswick, NJ: Rutgers University Press

Steans, J, Pettiford, L, 2005, *Introduction to international relations: Perspectives and themes*, London: Pearson Education

Stiehm, JH, 1982, The protector, the protected and the defender, *Women's Studies International Forum*, 5, 3/4, 367-76

Stoett, PJ, 1995, This age of genocide: Conceptual and institutional implications, *International Journal*, 1, 3, Summer

Strudwick, P, 2014, Why rape is as deadly a threat as the world has faced: Congo's cheap weapon of mass destruction, *Independent*, 30 December, www.independent.co.uk/news/world/why-rape-is-as-deadly-a-threat-as-the-world-has-faced-congos-cheap-weapon-of-mass-destruction-9950642.html

Swaine, A, 2009, Assessing the potential of national action plans to advance implementation of United Nations Security Council resolution 1325, *Yearbook of International Humanitarian Law*, 12, 405

Swiss, S, Giller, JE, 1993, Rape as a crime of war: a medical perspective, *Journal of the American Medical Association*, 270, 4 August

Tajfel, H, Turner, JC, 1986, The social identity theory of inter-group behaviour, in S Worchel and WG Austin (eds), *Psychology of inter-group relations*, Chicago, IL: Nelson Hall, 7-24

Thomas, DQ, Ralph, RE, 1994, Rape in war: Challenging the tradition of impunity, *SAIS Review*, 82-89

Tickner, A, 1997, "You just don't understand": troubled engagements between feminists and IR theorists, *International Studies Quarterly*, 41, 4, December

Tickner, A, 2001, *Gendering world politics: Issues and approaches in the post-Cold War era*, New York: Columbia University Press

True, J, 2001, Feminism, in S Burchill, R Devetak, A Linklater, M Paterson, C Reus-Smit and J True, *Theories of international relations*, New York: Palgrave Macmillan

True, J, 2003, Mainstreaming gender in global public policy, *International Feminist Journal of Politics*, 5, 3, November, 377

True, J, Mintrom, M, 2001, Transnational networks and policy diffusion: The case of gender mainstreaming, *International Studies Quarterly*, 45, 1

Tryggestad, TL, 2009, Trick or treat? The UN and implementation of Security Council resolution 1325 on women, peace, and security, *Global Governance: A Review of Multilateralism and International Organizations*, October–December, 15, 4, 552

Turner, T, 2007, *The Congo wars: Conflict, myth and reality*, London and New York: Zed Books

United Kingdom, High Level Plan, www.un.org/womenwatch/ianwge/taskforces/wps/nap/NAP_UK_2006.pdf

van Schaack, S, 1999, The definition of crimes against humanity: resolving the incoherence, Santa Clara University Legal Studies Research paper no 07-38, *Journal of Transnational law and Policy*, 37, 787

Viseur-Sellers, P, 2004, Individual('s) liability for collective sexual violence, in K Knop, *Gender and human rights*, Oxford: Oxford University Press, 153-95

von Clauswitz, C, 1968, *On War*, London: Pelican Books

von Clausewitz, C, 1980, *Vom Kriege*, 19th edn, Bonn: Werner Hahlweg

von Ragenfeld-Feldman, N, 1997, The victimization of women: Rape and the reporting of rape in Bosnia–Herzegovina, 1992-1993, Presented at the Fifth Annual Interdisciplinary German Studies Conference, 15-16 March

von Tigerstrom, B, 2006, International law and the concept of human security, in U Dolgopol and J Gardam, *The challenge of conflict: International law responds*, Leiden and Boston, MA: Martinus Nijhoff Publishers

Vulliamy, E, 1992, Shame of camp Omarska, *The Guardian*, 7 August, www.guardian.co.uk/world/1992/aug/07/warcrimes.edvulliamy

Walter, BF, 2010, *Conflict relapse and the sustainability of post-conflict peace*, September, http://web.worldbank.org/archive/website01306/web/pdf/wdr%20background%20paper_walter_0.pdf

Warburton, A, 1993, *European Council investigative mission into the treatment of Muslim women in the former Yugoslavia, Report to EC foreign ministers, December 1992-February 1993*, 28 January

Weiner, M, 1996, Bad neighbour, bad neighbourhoods: an enquiry into the causes of refugee flows, *International Security*, 21, 1, Summer

Weiss, TG, Daws, S (eds), 2007, *The Oxford handbook on the United Nations*, Oxford: Oxford University Press

Wildavsky, A, 1989, Choosing preferences by constructing institutions: a cultural theory of preference formation, in AA. Berger (ed), *Political culture and public opinion*, New Brunswick, NJ: Transaction

Williams, PD, 2010, Enhancing civilian protection in peace operations: Insights from Africa, *The Africa Center for Strategic Studies*, September, 53-4

Wolfe, L, 2013, "Take your portion": a victim speaks out about rape in Syria, 18 June, Women Under Siege, www.womenundersiegeproject. org/blog/entry/Take-your-portion-A-victim-speaks-out-about-rape-in-Syria

Wolfe, L, 2013, Syria has a massive rape crisis, 3 April, Women Under Siege, www.womenundersiegeproject.org/blog/entry/syria-has-a-massive-rape-crisis

Wood, EJ, 2009, Variation in sexual violence during war, *Politics & Society*, 34, 3, 307-42, http://pas.sagepub.com/content/34/3/307

Working Group on Women, Peace and Security, http:// womenpeacesecurity.org/media/pdf-2012-13_MAP_Report.pdf

World Bank, The, 2011, *World development report: Conflict, security and development*, Washington, DC: The World Bank, http://siteresources. worldbank.org/INTWDRS/Resources/WDR2011_Full_Text.pdf

Tribunal proceedings and judgments

ICTR (International Criminal Tribunal for Rwanda), *The Prosecutor v Jean-Paul Akayesu*, ICTR-96-4-T, Decision of 2 September 1998 [The Akayesu decision]

ICTY (International Criminal Tribunal for the former Yugoslavia), *Amended Indictment against Ratko Mladic*, IT-95-5/18-1, www.icty. org/x/cases/mladic/ind/en/mla-ai021010e.pdf

ICTY, *Amended Indictment against Radovan Karadžić Unsealed*, Press Release, 14 October 2002, www.icty.org/sid/8066

ICTY, *The Prosecutor v Tihomir Bla*, Judgment , Case No IT-95-14-T, 3 March 2000, www.icty.org/x/cases/blaskic/tjug/en/bla-tj000303e. pdf

ICTY, *Čelebići case: The Judgment of the Trial Chamber: The most significant legal aspects*, www.icty.org/sid/7617

ICTY, *Omarska, Keraterm and Trnopolje Camps* (IT-98-30/1), ICTY Press Release, www.icty.org/x/cases/kvocka/cis/en/cis_kvocka_al_en.pdf

ICTY, *Prosecutor v Delalić*, Indictment, IT-96-21-1, 19 March 1996

ICTY, *Prosecutor v Delalić*, Judgment, IT-96-21-T, 16 November 1998

ICTY, *Prosecutor v Delalić*, Judgment, IT-96-21-A, 20 February 2001

ICTY, *Prosecutor v Dragoljub Kunarac, Radomir Kovac and Zoran Vukovic*, Judgment IT-96-23-T and IT-96-23/1-T, February 2001

ICTY, *Prosecutor v Duško Tadić*, Decision on the Defence Motion for Interlocutory Appeal on Jurisdiction, 2 October 1995, Case No IT-94-AR72

ICTY, *Prosecutor v Furundžija*, Judgment, IT-95-17/1-T, 10 December 1998

ICTY, *Prosecutor v Kunarac*, Judgment, IT-96-23-T, 22 February 2001

ICTY, *Prosecutor v Kvočka*, Judgment, IT-98-30-T, 2 November 2001

ICTY, *Prosecutor v Radislav Krsti*, Judgment IT-98-33-A

ICTY, *Prosecutor v Tadić*, Judgment, IT-94-1-A (ICTY App. CH.15 July 1999)

ICTY, *Prosecutor v Furundžija*, Judgment, IT-95-17/1-A (ICTY App. CH. 21 July 2000)

ICTY, *Prosecutor v Kvočka*, Judgment, IT-98-30/1-T 2, November 2001

ICTY, *Kosovo, Croatia and Bosnia*, IT-02-54, www.icty.org/x/cases/slobodan_milosevic/cis/en/cis_milosevic_slobodan.pdf

ICTY, www.icty.org/x/cases/furundzija/cis/en/cis_furundzija.pdf

ICTY, *The Prosecutor of the Tribunal Against Radovan Karadžić and Ratko Mladic*, IT-95-5-I, www.icty.org/x/cases/mladic/ind/en/kar-ii950724e.pdf

ICTY, Trial Chamber, *Prosecutor v Tadić*, IT-94-1

ICTY, Gagovic & Others ('Foca') Indictment, confirmed 26 June 1996, IT-96-23-I322, 332

Special Court for Sierra Leone, 2007, *Prosecutor of the Special Court for Sierra Leone v Alex Tamba Brima, Brima Bazzy Kamara, Santigie Borbor Kanu* (the Africa accused) (judgment) SCSL-2004-16-T at 691, 19 July, www.refworld.org/pdfid/46a46d262.pdf

United Nations documents

Conventions and declarations

UN, 1948, *Convention on the Prevention and Punishment of the Crime of Genocide (the Genocide Convention)*

UN, 1948, *Universal Declaration of Human Rights*

UN, 1949, *Geneva Convention I for the Amelioration of the Condition of the Wounded and Sick in Armed Forces in the Field*

UN, 1949, *Geneva Convention II for the Amelioration of the Condition of the Wounded, Sick and Shipwrecked Members of Armed Forces at Sea*

UN, 1949, *Geneva Convention III Concerning the Treatment of Prisoners of War*

UN, 1949, *Geneva Convention IV Concerning the Protection of Civilian Persons in Time of War*

UN, 1966, *International Covenant on Civil and Political Rights*

UN, 1977, *Protocol Additional to the Geneva Conventions of August 12 1949, and relating to the Protection of Victims of International Armed Conflicts (Protocol 1)*, 8 June, 1125 U, NTS 3, 16 ILM 1331 (entered into force 7 December 1978)

UN, 1979, *Convention on the Elimination of All Forms of Discrimination Against Women*

UN, 1984, *Convention Against Torture and other Cruel, Inhuman and Degrading Treatment or Punishment*

UN, 1989, *Convention on the Rights of the Child*

UN, 1993, *Declaration on the Elimination of Violence Against Women*

UN, 2013, *Declaration of Commitment to End Sexual Violence in Conflict*

Letters

UN Security Council, 1994, Letter dated 1 October 1994 from the Secretary-General addressed to the President of the Security Council, S/1994/1125

UN Security Council, 1994, Letter dated 9 December from the Secretary-General addressed to the President of the Security Council, S/1994/1405

Press releases

UN News Centre, *DR Congo: UN envoy hails new pact with rebels in strife torn east*, 24 March 2009

UN News Centre, *DR Congo: More that 30,000 flee new attacks by splintered rebel factions*, 7 April 2009

UN News Centre, *Growing number of women falling victim to rape in DR Congo, reports UN*, 20 May 2009

UN News Centre, *UN, African Union sign landmark agreement to curb sexual violence in African countries*, 6 February 2014, www.un.org/apps/news/story.asp?NewsID=47095#.VRnEQvmUcU0

UN News Centre, *"As women thrive, so will we all," says Secretary-General as Women's Commission opens session, pointing to "unacceptably slow" progress since Beijing*, 9 March 2015, www.un.org/press/en/2015/wom2021.doc.htm

UN News Centre, *Society's attitudes must change worldwide to stop gender-based violence, says UN officials*, 11 March 2015, www.un.org/apps/news/story.asp?NewsID=50301#.VQZPkI6UcU0

UN, *Peace inextricably linked with equality between men and women says Security Council in International Women's Day Statement*, SC/6816, 8 March 2000, www.un.org/press/en/2000/20000308.sc6816.doc.html

UN, *Security Council concludes open debate on women, peace and security*, SC/6939, 25 October 2000, www.un.org/press/en/2000/sc6939.doc.htm

UN, *Stronger decision-making role for women in peace processes is called for in day-long Security Council debate*, SC/6937, 24 October 2000, www.un.org/press/en/2000/sc6937.doc.htm

UN, *Security Council, in Presidential Statement, condemns plundering of natural resources in Democratic Republic of Congo*, SC/7246, 4441st meeting, 19 December 2001, www.un.org/press/en/2001/SC7246.doc.htm

UN, *UN expert on violence against women expresses serious concerns following visit to Democratic Republic of Congo*, 30 July 2007, www.ohchr.org/EN/NewsEvents/Pages/DisplayNews.aspx?NewsID=5993&LangID=E

UN, *Security Council demands immediate and complete halt to acts of sexual violence against civilians in conflict zones, unanimously adopting resolution 1820 (2008)*, SC/9364, 19 June 2008, www.un.org/News/Press/docs/2008/sc9364.doc.htm

UN, *Security Council adopts text mandating peacekeeping missions to protect women, girls from sexual violence in armed conflict*, 30 September 2009, www.un.org/News/Press/docs/2009/sc9753.doc.htm

UN, *Security Council adopts resolution 2122 (2013), aiming to strengthen women's role in all stages of conflict prevention*, SC/11149, 18 October 2013, www.un.org/press/en/2013/sc11149.doc.htm

UN, *International Criminal Court receives mixed performance review, as General Assembly concludes discussion of body's annual report*, 31 October 2014, 69th session, www.un.org/press/en/2014/ga11577.doc.htm

UN Secretariat, *Special measures for protection from sexual exploitation and sexual abuse*, ST/SGB/2003, 9 October 2003, https://oios.un.org/resources/2015/01/ST-SGB-2003-13.pdf

Reports

UN, 1993, *Report of the Secretary-General pursuant to paragraph 2 of Security Council resolution 808*

UN, 1999, *Report of the Secretary-General to the Security Council on the protection of civilians in armed conflict*, S/1999/957, 8 September

UN, 2000, *Report of the Ad Hoc Committee of the Whole of the twenty-third special session of the General Assembly*, Supplement No 3, A/S-23/10/Rev1.

UN, 2000, *Resource requirements for implementation of the report of the Panel on United Nations peace operations: Report of the Secretary-General*, Addendum, 27 October, A/55/507/Add.1

UN, 2007, *Report of the International Tribunal for the prosecutions of persons responsible for serious violations of international humanitarian law in the territory of former Yugoslavia to the General Assembly and Security Council*, 1 August

UN, 2005, *UN system-wide action plan for the implementation of Security Council resolution 1325 (2005-07)*, S/2005/636.

UN, 2011, *Report of the Panel on Remedies and Reparation for victims of sexual violence in the Democratic Republic of Congo to the High Commissioner for Human Rights*, March

UN General Assembly, 1994, *Advancement of women*, A/49/587, 1 November

UN General Assembly, Committee 3, 1995, *Rape and abuse of women in the areas of armed conflict in the former Yugoslavia*, 99th plenary meeting, 22 December

UN General Assembly, 1997, *Report of the Economic and Social Council for 1997*, A/52/3, 18 September

UN General Assembly, 2010, *Home security*, A/64/701, 8 March

UN General Assembly, 2011, *Report of the International Criminal Court*, 19 August, A/66/309

UN General Assembly Security Council, 2010, *Report of the Secretary-General on the implementation of Security Council resolutions 1820 (2008) and 1888 (2009)*, S/2010/604

UN General Assembly Security Council, 2013, *Sexual violence in conflict*, S/2013/149, 14 March, www.refworld.org/pdfid/5167bd0f4.pdf

UNIFEM, 2009, *Workshop on gender and security sector reform*, Summary, September

UN International Research and Training Institute for the Advancement of Women, 2006, *Securing equality, engendering peace: A guide to policy and planning on women, peace and security (UN SCR 1325)*, Dominican Republic

UN Security Council, 1992, *Rape and sexual assault: A legal study, Final report of the United Nations Commission of Experts established pursuant to Security Council Resolution 780*, Annex II

UN Security Council, 1993, *Statute of the International Tribunal for the prosecution of persons responsible for serious violations of international law committed in the territory of the former Yugoslavia since 1991*, United Nations Doc S/25704 at 36, Annex (1993) and S/25704/Add.1 (1993), 25 May 1993, UN Doc S/RES/827

UN Security Council, 1994, *Rape and sexual assault – Final report of the United Nations Commission of Experts established pursuant to Security Council resolution 780 (1992)*, S/1994/674

UN Security Council, 2004, *The rule of law and transitional justice in conflict and post-conflict societies*, S/2004/616, 23 August

UN Security Council, 2009, *Twenty-seventh report of the Secretary-General on the United Nations Organization Mission in the Democratic Republic of Congo*, S/2009/160, 27 March

UN Security Council, 2009, *Women and peace and security*, S/2009/465, 16 September

UN Security Council, 2010, *Report of the Secretary-General on women and peace and security*, S/2010/498, 28 September

UN Security Council, 2012, *Conflict-related sexual violence*, S/2012/33, 13 January

UN Security Council, 2013, *Report of the Secretary-General on women and peace and security*, S/2013/525, 4 September

UN Security Council, 2014, *Conflict-related sexual violence*, S/2014/181, 13 March

UN Security Council, 2014, *Report of the Secretary-General on the situation in the Central African Republic*, S/2014/857, 28 November

UN Security Council, 2015, *Report of the Secretary-General on the United Nations organization stabilization mission in the Democratic Republic of the Congo*, S/2015/172, 10 March

UN Security Council, 2015, *Conflict-related sexual violence*, S2015/203, 23 March

UN Women, 1992, *Convention on the Elimination of All Forms of Discrimination against Women (CEDAW)*, General Recommendation No 19, 11th session, New York, www.un.org/womenwatch/daw/cedaw/recommendations/recomm.htm

UN Women, 2010, *Addressing conflict-related sexual violence – An analytical inventory of peacekeeping practice*, www.unwomen.org/en/digital-library/publications/2010/1/addressing-conflict-related-sexual-violence-an-analytical-inventory-of-peacekeeping-practice

UN Women, www.unwomen.org/en/what-we-do/post-2015

UN Women, www.unwomen.org/en/news/stories/2015/01/ending-gender-inequality-through-the-post-2015-agenda

UN Women, 2015, Gender consideration in security management: a speech by Lakshmi Puri, www.unwomen.org/en/news/stories/2015/01/gender-consideration-in-security-management-a-speech-by-lakshmi-puri#sthash.B7u2g7zq.dpuf

UN Women, Women and security sector reform, www.womenwarpeace.org

UN Women, Transitional justice, www.womenwarpeace.org

Resolutions

See www.un.org/en/sc/documents/resolutions/ for information on each resolution.

UN General Assembly, *Resolution 217A(III) (1948), Universal Declaration of Human Rights*, 10 December 1948

UN General Assembly, *Resolution 1994/205, Rape and abuse of women in the territory of the former Yugoslavia*, 6 March 1994

UN Security Council, *Security Council resolution 770 (1992) [on Bosnia and Herzegovina]*, 18 December 1992

UN Security Council, *Security Council resolution 808 (1993) [on former Yugoslavia]*, 22 February 1993

UN Security Council, *Security Council resolution 827 (1993) [on former Yugoslavia]*, 25 May 1993

UN Security Council, *Security Council resolution 929 (1994) [on Rwanda]*, 22 June 1994

UN Security Council, *Security Council resolution 935 (1994) [Commission of Experts to examine violations of international humanitarian law committed in Rwanda]*, S/RES/935, 1 July 1994

UN Security Council, *Security Council resolution 955 (1994) [on Rwanda]*, S/RES/955, 8 November 1994

UN Security Council, *Security Council resolution 1265 (1999) [Protection of civilians in armed conflict]*, S/RES/1265, 17 September 1999

UN Security Council, *Security Council resolution 1296 (2000) [protection of civilians in armed conflict]*, S/RES/1296, 19 April 2000

UN Security Council, *Security Council resolution 1325 (2000) [on women and peace and security]*, S/RES/1325, 31 October 2000

UN Security Council, *Security Council resolution 1503 (2003) [International Criminal Tribunal for the former Yugoslavia (ICTY) and International Criminal Tribunal for Rwanda (ICTR)]*, S/RES/1503, 28 August 2003

UN Security Council, *Security Council resolution 1820 (2008) [on women and peace and security]*, S/RES/1820, 19 June 2008

UN Security Council, *Security Council resolution 1888 (2009) [on women and peace and security]*, S/RES/1888, 30 September 2009

UN Security Council, *Security Council resolution 1889 (2009) [on women and peace and security]*, S/RES/1889, 5 October 2009

UN Security Council, *Security Council resolution 1960 (2010) [on women and peace and security]*, S/RES/1960, 16 December 2010

UN Security Council, *Security Council resolution 1969 (2011) [on Timor-Leste]*, S/RES/1969, 24 February 2011

UN Security Council, *Security Council resolution 2106 (2013) [on women and peace and security]*, 24 June 2013

UN Security Council, *Security Council resolution 2122 (2013) [on women and peace and security]*, S/RES/2122, 18 October 2013

Statements

UN Security Council, Statement by the President of the Security Council, S/PRST/1999/6, 12 February 1999

UN Security Council, Statement by the President of the Security Council, S/PRST/2004/40, 28 October 2004

UN Security Council, Statement by the President of the Security Council, S/PRST/2005/52, 27 October 2005

UN Security Council, Statement by the President of the Security Council, S/PRST/2010/22, 26 October 2010

Other UN documents

UN-APPG meeting on protecting women and girls in emergencies, *Tackling violence against women and girls: A joined-up response*, London, 13 November 2013

UN, Department of Public Information, *United Nations peace keeping*

Index